A PRIVATE WAR

ALSO BY MARIE BRENNER

A

PRIVATE

WAR

MARIE COLVIN AND OTHER
TALES OF HEROES, SCOUNDRELS
AND RENEGADES

MARIE BRENNER

**SIMON &
SCHUSTER**

London · New York · Sydney · Toronto · New Delhi

A CBS COMPANY

First published in the United States by Simon & Schuster, Inc., 2018
First published in Great Britain by Simon & Schuster UK Ltd, 2018
A CBS COMPANY

The pieces in this collection were originally published in *Vanity Fair*.
The piece 'Judge Motley's Verdict' was originally published in the *New Yorker*.

1 3 5 7 9 10 8 6 4 2

Simon & Schuster UK Ltd
1st Floor
222 Gray's Inn Road
London WC1X 8HB

www.simonandschuster.co.uk
www.simonandschuster.com.au
www.simonandschuster.co.in

Simon & Schuster Australia, Sydney
Simon & Schuster India, New Delhi

A CIP catalogue record for this book is available from the British Library.

Paperback ISBN: 978-1-4711-8070-5
eBook ISBN: 978-1-4711-8071-2

Interior design by Paul Dippolito
Printed and bound by CPI Group (UK) Ltd, Croydon, CR0 4YY

MIX
Paper from
responsible sources
FSC® C020471

Simon & Schuster UK Ltd are committed to sourcing paper
that is made from wood grown in sustainable forests and support the Forest
Stewardship Council, the leading international forest certification organisation.
Our books displaying the FSC logo are printed on FSC certified paper.

For Ernie and for Peggy, and always for Casey
and
for Marie Colvin and all who put
themselves in harm's way to report the truth

"There is always one moment in childhood when the door opens and lets the future in."

—Graham Greene

Contents

Introduction

To understand the arc of her career, you have to know how it ended.

Marie Colvin's last assignment was in February 2012, in a ravaged war zone in Syria. She operated from what she called "a media center" in the town of Baba Amr, crouched with a few other journalists in a small building in narrow streets. The top floor had been blown off by the deluge of rockets and shells raining down from the forces of the dictator Bashar al-Assad. Now, on a Wednesday morning in the early hours, the American-born foreign correspondent who worked for decades for the *Sunday Times of London* awakened to the convulsions of rockets and shells around her.

The night before, she'd left her shoes outside in the hall—the gesture, her longtime colleague and friend Jon Swain noted later, would cost her life. With her was *Sunday Times* photographer Paul Conroy, fraught with anxiety because he was certain Colvin's insistence on returning to Baba Amr could end in catastrophe. But Colvin was there to record it all: "Snipers on the rooftops of al-Baath University . . . shoot any civilian who comes into their sight. . . . It is a city of the cold and the hungry, echoing to exploding shells and bursts of gunfire." There was, of course, no telephone or electricity. Freezing rain filled potholes and snow drifted through the

1

windows during the coldest winter anyone in Baba Amr could remember, Colvin wrote. "Many of the dead and injured are those that risked their lives foraging for food," Colvin wrote.

The essence of that detail was what mattered to Colvin most: the need to bring to vivid life the human costs of war. Sprinting through a barrage of rockets, Colvin spent a day in a makeshift clinic, interviewing victims. The *Sunday Times* bannered her report across two pages. Later it would be noted that hers was one of the first convincing reports predicting al-Assad's genocide, which would overtake Syria. After her first piece was filed, Colvin mailed her colleague Lucy Fisher, "I did have a few moments when I thought, 'What am I doing? Story incredibly important though.'" Mx. She demanded to return to Baba Amr and would not hear otherwise. "It is sickening that the Syrian regime is allowed to keep doing this," she wrote her editor when she returned three days later. "There was a shocking scene in an apartment clinic today. A baby boy lay on a head scarf, naked, his little tummy heaving as he tried to breathe. The doctor said, 'We can do nothing for him.' He had been hit by shrapnel on his left side. They just had to let him die as his mother wept."

"This is insane, Marie," Conroy told her angrily when she announced she had every intention of returning. "Assad has targeted you and all the journalists." Trained in the British military, Conroy understood the peril. He also had an acute sense of Marie's vexed tech skills. She was a woman of a certain age, who had started her career when you dictated a story over the phone to an editor. Often, in the field, Conroy would retrieve lost files that had vanished into the nether land of her laptop. How could she ever truly understand the consequences of dialing from a SAT phone in an area where an enemy was trying to track her location? He argued with her in the tunnel, until she stalked off, saying, "Save a place for me at the bar." Then he followed her, terrified of what could happen if he was not, as always, by Marie's side.

I arrived in London a few days after Colvin died to write about her life for *Vanity Fair*. Conroy was still recovering from the explosions that almost cost him his leg. Dragging his IV poles, he forced himself to speak about Colvin at a reception at the Frontline Club, where London's foreign correspondents meet. The next day, at the hospital, I spent hours by his bed. One of the first stories he told me took place outside Sirte in the Libyan civil war. Colvin and Conroy had been trapped for days as the troops who surrounded Libya's strongman Muammar Qaddafi fought with those who were trying to depose the vicious despot. Minutes from deadline, in a speeding car heading for the border, there wasn't a whisper of power they could use to transmit Marie's copy from her laptop. The driver screamed as Conroy crawled onto the back of the car with his gaffer tape to place a booster, with sand and dust blowing in his eyes. Marie hit send. Then, both Paul and Marie screamed with relief as the car streaked down the highway. "I have never seen journalists who worked this way," the driver told them. "Well, you have never worked with the *Sunday Times*," Marie yelled.

A few words of context: For years, Colvin had dined out on her early days as a thirty-year-old reporter for the Associated Press posted to Beirut in 1986. Her first real scoop was the penetration of Qaddafi's underground lair at the moment he was in a tense stand-off with then-president Ronald Reagan. Qaddafi was at this point an eccentric under-the-radar autocrat who posed as a Bedouin chief, then anointed himself a colonel, directing bombings across Europe from subterranean rooms underneath his palace. Colvin refused to stay with the small press pack that had converged on Tripoli, hoping to get an interview. Arriving at his palace gate, she pretended to be French and captivated Qaddafi's guards with her dark, curly hair and reporter's moxie. At 3 a.m., she was summoned to a hideout three stories beneath his palace garden. It contained an underground medical clinic, armored doors with automatic locks, and a throne room where Qaddafi would later lay out green shoes for her to wear. After one interview, he sent a nurse to her hotel room with a hypodermic needle. The nurse announced, "I Bulgarian; I take blood," before Colvin could flee with her cassette tapes. The scoop made her name and brought Colvin to the attention of the *Sunday Times,* where she quickly rose to become one of the most acclaimed war reporters of her generation.

Colvin never wavered in the essential understanding of who she was and the importance of what she did. She could somehow use the term "bear witness" and get away with it. You can call a phrase like that grandiose and self-inflated, and sometimes people did, but Marie had a mission that she turned into a vocation, and that was to go to the most violent and dismal places on earth and bear personal witness to what man does to man. She was glamorous, but there was nothing glamorous about what she did. She was a paradox—a girl's girl with a posse of devoted friends. From time to time, she would appear at someone's door with fabulous shoes or clothes that she had spotted as a gift for a friend or cook midnight feasts for a crowd. She was a romantic drawn to another world reality, a ferocious war correspondent who refused to recognize obstacles when she went into the field. Nothing deterred her—not rocket strikes, or military censors, or the loss of balance from her vision problems. Colvin did not think in gender terms; she just got the job done and used whatever means she had. She regaled her friends with stories from the field, shaped into performances that camouflaged the raw truth of her existence. After being rescued from bombings in the mountain of Chechnya—where she existed on snow and one jar of jam—she teased a friend that she could not have survived without the pricey fur the friend had pushed her to buy.

Colvin's sangfroid and wit fit beautifully in London media and political circles, but there was a price: She battled PTSD and alcohol, and fiercely maintained a size 4, determined never to be fat, wearing La Perla in the field. She made no secret of her love of men—and she was faithful to the ones she loved. In that way, she was often and easily betrayed. Her north stars were the glamorous war correspondents who came before her. At all times, she carried Martha Gellhorn's *The Face of War,* a masterwork of dispatches from Gellhorn's decades in the field, including her on-the-ground reporting from the liberation of Dachau, where her view of corpses stacked like kindling haunted the rest of her days. Colvin, too, had a recurring nightmare—of a twenty-two-year-old Palestinian girl gunned down in a refugee camp in Lebanon. She was not interested in the strategy of war or its artillery, but rather the very real human dramas of those who suffered the consequences of what wars actually do to those who are somehow able to survive them.

A theme of basic justice links the cluster of profiles in this collection. It seems almost unnecessary to observe the obvious: I don't like to see the innocent get railroaded or the perpetrators of evil get away with it. The length of these stories and the months spent reporting them were a gift of what is now called the golden age of magazine reporting. My editors were generous with time and resources. The essence of the craft is always the same—obsession. As a reporter, I am drawn to others as obsessed. In 1993, on assignment for *The New Yorker,* I wrote of Constance Baker Motley, who had helped draft *Brown* v. *Board of Education* with NAACP founder Thurgood Marshall and went on to become the first African-American woman to be appointed to the federal bench. She was a woman of quiet elegance who shopped at Lord & Taylor for a new suit before she flew to Jackson, Mississippi, to face down racist crowds outside a segregated courthouse where she argued her case to integrate the University of Mississippi in front of a mural of a plantation and its slaves memorialized on the courtroom wall. She argued case after case in Mississippi, Alabama, and Georgia, bringing in crowds of African-Americans who would marvel that a woman of color was at last causing real change. In Jackson, the local paper referred to her as "that Motley woman."

Her pursuit of justice did not incite the murderous violence that came out of the quest, twenty-five years later, of a school teacher in the Swat Valley of Pakistan who attempted to alert the world to the sadism being perpetrated by the Taliban in collusion with the powers inside Pakistan. Ziauddin Yousafzai, the father of Malala Yousafzai, almost lost his daughter in an attack that galvanized the world and turned the then-fourteen-year-old Malala into an international heroine who won the Nobel Prize.

I am also drawn to those who have been somehow caught in the vise of public events and have been shredded by overwhelming forces. The death threats and the smear campaign waged against tobacco whistleblower Jeffrey Wigand and CBS's *60 Minutes* producer Lowell Bergman as they attempted to break the story of the corporate malfeasance being perpetrated by Big Tobacco preoccupied me for months. The chilling winds that could come from corporate big footing at news organizations could only lead to censorship—as it had at CBS, which had killed Bergman's story. Not long after, I was in Atlanta, spending days with the hapless security guard Richard Jewell, wrongly accused by the F.B.I., NBC, and the *Atlanta Journal-Constitution* of a terrorist attack on the 1996 Atlanta Olympics. It took Jewell months to escape from the machinations of the F.B.I. He was rescued by a quirky contrarian local lawyer named Watson Bryant who had once employed Jewell as an office boy. How could the news outlets have gotten it so wrong? Why was I not surprised?

The answer is perhaps rooted in my childhood in San Antonio. My father, feisty and opinionated, styled himself as a self-appointed one-man district attorney's office. He was a businessman; his day job was running a small chain of discount department stores, but his hobby was exposing, as he phrased it, "the god damn hypocrites and corrupt sons of bitches" who lived around us in our leafy garden suburb. I have written before of my gratitude for the background music of my growing up years—the pounding of my father's typewriter keys churning out furious letters to editors and the heads of the Federal Trade Commission, and the copy for the thousands of handbills that every day would be placed in the shopping bags of Solo-Serve, the discount store that was started by my grandfather, a Mexican immigrant by way of the Baltic. His mission in 1919 was revolutionary: Solo-Serve was South Texas's first "clerkless store" and welcomed all customers, especially the Mexican-Americans who were forced to use separate entrances at Texas schools.

Who and what didn't my father take on? The tax frauds and attempts to demolish historic Mexican-American neighborhoods for real estate development that were being perpetrated by San Antonio's social set; the escalation of South Texas electrical power rates that would implicate a prominent local lawyer and his client, Houston's oil magnate Oscar Wyatt, the chairman of Coastal States, who was often splashed in *Vogue* and *Town and Country*, with his wife, the ebullient social swan Lynn. Wyatt later pleaded guilty to foreign trading violations for his relationship with Saddam Hussein.

My father's own command post was a glassed-in office on the second floor of his downtown store where he loved to bark into the public address system. "Attention, shoppers," he once announced in his deep Texas drawl, "the chairman of the Estée Lauder Company is in our stores today in the cosmetics department trying to find out how we are able to sell his products at 50 percent off what you buy them for in New York. I want y'all to go and tell him a big Texas hello!" He came home gleeful at the melee he had caused. As an advertiser responsible for multiple pages of weekly Solo-Serve coupon specials, he was tolerated by the local newspaper editors and publishers, and beloved by reporters, who relied on him for scoops, but loathed by many of the husbands of my mother's friends and members of our temple who were occasionally the targets of his investigations. The implicit message of my childhood was that it was our moral duty to speak out against injustice loudly and often, no matter who might be offended. I'm not sure this lesson did me any favors beyond the essential one of setting me on my path as a reporter.

There was no other profession I could choose. Tom Wolfe had thrown down the gauntlet and lured in just about anyone who had ever thought about lifting a pen, hooking us with his neon language and Fourth of July word explosions that made vivid the race car drivers and the follies of the nouveau riche and limousine liberals, including the art collector Ethel Scull, whose pineapple-colored hair and taxi fleet owner husband allowed her to buy walls of Andy Warhols. And there was Wolfe himself in Austin, speaking to a standing-room-only crowd at the University of Texas in 1969. I jammed myself into the room to hear my idol and, during the question and answer session, waved my hand until Wolfe looked my way. Then, nerves overcame me. All I could stammer was, "What did Ethel Scull think of the story you wrote about her?" The question, fifty years later, still mortifies with its naïve assumption that what anyone thinks matters, but Wolfe, always so kind and impeccable, took the time to answer. "Well, she did not like it very much," he said. The assertion of fact with its unspoken corollary—what difference does it make?—delivered by this god in his white linen suit was, for me, the beginning of liberation.

———

Like Marie Colvin, I fell in love with the exhilaration of reporting, the flow state where your obsession to Get the Story makes all distractions melt away. My father lived to be almost ninety and encouraged me to go after the corporate scoundrels of the 1990s—the Brown & Williamson Tobacco Company, which poisoned its products; the Houston thugs who ran Enron; Michael Milken and his junk bond schemes; the F.B.I. and its false accusation and tarnishing of the reputation of Richard Jewell; and the crass opportunism of New York real estate con man Donald Trump and his mentor, the moral monster and rogue darling of the New York establishment Roy Cohn. "Those sons of bitches!" he said in his last years. "How do they get away with it?"

"I would fly to Canada for a bobby pin," one writer told me, describing her research methods, not long after I joined *Vanity Fair* in 1984. We were given the expense accounts and salaries to be able to do such things and were ferried about the city in sleek black town cars from a company called Big Apple. All day long they idled, tying up the traffic, firmly double-parked outside the Condé Nast Building at Madison Avenue and Forty-fourth Street. Take a subway? Why bother? It was boom time in the world of media. Anyone who had a major role in what we now quaintly refer to as "a content company"—then defined as a movie studio, a network, a talent agency, or a newspaper or magazine—was treated as if he or she was a god on Mount Olympus. Incredibly, in the atmosphere of surging magazine sales and new magazine start-ups that all attempted to describe the bonfire of 1980s vanities, we traveled the world and would linger for weeks, hoping to get a source to talk, turning in five-figure expense accounts for stories that could run eighteen thousand words. Fly to the South of

France with one of the editors in hopes of snaring an interview with the deposed Haitian dictator Jean-Claude Duvalier? Not a problem. Weeks were spent near Moulin de Mougins, three-star meals charged without a thought. The interview was finally secured because of the intense vanity of Michelle Duvalier, the wife of "Baby Doc" Duvalier—*Madame le President,* as she insisted we call her. "Why didn't you tell me that I would be photographed by Helmut Newton?" she asked (referring to that decade's most celebrated chronicler of the beau monde) when we stuffed a final note inside her gate. The brazen larcenies of Michelle Duvalier, a former fashion model who appeared at our interview in a jewel-encrusted appliquéd jacket, had taken $500 million from a country where the average yearly income was $300. Mired in splendor on the Riviera, she spent much of our interview complaining because the locals hated her and she had to make dinner reservations under an assumed name—and she was forced to give her husband a manicure every fortnight.

On the same trip, I visited Graham Greene, perhaps the finest literary stylist of the century, in his modest one-bedroom flat in the port of Antibes. Greene wrote on a card table and was mildly irritated when I expressed surprise. "What else would I need?" he asked me. Then the man who had defined the barbaric Haiti of the Duvaliers in his masterpiece, *The Comedians,* said, "You can kill a conscience over time. Baby Doc proves that."

It was not all glamorous or luxe. From time to time I felt in some degree of danger. Landing in Kabul in the summer of 2004, there were explosions nightly and a guard posted outside my door. "Keep your windows closed," my fixer, Samir, cautioned as we drove into Herat in search of a warlord and anyone who could tell us anything about the location of Osama Bin-Laden. My reporting in that period as well took me to the most dismal areas in the outskirts of Paris, where the police often failed to respond to crime. There, I found a terrified group of Muslim women trying to assimilate. Their terror was of their families, who insisted that they marry and return to Algeria or Tunisia, to remain in a more traditional life. Their fear was real—already five thousand French women reportedly had been virtually kidnapped, as France grappled with its failure to come to embrace their immigrant population.

As I write in June of 2018, America and the world are in the grip of a political and cultural civil war, ramped up by the machinations of a president who appears untethered from any sense of legal reality, respect for our institutions, or moral core. As corrupt as the Duvaliers, he has installed his children in positions of power and enrichment. The frame of our daily life is now dictated by the scolds and pronouncements of cable TV and the urgencies of infotainment news that helped to create Trump and define the era. All of this was done with the implicit acquiescence of a New York establishment that helped Trump rise to power, pushing his buffoon antics into frequent headlines in the 1980s and 1990s while reporting in whispers to each other his vulgar asides, as if the display of his id was somehow an art form.

Perhaps it was. His ghostwriter Tony Schwartz perpetrated the Trump myth in *The Art of the Deal,* baffling his colleagues for his willingness to sign on as a Trump biographer. Eventually he realized that he had helped to create "a Frankenstein who got up from the table," as former *New York* editor Edward Kosner phrased it.

That phrase would be used and used again, as well as all the others that have defined this era—"we are beyond the tipping point"; "we are in uncharted territory"; "he doesn't know what he doesn't know"—and have been rendered meaningless by the constant barrage of cable TV against forces that cannot be shamed or, as of this moment, stopped.

I was reporting for Ed Kosner and his *New York* in 1980, just after Trump burst onto the scene. It was a moment when the city still hovered in the twilight of a world controlled by the Tammany bosses and the Favor Bank politics of the party bosses. The elite old-money values of the WASP power structure were evaporating. Few would mourn the passing of their predatory monopolies and quotas—or almost complete exclusion of women and minorities in jobs, clubs, and real estate. The ad "You don't have to be Jewish to love Levy's Rye Bread" seemed revolutionary when it appeared in the 1960s, but the snobberies and anti-Semitism depicted in *Gentleman's Agreement* seemed almost as relevant a decade later. Soon all of that would change: We were hovering on the edge of the volcano of deregulation brought by newly elected president Ronald Reagan and the greed and glory of the Wall Street buccaneers. Trump rode the gossip columns, shamelessly called the columnists pretending to be a Trump PR man, and charmed his way into Manhattan with his rogue antics. For a generation that had grown up in the sixties, the kid from Queens sticking his fingers in the eyes of authority was catnip, and we could not get enough of him. "I called Trump every time I wanted to juice up my copy," the *New York Times* reporter Maggie Haberman said recently.

Trump was, for all of us, irresistible, even as a target. Everything about him was fishy, I wrote in 1980, not least his antics in getting the Hyatt hotel developed in a desolate part of Forty-second Street near Grand Central Terminal. He spoke to his lawyer Roy Cohn at least "a dozen times a day," Cohn preened from his shambles of an office with dusty stuffed frogs decorating every surface. He was obsessed with his young protégé. "Donald can't make a move without me," Cohn said, as if he wished they were lovers. Trump had transferred from Fordham to the Wharton School, where my older brother Carl was in his class. Learning I had been assigned to write about him, my brother laughed. "That jerk. He had no friends and rode around in a limousine talking about his father's deals in Queens." At the time, the future actress Candice Bergen was also at Penn. Trump called her for a date and appeared, she later remembered, in a maroon jacket that matched his limousine. "I'm a vegetarian," she told him. "That's good," he said. "We are going to a steak house." He was all id, even then, a man-child trying to hide what seemed to be anxiety about himself. By the time he was in his thirties, the bully-boy tactics and flouting of all rules began to leak into public view, but the lack of censure of his corrosive persona was impossible to predict. The bankruptcies and financial shenanigans that sank his empire in 1990 will be seen as predictive when the Trump bubble finally bursts. America will be affected for decades to come.

I mentioned the ways subjects respond to profiles. I wrote a piece about Donald Trump in *Vanity Fair* in 1990, as Trump's world seemed about to collapse. He was close to bankruptcy and had left his wife Ivana, moving to a separate apartment at the Trump Tower, where he was reportedly spending his day eating hamburgers and fries in front of a large TV. I have never written about Trump's reaction to my reporting. Upset that I reported for *Vanity Fair* that he kept a copy of *My New Order*, Hitler's speeches and pronouncements, by his bed, Trump went on a rampage, appearing with anchorwoman Barbara Walters in prime time to announce he was suing me. Of course he never did. Instead, for a decade, he attacked me as "an unattractive reporter with men issues" in the tabloids, and in his own book, *Trump: The Art of the Comeback*. I am happy to report that he described "After the Gold Rush" as "one of the worst stories ever written about me."

And that brings us to the wine. Since 1991, the wine Trump may or not have poured down my dress—or over my head, in one Trump retelling—has changed color and amount depending on who recounts the tale. Trump told *New Yorker* writer Mark Singer that he threw red wine on me. Singer was gallant enough not to report whatever else he said.

Trump's inability to tell the truth extended even to misstating his form of revenge on my reporting.

At a charity dinner, almost a year after my twelve-thousand-word story appeared, Trump slipped behind me as I sat with friends and took a half glass of white wine and poured it down my black jacket. I thought it was a waiter and did not flinch, but the faces at the table froze in horror. Trump scurried out the door, a coward's coward, incapable of even facing me. I will never be able to express my gratitude for Trump's remark to Mark Singer. That half glass of wine has become a badge of honor.

What was it that really angered Donald Trump in "After the Gold Rush"? The fact that he had grifted—among others—his close associate Louise Sunshine, who had to borrow $1 million from her friend the developer Leonard Stern to retain property rights in one of his buildings? Or that his children did not speak to him? The detail that stays with me occurred in the press room of the New York State Courthouse in lower Manhattan. Trump was fighting a brutal case brought against him by scores of Polish immigrant workers who allegedly had been paid under the minimum wage to build the Trump Tower. The tabloids had turned on Trump, accusing him of paying "slave wages," exploiting the Polish workers. Trump settled, at a cost, it was said at the time, of millions of dollars. I made my way to the press room to hear my colleagues erupt in rage, at themselves and at the man to whom they had devoted so much ink. The babble in 1990 seemed definitive: "We made this monster. We gave him the headlines. We created him. Never again."

The piece I wrote about Marie Colvin—"A Private War"—has been made into a movie. In January of this year, I visited the set. It was snowing in England that day outside London. The movie *A Private War* was being directed by Matt Heineman, adapted from my piece. Heineman, just 34, had been nominated for an Oscar for his documentary *Cartel Land*, but had never made a feature. He had however directed a searing film—*City of Ghosts*—detailing the lives of several of Syria's citizen reporters. He was galvanized by Marie's career and for three years had worked tirelessly to bring her life story to the screen.

The newsroom of the *Sunday Times of London* had been meticulously re-created to look like the newsroom that Marie Colvin worked from. I was there to see the actress Rosamund Pike playing Colvin. On the day I visited, a pivotal scene was being filmed. Colvin was determined to get herself assigned to Sri Lanka in April of 2001 to cover a yet unreported scene of hundreds of thousands of refugees who were under siege by government forces. She had a shouting match with her editor in the newsroom. He wanted her to write about the leader of the PLO, Yasser Arafat; she insisted she would go to Sri Lanka. He was furious she had run up $56,000 in SAT phone charges. The Sri Lanka decision was catastrophic for Colvin: She would lose the sight in an eye to a grenade thrown at her when she announced she was a reporter and wear an eye patch for the rest of her life.

The afternoon I spent on the set was unnerving, as I knew what was coming for Colvin once she left the safety of the London newsroom. It was for me a time warp on many levels, not least of which was the atmosphere of the *Sunday Times*. Struggling as a freelance foreign correspondent in the London of the late 1970s, I had the immense good fortune to be befriended by the legendary *Sunday Times* editor Harold Evans, whose investigations into the horrors of thalidomide and the unmasking of the elite spies Kim Philby and Anthony Blunt inspired not only my reporting but also Colvin's. Evans had fallen in love with a young writer, Tina Brown, and had brought her to dinner. "Use my telex room any time you want to send your copy," Evans told me. "Just take the telex operator a bottle of scotch and tell them I said it was okay." Evans was at the top of his game—the foreign correspondents of the *Sunday Times* were dispatched to every remote war in the world.

That night would begin a long and enduring friendship and two decades of reporting for Tina during her eventual tenure at *Vanity Fair*. Two of these stories—including "After the Gold Rush"—were written with Tina's strong encouragement and editorial hand, Wayne Lawson's sharpened red pencils and rigor enhanced every word I wrote for three decades at the magazine. Trying to close

Trump, my fax machine blipped out all hours of the night with Tina's notes. "Not there yet—" "What does——prove?" "You need more sources." I tried to sleep but heard the beep of the fax machine until dawn. "Can you get more inside?" "Can you go deeper and more reflective? It needs more you." She was right—and is responsible for the macabre final scene at the courthouse.

If you are lucky as a reporter, you get that kind of editing—and the ethical judgments that accompany it. In 1995, I returned to *Vanity Fair* from *The New Yorker* to write about the hypocrisy of CBS killing a *60 Minutes* episode that featured a mysterious tobacco whistleblower—so as-yet-unknown that we called him Jeffrey "Wee-gand." I had gone back to work at *Vanity Fair* at the gracious invitation of Graydon Carter, whom I had only briefly worked with before. At a lucky lunch with a close friend named Andrew Tobias, an anti-tobacco activist and later the Democratic National Committee treasurer, Andy quickly set me on the right course on the subject of Jeffrey Wigand. "It's not about CBS. It's about who is the whistleblower and what does he know?" he said. I took that back to Carter, who said, "Christ. Let me find out how much advertising we get from Brown & Williamson." He came back the next day. "Go for it. It's only $500,000."

It took weeks to discover that "Wee-gand" was in fact pronounced "WY-gand," and that he was being smeared by John Scanlon, a genial public relations man who had taken $1 million from Brown & Williamson to demolish Wigand's reputation. Scanlon was a close friend of Carter's as well as a *Vanity Fair* consultant. "I can't go forward with this unless John is put on leave," I told Carter, unsure of his reaction. He did not hesitate. "He is out as of now," he said. Their friendship would never fully recover, but Carter did not change a word of the lengthy description of Scanlon and his machinations detailed in the eighteen-thousand-word "The Man Who Knew Too Much."

Carter stayed at *Vanity Fair* for twenty-five years and sent me to India to report on 26/11 and the terrorists who overtook the Taj Palace in Mumbai; to France, on multiple occasions, to report on the rise of anti-Semitism; to Afghanistan; and to England to chronicle the life of Marie Colvin. He knew legal dramas attracted me and called when one caught his attention—Richard Jewell; the savaging of the Haitian immigrant Abner Louima by a New York City police detective; the build up to the Iraq War in 2003. Over the years, we did dozens of stories together, several of which would be beautifully edited by Wayne Lawson's successor, Mark Rozzo. A few years ago, Graydon collected them and presented them to me in a stylish leather-bound volume that he had archly titled *Dynasties, Angels and Compromising Positions*. On the spine, I saw his display title: *The Brenner Years in Vanity Fair*. The reporter in me wondered: *was he telling me to retire?* He was not.

Our last story together was the profile that closes this collection: Graydon and my current editor David Friend divined it was time to revisit the history of Trump's mentor Roy Cohn and his long, sordid association with his final prodigy, Donald Trump. As always with Graydon, an elegant typed thank-you on a Smythson's card appeared after the story was published. This one was particularly poignant. Graydon had made the decision to retire, but I did not know it yet. He had written profoundly and at length, month after month, in his editor's letter, about the rise of the moral monsters around Trump and felt the time had come to move on. In his note, he seemed almost sentimental about the rogues and con men that had fed both our careers. How had we both started out thinking and writing about Roy Cohn and Donald Trump, and how could we still be grappling decades later with their legacy? "To think it would all resurface today," he noted, restraint hardly disguising the emotions he kept in check.

MARIE COLVIN'S
PRIVATE WAR

AUGUST 2012

"They just don't make men like they used to."

“W hy the fuck is that guy singing? Can't someone shut him up?" Marie Colvin whispered urgently after dropping into the long, dark, dank tunnel that would lead her to the last reporting assignment of her life. It was the night of February 20, 2012. All Colvin could hear was the piercing sound made by the Free Syrian Army commander accompanying her and the photographer Paul Conroy: *"Allahu Akbar. Allahu Akbar."* The song, which permeated the two-and-a-half-mile abandoned storm drain that ran under the Syrian city of Homs, was both a prayer (God is great) and a celebration. The singer was jubilant that the *Sunday Times* of London's renowned war correspondent Marie Colvin was there. But his voice unnerved Colvin. "Paul, do something!" she demanded. "Make him stop!"

For anyone who knew her, Colvin's voice was unmistakable. All her years in London had not subdued her American whiskey tone. Just as memorable was the cascade of laughter that always erupted when there seemed to be no way out. It was not heard that night as she and Conroy made their way back into a massacre being perpetrated by the troops of President Bashar al-Assad near Syria's western border. The ancient city of Homs was now a bloodbath.

"Can't talk about the way in, it is the artery for the city and I promised to reveal no details," Colvin had emailed her editor after she and Conroy made their first trip into Homs, three days earlier. They had arrived late Thursday night, thirty-six hours away from press deadline, and Colvin knew that the foreign desk in London would soon be bonkers. The day before she walked into the apartment building in Homs where two grimy rooms were set up as a temporary media center, the top floor had been sheared off by rockets. Many thought the attack had been deliberate. The smell of death assaulted Colvin as mutilated bodies were rushed out to a makeshift clinic blocks away.

At 7:40 a.m., Colvin had opened her laptop and emailed her editor. There wasn't a hint of panic or apprehension in her exuberant tone: "No other Brits here. Have heard that Spencer and Chulov of the Torygraph [*Private Eye*'s nickname for the *Telegraph*] and *Guardian* trying to make it here but so far we have leapfrogged ahead of them. Heavy shelling this morning."

She was in full command of her journalistic powers; the turbulence of her London life had been left behind. Homs, Colvin wrote a few hours later, was "the symbol of the revolt, a ghost town, echoing with the sound of shelling and crack of sniper fire, the odd car careening down a street at speed. Hope to get to a conference hall basement where 300 women and children living in the cold and dark. Candles, one baby born this week without medical care, little

22

food." In a field clinic, she later observed plasma bags suspended from wooden coat hangers. The only doctor was a veterinarian.

Now, on her way back into Homs, Colvin moved slowly, crouching in the four-and-a-half-foot-high tunnel. Fifty-six years old, she wore her signature—a black patch over her left eye, lost to a grenade in Sri Lanka in 2001. Every twenty minutes or so, the sound of an approaching motorcycle made her and Conroy flatten themselves against the wall. Conroy could see injured Syrians strapped on the backs of the vehicles. He worried about Colvin's vision and her balance; she had recently recovered from back surgery. "Of all the trips we had done together, this one was complete insanity," Conroy told me.

The journey had begun in a muddy field, where a concrete slab marked the entrance to the tunnel. They had been taken through orchards by former military officers fighting against al-Assad. "We move when it's dark," one of them said. "After that, just hand signals. No noise until we are in the tunnel."

The night was cold, the sky lit with hundreds of rocket missiles. Inside Homs, twenty-eight thousand people were surrounded by al-Assad's troops. Food supplies and power had been cut off, and foreign reporters had been banned. In Beirut earlier, Colvin had learned that the army was under orders to kill journalists. They had two options for penetrating the occupied area: race across a highway swept by floodlights or crawl for hours through a frigid tunnel. "Paul, I don't like this," she said.

Syria under al-Assad broke all rules of war. In Libya in 2011, Colvin and Conroy had spent months sleeping on floors in the besieged city of Misrata, living on "the war-zone diet"—Pringles, tuna, granola bars, and water—relying on each other for survival. Their arena was the closed world of war: one-room concrete safe houses with cheap Bokhara carpets and a diesel stove in the middle, mint tea offered by Free Syrian Army soldiers.

They were an unlikely pair. Conroy, a decade younger and a natural comedian, was called "the Scouser" by his colleagues for his working-class Liverpool accent. His sharp cheekbones and high brow reminded them of the actor Willem Dafoe. Colvin was the daughter of two Long Island public-school teachers, but she had the air of an aristocrat. Her nails were a perfect scarlet, and her double strand of pearls was a gift from Yasser Arafat. In a war zone, Colvin always wore a brown jacket with "TV" in large letters of silver gaffer tape on the back. Not this time: She was well aware that she could be a target for al-Assad's soldiers, so she wore a Prada black nylon quilted coat as camouflage.

As they left for the second trip, they learned that there would be no space for them to carry flak jackets, helmets, or video equipment. Trained as an artillery officer in the British army, Conroy counted the rockets coming down and clocked forty-five explosions a minute. "Every bone in my body is telling me not to do this," he said. Colvin listened to him carefully, her head cocked to one side. "Those are your concerns," she said. "I'm going in, no matter what. I'm the reporter, you're the photographer. If you want, you can stay here." It was the first argument they had ever had. "You know I'll never leave you," Conroy said.

For Colvin, the facts were clear: A murderous dictator was bombarding a city that had no food, power, or medical supplies. NATO and the United Nations stood by doing nothing. In a nearby village, hours before they left, Conroy had watched her trying to get a signal and file her story for the next day's paper on her vintage satellite phone. "Why is the world not here?" she asked her assistant in London. That question, posed by Colvin so many times before—in East Timor, Libya, Kosovo, Chechnya, Iran, Iraq, Sri Lanka—was the continuing theme of her life. "The next war I cover," she had written in 2001, "I'll be more awed than ever by the quiet bravery of civilians who endure far more than I ever will."

Surrounded by members of the Free Syrian Army, Colvin had gathered the essentials for the return trip: the Thuraya SAT phone, a battered laptop, La Perla briefs, and her lucky copy of Martha Gellhorn's *The Face of War*, essays detailing wars, many of them waged before Colvin was born. At night, she would often reread Gellhorn's leads: *War started at 9:00 o'clock promptly.*

"Hey, Marie, welcome back to hell," said a Syrian activist huddled on the floor of the media center. All the other reporters had left. As always, when she was in a Muslim country, the first thing Colvin did was take her shoes off and leave them in the hall. In Syria, she found herself in a still-uncharted arena for war reporters—a YouTube war. She and Conroy watched as Syrian activists uploaded videos of the battle of Homs. "I am in a place where the locals are uploading videos etc so I think internet security is pretty much out the window," she had emailed her editor.

At 11:08 p.m., she emailed Richard Flaye, the current man in her life:

My darling, I have come back in to Baba Amr, the besieged neighbourhood of Homs, and am now freezing in my hovel with no windows. I just thought, I cannot cover the modern day Srebrenica from the suburbs. You would have laughed. I had to climb over two stone walls tonight, and had trouble with the second (six feet) so a rebel made a cat's cradle of his two hands and said, 'Step here and I will give you a lift up.' Except he thought I was much heavier than I am, so when he 'lifted' my foot, he launched me right over the wall and I landed on my head in the mud! . . . I will do one more week here, and then leave. Every day is a horror. I think of you all the time, and I miss you.

It was the last email she would ever send him.

THE SILVER GIRL

I arrived in London a few weeks after Colvin's death forced the world to pay attention to the atrocities in Syria. It was a brutal winter for journalists: Anthony Shadid, forty-three, of the *New York Times*, had died while attempting to cross the Syria-Turkey border. The French photographer Rémi Ochlik had been killed along with Colvin. At Rupert Murdoch's press empire, there were charges of hacking phones, bribing police, and trading favors with prime ministers. The company was in desperate need of a Joan of Arc, and in Colvin it found one. As foreign staffs around the world had been disbanded because of budget cuts and threats to reporters' security, Colvin's process still resembled Martha Gellhorn's. Her notes were meticulously kept in spiral notebooks lined up on her office shelf at her house in Hammersmith, on the Thames. Nearby, a stack of business cards: Marie Colvin, foreign affairs correspondent. The role had defined her and had become, tragically, irrevocable.

Colvin's boldness in war zones across the world could appear like a form of derring-do or addiction to the poison elixir of battle, as one reporter called it, but the truth was more complex. For years, the ferocious competition for scoops in the British foreign press thrilled Colvin and completely suited her nature. More, she had a deep commitment to reporting the truth.

By accident, I was an hour early for the celebration in Colvin's honor at the Frontline Club, a gathering spot for journalists near Paddington Station. Organizers were trying to make the sound system work, and suddenly Colvin's voice filled the room. She appeared on a TV monitor in a car outside an Iraqi prison in 2003. To her fixer in the backseat, Colvin says with fierce quiet, "Calm down. You getting excited makes the situation worse." Then, to the driver, "Get out of here!" The steadiness of her gaze stops all debate. The footage came from Barbara Kopple's 2005 documentary, *Bearing Witness*.

Among the scores of guests were Colvin's editors John Witherow and Sean Ryan, the actress Diana Quick, and *Vanity Fair*'s London editor, Henry Porter. The historian Patrick Bishop, an ex-husband, and a number of former lovers were there, along with Flaye, as well as intimate friends, including the author Lady Jane Wellesley; two Bonham Carter sisters, Virginia and Jane; Rosie Boycott, the former editor of the *Daily Express* and the *Independent*; and British *Vogue* editor Alexandra Shulman. The room also held dozens of young reporters whom Colvin had mentored with her astonishing generosity. "You always have to think about the risk and the reward. Is the danger worth it?" she had once advised Miles Amoore in Afghanistan.

From her earliest days as the American girl in the small, clubby world of British journalism, Colvin appeared to play beautifully into the paradigm of reporting as a bit of a lark, not to be taken too seriously, as if she had parachuted in from the pages of Evelyn Waugh's *Scoop*. In truth, Colvin identified with her subjects and found her own emotions in their plights. Her particular talent was giving voice to the voiceless—widows holding their mangled husbands in Kosovo, Tamil Tigers rebelling against the government in Sri Lanka. "The first sound of trouble was the screams of two little old ladies who slashed themselves on the razor coils topping the walls of the United Nations compound, desperate to enter," Colvin had reported from the East Timor city of Dili in 1999. It was, she always believed, her finest hour. For four days straight, she broadcast the plight of a thousand victims, mostly women and children, trapped in a siege that had killed thousands of Timorese. "Who's there? . . . Where have all the men gone?" her editor in London asked when she announced that she and two female Dutch journalists had stayed behind to help the stranded refugees. "They just don't make men like they used to," she replied. The line would become part of her growing legend.

Colvin's story recounting the river of blood that flowed out of her mouth when she was left to die in Sri Lanka in 2001 also became part of her myth, as would the quiet eloquence that set her apart from the cliché of the war correspondent as adrenaline junkie with a death wish. "Bravery is not being afraid to be afraid," she said when she accepted an award for her work in Sri Lanka.

Though her dispatches brought her numerous awards and fame in England and in every major conflict zone in the world, she was less known in her own country. Unlike Gellhorn, she did not leave a literary legacy; her genius was for low-to-the-ground news-paper reporting. Her writing had a strong moral undertow. She functioned best when she was on the scene. In spite of the massive changes of the last twenty-five years brought on by the high-tech presence of Twitter and YouTube, Colvin continued to believe that war reporting remained the same: You had to be there. "How do I keep my craft alive in a world that doesn't value it? I feel like I am the last reporter in the YouTube world," she told her close friend Katrina Heron. "I am inept with technology." Heron, the former editor of *Wired*, sent her frequent tech advice.

She pushed into combat zones that made her drivers sometimes vomit from fear. Yet she dreaded becoming "this smelly, exhausted pseudo-man," as she wrote in British *Vogue* in 2004 when explain-ing her "defiant preference" for satin and lace underwear in the trenches. In the hospital recovering from shrapnel wounds in the head and chest in Sri Lanka, she received a missive from her editor, who had seen pictures of her wounded and seminaked in the field. He asked her to "tell us about your lucky red bra." He did not real-ize that the bra was "cream (lace cups, double satin straps) but had turned red because it was drenched in my blood," Colvin wrote. She added that militia had broken into her hotel room in East Timor and that "all my La Perla knickers and bras had been stolen. How weird is that?" They had "left behind a radio, tape recorder . . . even a flak jacket." Not long before she left for Homs, she told Heron, "I would like to have a saner life. I just don't know how."

In London, she rarely talked about her fieldwork. "Hornet, make me a huge martini right this second!" she would demand as she breezed into the kitchen of *Chariots of Fire* director Hugh Hudson, whom she had nicknamed after the vintage car. If she talked about her travels, she would lighten them with a flawless imitation of a despot guaranteed to get a laugh. "I don't want to be the kind of person about whom they say as you move up to the bar, 'Oh, god, here comes the experiences in Beirut again,'" she once wrote. Former *Sunday Times* editor Andrew Neil recalled the day in 1994 he got swept up in his star reporter's carousel: "Suddenly I found myself in a taxi being uprooted from my hotel to a secret and god-awful place in downtown New York where I was to meet the most astonishing Saudi defector. How would she do it? I have no idea. There I was, powerless under Marie's spell."

There were no boundaries in her friendships; guerrilla fighters, refugees, movie stars, and writers would appear at her parties. "She stayed in many ways a wayward teenager," one friend said. She was careless when it came to bills, taxes, and expense-account receipts, and she failed to deliver books she promised publishers. In Iraq in 2003, Colvin accidentally left her SAT phone on, and the paper had to cover a $37,000 bill. She laughed loudest at herself—chain-smoking, starting to serve supper at midnight, drunk, and realizing she had forgotten to turn on the stove.

"THE SILVER GIRL SAILS OFF INTO THE NIGHT," the *Sunday Times* headlined the inside spread of its special section, where Colvin was pictured in a tiny bikini on Richard Flaye's sailboat. A fierce dieter, she would have been delighted to see her sveltest self taking up almost half a page. Several memorials referred lightly to Colvin's long nights of drinking. The reality was darker. Often she would disappear for days. "I'm in the hole," she once confided to producer Maryam d'Abo, and she would say the same to friends when they drove to her house, worried that she had slipped back into the terrors of post-traumatic stress disorder (PTSD). An extreme reaction to psychological trauma, PTSD has become a regular news feature, afflicting returning soldiers from Iraq and Afghanistan. The complications—paranoia, alcohol and drug abuse, night terrors—are often slow to appear.

At the Frontline Club, I detected a strong undercurrent in the room. "The *Sunday Times* has blood on its hands," I overheard one writer say. In the days following Colvin's death, there were many unanswered questions: Why didn't she wait to file her copy until she had safely crossed the Lebanese border? What drove her back, knowing that her SAT phone had been compromised and journalists had been targeted? What was a fifty-six-year-old woman with a drinking problem and PTSD doing in the center of a massacre?

A RISING STAR

"Are we really going to do this?" Colvin asked the photographer Tom Stoddart as they stood outside the refugee camp of Bourj el Baranjneh, in West Beirut, in 1987. Beirut was divided by a "Green Line" battle zone—Christians on the east, Muslims on the west. Colvin and Stoddart were recent hires at the *Sunday Times*, covering the conflict between Lebanon and Yasser Arafat's Palestinian Liberation Organization. In the camps, the Palestinians were being starved and were under siege by Amal, the Syrian-backed Shiite militia. Almost seventy women had been gunned down, and sixteen had died.

"Every reporter in Beirut was trying to get into the camp," Stoddart said. "But Marie, with her American charm, had convinced a

31

commander not to shoot us. We had a plan." They would run two hundred yards across a road manned by Amal commanders with rockets. "The idea was that we would hold hands. In case one of us was shot, we could rescue each other." Colvin hesitated, then took Stoddart's hand. "This is what we do," she said calmly, then ran.

The next morning, snipers turned their guns on Haji Achmed Ali, a twenty-two-year-old Palestinian woman, who lay near a pile of rocks by a burned-out car. Blood poured from the wounds in her head and stomach. Colvin took in and described the young woman's tiny gold earrings and "the handful of blood-soaked dirt she had clenched in her pain."

Stoddart captured Colvin by the makeshift operating table, her face glazed with incomprehension. Colvin and Stoddart then had to smuggle the film out of Bourj el Baranjneh. Colvin put the canisters in her underwear, along with a letter Dr. Pauline Cutting, a British surgeon trapped in the camp, had written to Queen Elizabeth, urgently appealing for her help. They fled Beirut on an all-night ferry to Cyprus. Colvin filed her story on a telex. The headline would read "Snipers Stalk Women on the Path of Death." Inside were two full pages of photographs of the young Palestinian woman leaking blood. It was the Ur-moment of Colvin's early London career. But the image of Haji Achmed Ali and her earrings would haunt Colvin's nightmares.

By the time she arrived in London, Colvin had already worked as the Paris bureau chief of UPI. Not long out of Yale, she had so impressed her UPI bosses in Washington that when she threatened to quit if they didn't send her to Paris they did. "I was the bureau chief and everything else, including the desk assistant," Colvin later said of that assignment. But her vision of the future had been shaped by Vietnam and Watergate and fueled by reading the *New York Times* war correspondent Gloria Emerson and the political philosopher Hannah Arendt. Soon, bored by the *jeunesse dorée* of Paris, she realized she was missing a bigger story—a possible war in Libya. In Tripoli, Muammar Qaddafi, an epic thug in a desert filled with oil, was poised in his underground lair, planning terror strikes. "Just go," the then *New York Times* reporter Judith Miller told Colvin, giving her a list of contacts. "Qaddafi is crazy, and he will like you."

When the sleek young reporter appeared at Qaddafi's estate—avoiding any press-corps briefing—the startled guard believed she was French. At forty-five, Qaddafi lived in a palace at the Bab al Azizzia compound, and he had an endless appetite for beautiful women. That night, she was summoned to his chambers.

"It was midnight when Col. Moammar Gadhafi, the man the world loves to hate, walked into the small underground room in a red silk shirt, baggy white silk pants and a gold cape tied at his neck," Colvin began her story, a scoop that went around the world. She had an exquisite eye for detail—Qaddafi's "stack-heeled gray lizard skin slip-ons," TVs replaying his speeches continuously. "I am Qaddafi," he said. She remembered saying to herself, "No kidding," and then spent the next hours fending off his advances.

The UPI bannered the story, and Qaddafi's ardor for her grew stronger. In a later interview, he pressed her to wear "petite green shoes"—his favorite color—and on one occasion he sent a Bulgarian nurse to draw her blood. Colvin refused and soon fled the country.

———

Colvin's mother was visiting her in Paris in 1986 when the invitation came from the *Sunday Times*. "I'm not going to work there!" Marie said. "All my life I wanted to live in Paris, and I'm finally here." Besides, the *Sunday Times* of London had been in turmoil since the Rupert Murdoch takeover. Former editor Harold Evans, whose investigative reporters had revolutionized British journalism, was gone, as was the former owner, Roy Thomson, who had backed the vigorous disclosure of corruption. The new, young editor, Andrew Neil, persuaded Colvin to take the job.

"Who could ever forget the first time they saw Marie? She was a whirl of black curls," said John Witherow. "The impression she gave was quiet authority and immense charm." Colvin, who had just turned thirty, was absorbed into Neil's new team, which included a platoon of dynamic women reporters and one of the finest foreign staffs in the world, known for the vivid, personal style he exacted from them.

Colvin quickly became the Middle East correspondent. Patrick Bishop, then the paper's diplomatic correspondent, encountered her in Iraq, in 1987, monitoring the Iran-Iraq War. Bishop recalled, "There was a bit of shelling going on, and I was anxious to impress her by pointing out the distinction between outgoing and incoming fire. I explained that the bang we had just heard was outgoing and therefore nothing to worry about. Then there was another explosion. 'And that one,' I said, 'is *incoming!*' and threw myself headlong on the ground. As the shell exploded some distance away, I looked up to see the woman I had been trying to show off to, gazing down at me with pity and amusement."

As Bishop was leaving Iraq, he spotted Colvin trying to sneak off to the front. "Don't think of going there," he told her. "It's much too dangerous." She ignored him. "The next thing I know is I see the *Sunday Times*, and there was Marie, inside the lines in Basra," said Bishop.

Next, disguised as a Jewish settler, she got her nose broken when Palestinian demonstrators threw a rock through the window of her car. Then she interviewed Yasser Arafat, who invited her to travel with him on his plane. Those interviews would be part of a BBC documentary on his life that Colvin wrote and produced. He would give her twenty-three more interviews, and she accompanied him to the White House with Yitzhak Rabin. "Just put the pencil down and sign it already," she reportedly told Arafat during the Oslo peace accords of 1993.

She and Bishop were married in August 1989, and the marriage looked like a true love match. Both reared as Catholics, the couple shared a solid middle-class background, parents who were teachers, and families who stressed intellectual achievement. The pressure of war reporting, however, affected them in different ways. Not long after they were married, Colvin discovered that Bishop was having a dalliance with a European journalist. In Iraq, she struggled with reports of his betrayal, but they stayed together. "She would howl into the phone, shouting at him," recalled the reporter Dominique Roch. Colvin never unpacked her wedding presents, which remained in a jumble under the staircase in her home.

That marriage was followed in 1996 by another, to Juan Carlos Gumucio, a well-born Bolivian journalist working for the Spanish newspaper *El País*. "I'm going to have a baby!" Colvin announced to her friends. "That is my dream." Instead, she had two miscarriages, and her volatile new husband proved to have a massive appetite for disputes and alcohol. They separated, and in 1999 Bishop flew to Albania, worried about Colvin's safety in covering Kosovo. "I arrived convinced she was in desperate trouble only to be told that she was at the bar briefing young reporters on the local dangers." They quickly reunited.

Later, in East Timor, the writer Janine di Giovanni saw them happily sitting on a wall in Dili in the midst of the turmoil in the burning capital. "Marie was wearing a pair of white short-shorts and calmly reading a thriller. She looked like an Irving Penn portrait of Babe Paley."

In 2002, Bishop and Colvin were still together when they learned that Gumucio had committed suicide.

"I wake up now many mornings with a slab of cement on my chest," said *Sunday Times* foreign editor Sean Ryan the day we met, not long after Colvin died. The hardworking Ryan was elevated to run the foreign desk in 1998. Though he had done some feature writing from Kosovo and Israel, he had never actually been posted in a war zone. He had occasionally worked on Colvin's stories from Iraq in 1991, when they appeared on the features pages, but soon they were speaking every day, sometimes for an hour. Ryan would now supervise the foreign staff as the paper intensified its personal coverage in order to compete with cable news and the tabloidization of the Murdoch press.

One morning in December 1999, he heard Colvin's voice on the BBC, describing the siege going on in East Timor. "My stomach started churning," he told me. For the next four days, he demanded copy, but Colvin never filed. She was, she said, too busy helping refugees contact their families. "That was life with Marie," he said. "She was a crusader most of all."

A few months later, Ryan's phone rang. "Hey, Sean, I'm lying down in a field, and there's a plane circling overhead. I'll call you back." Colvin was in the middle of another bloodbath, on the Russian border with Chechnya. Before she left, Bishop had angrily warned her, "You will get stuck there if you go to that massacre. The Russians are targeting journalists." Bishop was frightened about the danger Colvin would face. For years he had called his friend Witherow repeatedly to pull her out of battle areas. "You cannot allow Marie to do this," he had said in 1991, when she was one of the first British journalists inside Iraq in the early stages of the Gulf War. "She doesn't want to come back," Witherow answered. "Order her," Bishop said.

When she landed in Georgia, she was drunk, her Russian photographer, Dmitry Beliakov, later told the *Sunday Times*. "The Chechens who came to take us were shocked. She was a woman, and it was Ramadan. The next morning she knocked on my door, pale from a hangover, and we talked. Or she talked and I listened. It was clear she knew what she was doing. She said, 'If you aren't sure of me, don't go.'"

After Colvin was smuggled into Chechnya, the leader would not shake her hand, because she was a woman. Colvin told him, "There is no woman in this room, only a journalist." She found children who had been shot by drunken Russians for their amusement. When the car she was in was blasted by shrapnel at night, she fled into a field of beech trees. It "felt like a death trap," she wrote in her report. "I spent 12 hours yesterday pinned down in a field by a road The planes, evil machines . . . circled again and again . . .

dropping bombs that whined as loudly as high-speed trains as they fell."

Bishop flew to Tbilisi, the Georgian capital, to help with her rescue. Colvin's only way out in subzero temperatures was across a twelve-thousand-foot mountain range. A Chechen guide took her and Beliakov zigzagging up sheets of ice. Colvin was carrying a computer and a satellite phone and wearing a flak jacket, a weight of thirty pounds. At one point, Beliakov threatened suicide. At another, Colvin plunged into icy water. She jettisoned the flak jacket and kept the phone. It took them four days to reach the border and cross over into Georgia. They found an abandoned shepherd's hut, but their only food consisted of three jars of peach jam and some flour, which they mixed with fetid melted snow into a paste.

Bishop and the senior correspondent Jon Swain beseeched the American Embassy for help as Colvin fled the hut. Her party stumbled for days through a series of deserted villages. Suddenly she saw "an Ernest Hemingway figure," who said, "Jack Harriman, American Embassy. Are we glad to find you." Reunited with Bishop, Colvin later made light of it all. When she joined her friend Jane Wellesley at her country house for New Year's, she said, "If I hadn't had this hideously expensive anorak you made me buy, I wouldn't have made it."

"YOU ONLY CRY WHEN YOU BLEED"

"So, this Oyster Bay—what kind of place is it?" the poet Alan Jenkins once asked Colvin of the town near where she grew up. "Oyster Bay? It's just a little fishing village," she said, and laughed when Jenkins later discovered it was an area filled with the very rich and social. In fact, Colvin came from East Norwich, the solidly middle-class next town over. At Yale, Colvin confided to close friends that she often felt insecure among her classmates. During high school, she had worked at the local yacht club for spending money. Her mother, Rosemarie, the first college graduate in her family, had grown up in Queens and fallen in love with a handsome Fordham student who was also studying to be an English teacher. Just out of the Marines in World War II, Bill Colvin was passionate about literature and Democratic politics. "My parents had a storybook marriage," Marie's younger sister Cathleen, known as Cat, now a corporate lawyer, told me. "Our father doted on Marie." The oldest of five children, Marie filled the house with her projects—fruit flies, architectural models. At night, Bill read his children all of Dickens and James Fenimore Cooper. Weekends, he packed the family into the car and drove to political rallies. A passionate Kennedy supporter, Bill later worked briefly for New York governor Hugh Carey.

"You only cry when you bleed," Rosemarie told her children, a mantra Marie took to heart. By the time she was a teenager, she had the confidence and moxie of a daddy's girl, but her relationship with her father became stormy as she battled for independence. Determined to have her own sailboat, she saved up money from babysitting. A girl of her era—the late 1960s—she would sneak out the window and spend nights smoking pot with her friends. "Bill did not know what to do with her," Rosemarie said. She made straight As, was a National Merit finalist, and took off for Washington to protest the war in Vietnam. "She and my father were so much alike in their visions that it was destined that they collide," Cat said. Years later, in London, Colvin would tell Patrick Bishop that she had run away to Brazil—a classic Colvin dramatization of the facts. She actually went as an exchange student and lived with a wealthy Brazilian family. "She came back sleek and chic and determined she was going to live out of East Norwich," Cat recalled.

In Brazil, Colvin had neglected to apply to college. When she returned, in the middle of her senior year, the deadlines were long past. As the family story has it, she said, "I'm going to Yale," and took the car to New Haven. "With her was her high-school transcript and her test scores—two 800s," said Rosemarie. The next day she was back. "I'm in." Soon after she entered Yale, she met Katrina Heron, and they quickly became a trio with Bobby Shriver, the son of Sargent Shriver, the founder of the Peace Corps. For a class taught by John Hersey, Colvin read his masterpiece, *Hiroshima*, and she began to write for the *Yale Daily News*. That fall, Bill Colvin discovered an advanced cancer. Marie was inconsolable when he died. "It broke something in her," Heron said. To all of Colvin's friends, her father remained a mystery figure. It was as if a part of her froze at the moment he died. Her guilt about their unresolved relationship haunted her, Bishop told me. But with Cat, her closest confidante, she frequently talked about her anger and her failure to restore the special affection they had had when she was a child.

Sent to Sri Lanka in April 2001, Colvin delivered an interview with a commander of the controversial and brutal antiregime Tamil Tigers, in which she highlighted that there were 340,000 refugees in what she described as "an unreported humanitarian crisis—people starving, international aid agencies banned from distributing food . . . no fuel for cars, water pumps, or lighting."

"She could have spent the night and probably have left safely the next morning," Jon Swain said. Instead, she fled through a cashew plantation and had to dodge army patrols. Trapped as flares from a nearby base swept the ground, Colvin had to make a difficult decision: Should she identify herself as a journalist? Had she not, she later said, she would have been slaughtered as a Tamil rebel. "Journalist! American!" she yelled as she felt searing heat in her head. A bursting grenade had punctured one of her lungs and destroyed her left eye. "Doctor!" she shouted when soldiers arrived and tore off her shirt, searching for weapons. "Admit that you came to kill us," an officer demanded and threw her into the back of a truck.

"I was uninjured until I yelled 'journalist' and then they fired the grenade. The nightmare for me is always that decision about yelling. My brain leaves out the pain," Colvin told the author Denise Leith. "They made me walk to them. I knew that if I fell they would shoot so I had them put a light on me before I would stand up, but I lost so much blood that I fell down, literally I replay that whole walk endlessly in the nightmare. I know that it is my brain trying to find a different resolution. 'This body didn't have to be shot.'"

On the phone, Sean Ryan could hear Marie screaming in a hospital, "Fuck off!" Ryan said he was relieved, at least, "that she sounded like Marie." Later she told him that she had fended off a doctor who was trying to take out her eye. Flown to New York to be operated on, she filed three thousand words from her hospital bed. "My God, what will happen if I go blind?" she asked Cat. "I wish I could cry," she told the TV news editor Lindsey Hilsum. "So many Tamils have called to offer me their eyes." As she was slowly recuperating, a worried Ryan told Rosemarie to get her psychological support, but Colvin resisted.

Back in London, Colvin was convinced that work would cure her. "I started to worry that she was self-medicating with alcohol," Heron told me. Meanwhile, her editors gave her a heroine's welcome and praised her stiff-upper-lip valor.

Ryan became alarmed when she called him, yelling, "Someone at the paper is trying to humiliate me!" A story of hers had run with a headline that used the term "evil eye," and Colvin saw that as a plot against her. "It was bewildering, and the first sign that Marie was having a stress reaction," Ryan remembered. Alarmed, Cat could not get her on the phone. "I've thrown my cell phone into the river," Marie told her. "I'm not getting out of my bed ever."

Two close friends encouraged her to get counseling, and she sought treatment at a military hospital by someone who understood PTSD. "When I look at you," one doctor told her, "no soldier has seen as much combat as you have." Sean Ryan recalled a lunch with her at about that time: "Marie gripped the table and said, 'Sean, I have PTSD. I am going to hospital to be treated.'" She seemed relieved by the specific diagnosis. According to Rosie Boycott, "While the PTSD was absolutely true, it was as well for Marie a way she did not have to confront her drinking." Bishop begged Colvin to stop; she refused.

For years in England, with its high tolerance of alcoholism and its reluctance to force confrontation, Colvin's friends and editors often resorted to evasion—*Marie is feeling fragile. Marie does not sound like herself.* When they tried to intervene, she would tell them, "I have no intention of not drinking. I never drink when I am covering a war." Her attempts to find help were always short-lived.

She would wake up drenched in sweat. The desperate reel of horrors that played over and over in her mind kept returning to the refugee camp in Beirut, where she saw the twenty-two-year-old Palestinian woman lying in a heap with half her head blown off. As recently as last year, Colvin was staying with her nieces and nephews in East Norwich when the doorbell suddenly awakened her. The next morning Rosemarie discovered that Marie had gotten up and put a knife in her sleeping bag. When Rosemarie mentioned it, Marie said, "Oh, that," and changed the subject.

Colvin worked at the paper two days a week and hated it. Robin Morgan, then the editor of the paper's weekly magazine, begged her to write long stories, but Colvin pressed to return to the field. She called the office "the chamber of horrors," and she hounded Ryan and Witherow to let her get back to work. She went to the Palestinian cities of Ramallah and Jenin in 2002 to cover the intifada. Arriving in Jenin, Lindsey Hilsum was convinced that her TV team had the scoop:

"And there was Marie, popping out of the rubble, smoking a cigarette. 'Hey, you guys, can I get a ride out?'" Recalling the decision to allow her back into war zones, one correspondent recently could not contain his anger. "They would put us all in this kind of danger," he said. Colvin was never out of the field again.

In 2003, as George Bush prepared to go to war with Iraq, Colvin was sent to assess the scene. After witnessing Saddam's brutalities, she would fiercely defend the war at parties, declaring that no reasonable person could allow the genocide to continue. In dispatches from Baghdad, she described the mass graves of dismembered

Iraqis and the atrocities Saddam's son Uday had committed on his own family. Not long after that, while visiting her family on Long Island and seeing her nine-year-old niece with a collection of Barbie dolls, she said, "Justine, are you playing dead babies' mass grave?" She then realized that she was slipping into another reality. She told Cat, "I know things I don't want to know—like how small a body gets when it is burned to death." She continued to struggle. "I couldn't feel anymore," she told an interviewer. "I'd gotten into too black a place. I needed to say 'I'm vulnerable.'"

In the weeks after Colvin's death, angry emails circulated among the correspondents, blasting the attitude of the paper. The *Sunday Times* mounted an internal investigation into its responsibility. Several members of the foreign staff confided to me their rage at what they considered the danger they now faced in the paper's frenzy for press awards. "Are you aware that there is a tremendous anger about what happened to Marie, and that you are taking a bit of the heat for it?" I asked Sean Ryan. Ryan hesitated and then answered carefully: "There have been a couple people who have expressed concern about it. . . . I initiated a debate about what lessons could be learned. There were some reporters who think there shouldn't be war reporting. There were some reporters who think that any reporter who has ever had PTSD should be retired. . . . There are those who think that reporters on the ground should be allowed to make their own judgment. My view is in the middle, as is the majority of the staff's." Then Ryan surprised me, adding, "It is illegal not to allow reporters to return to work with PTSD after they have been cleared." I asked him, "Is this a British law?" He hesitated again. "Yes," he said.

"If the *Sunday Times* had not allowed Marie to continue the work she loved, it would have destroyed her," said Colvin's executor, Jane Wellesley.

THE BOATMAN

"My God, they are drugging the fucking journalists," Colvin cracked when she landed in the town of Qamishli, on the northeastern border of Syria, as the 2003 war in Iraq began to build. It was March, and Colvin, like scores of other reporters, was trying to get a visa into the country. Paul Conroy told me, "For days the journalists camped out, sleeping on plastic chairs in the office of the consul closest to the border. That was the first time I clapped eyes on her. She walked into that room and then just turned and walked out the door."

Shortly after that, he recalled, "She whirled into the lobby of the Petroleum Hotel and called out, 'Where is the boatman?'" Conroy, then a freelance cameraman, had been so determined to get into Iraq that he built a raft in his room and launched it with a stringer from the *New York Times*. "We were arrested almost immediately by the Syrians," he told me. "They held us a few hours and then let us go, telling us they believed in free speech."

"You built a fucking *boat*?" Colvin asked Conroy when she tracked him down. "I fucking love that! Everyone else here looks dead. Let's sail!" That night they stayed out drinking until dawn. Conroy did not see her again for seven years.

Back in London, for therapy she rediscovered the thrill of ocean racing. "It focuses my mind completely," she told Rosie Boycott. "Three hours on deck, three hours asleep—that was how she destressed!" Boycott told me. Through a friend, she met Richard Flaye, a director of several companies. Soon she was introducing him as "the love of my life." Flaye, who grew up in the privileged world of white Uganda, has a colonial elegance and a macho demeanor. Like Colvin, he is a fierce ocean sailor. "We worked out an exit strategy for her," Flaye told me. Colvin happily agreed to work half of the year and sail with her new love the rest of the time. "I hope you don't mind if I buy a house a few blocks from you," he said several months after they met. Colvin spent time designing a new kitchen for her own house, planting her garden, and finally unpacking her wedding presents. At night she cooked elaborate dinners for Flaye and his teenage children. "I warned her when we got together, I am a leopard with spots," Flaye said. "Marie herself was strongly independent by nature and recognized that she had to give me my independence as well."

Then came the Arab Spring. In January 2011, Sean Ryan was at the gym looking at the news from Tahrir Square, in Cairo, when his cell phone rang. "Are you watching this?" Colvin said. "It looks to be a small crowd," he told her. "No, Sean, this is really important," she said. "I think I should go." Once there, she learned of the attack on CBS's Lara Logan and had a call from Ryan. "What can you do to add to this story?" he asked.

The next time Colvin called, she sounded terrified. She was locked in a shop, where people from the neighborhood had turned violently on her as a foreign woman. In the background, the editor on duty could hear a crowd trying to break in. She was barely able to get out with her translator. The *Sunday Times* headline read: "Trapped in an Alley by a Mob After My Blood." "Shaken but okay," she wrote Judith Miller. "This is not our Egypt."

Concerned about Colvin's state of mind in Cairo, her colleague Uzi Mahnaimi sent a warning email to London. Despite the alarm of some at the *Sunday Times*, Sean Ryan says, if he had thought Colvin's condition was serious he would have gotten her "on the first plane home."

Colvin's romantic life had once again collapsed. She and Flaye had separated when she discovered in his emails a trail of other women. One afternoon she read all of the emails to two of her closest friends, sobbing. She went to a new therapist, who tried to get her to a center in Cottonwood, Arizona, that treats alcohol addiction and trauma. "There was no longer hiding in euphemisms what she had," one friend said. But it was even more complicated than that. Work was where she felt competent and safe. She would say, "I have no problem with drinking when I am in the field." Inside the paper, however, others disagreed.

"Are you happy to work with Marie Colvin?" Paul Conroy was asked by his editor in the winter of 2011 as war raged in the city of Misrata, Libya. "Are you kidding?" he said. "She's a bloody legend." Conroy, by then on the staff of the *Sunday Times*, was caught up in the frenzy of antigovernment demonstrations in the Arab world. When Colvin spotted him in the lobby of his hotel in Cairo, she cried, "Boatman! I don't believe it!" It was as if no time had passed. They flew to Tripoli and found their way by ferry to Misrata, which was being shelled by Qaddafi loyalists.

As rockets ripped nearby buildings apart, Colvin and Conroy made it to their destination, the clinic where Colvin knew victims were being taken. Just as they arrived, they saw stretchers being carried in. Inside they learned that *Vanity Fair* contributing photographer Tim Hetherington had just been admitted. "Marie suddenly turned white," Conroy said. She rushed off to find Hetherington, and later that night she told Flaye that she had cradled the dying man in her arms.

Colvin and Conroy had planned to stay in Misrata five days, but they remained for nine weeks. Colvin often slept on the floor of the clinic, where she felt protected.

"Hornet!" she wrote Hugh Hudson:

I am now like a character in a modern remake of Stalingrad I pause in my race to the shelling at the front and veer over to the roadside when I spot someone selling onions from a wooden table on the verge But when I hear a chorus of "*allahu akbars*" . . . shouted from the doctors, medics and rebels in the parking lot, I know a body or severely injured person has arrived and I head down There is always a story at the end of a rocket. On the positive side, this is like a health reservation without the counselling. No booze, no bread. Off to the front in my Toyota pickup. Handful of dried dates, can of tuna.

"I MUST SEE WHAT IS GOING ON"

"Every week, she would convince me they had a good story for the following week," Ryan said. Colvin outdid herself. She delivered a rapist's confession and a profile of deserters from Qaddafi's army, and from time to time she accompanied Conroy to the front. In London, Ryan was now concerned. "Do not go to the front," he emailed her. One day, she mentioned that she had been there. "Didn't you get my emails?" he demanded angrily. "I thought you were joking," she said.

"What did you live on?" I asked Paul Conroy. "Pringles, water, and cigarettes. One day, Marie shouted, 'Paul, I have eggs!' She had found them at a farmer's stand and was balancing them on her head." He added, "Marie quit smoking completely. She was losing all of her teeth. Whenever I would light up, she would say, 'Blow the smoke at me, Paul. I miss it so fucking much.'" He was in a London hospital, still recovering from injuries suffered in the attack in Homs that killed Colvin.

On October 20, 2011, as the first reports of Qaddafi's death made the news, Conroy and Colvin got frantic calls from their editors to take a plane to Tripoli and get a story for page one in seventy-two hours. "Hey, boatman, we are on the move!" Colvin said as she scrambled to find her passport, which she had misplaced. Landing in Tunis, they realized that all they had was a possible lead on Qaddafi's body in the morgue. "That is nothing. Everyone will have that," the picture editor told Conroy. With only twelve hours to go, Colvin was tipped that Qaddafi had last been seen in his childhood home of Sirte, a besieged city, once a faux Beverly Hills in the desert. In a frenzy, she ordered up another driver to take them through the desolate landscape. "You'll never get in," the driver said. "Trust me. If Marie says we will, we will," Conroy said.

"Libya is my story," Colvin said as she fell asleep on Conroy's shoulder. She was on a high, with the possible thrill of a scoop ahead of her and no sign of any competition. They had four hours left to file. Conroy crawled out of the car's back window, hoping for a satellite signal, and found a way to put gaffer tape on a makeshift antenna to transmit their copy and photos. "We were screaming at each other to share the laptop," he recalled. "Marie was typing madly, and I was trying to send my pictures. The driver looked at us and said, 'I have never seen anyone act like this before.' And Marie shouted, 'Well, you have never worked with the *Sunday Times.*'"

"My God, what should I do?" Colvin asked Flaye, with whom she was back together, on Skype not long after she reached Homs. "It is a risk. If I go on the BBC and CNN, it is very possible that we will be targeted." It was late in the afternoon on February 21. "I watched a little baby die today," she told Ryan, a line she would repeat on television. "This is what you do," Flaye assured her. "You get the story out." Her editors agreed and cleared her to broadcast.

"It is absolutely sickening," Colvin said on the BBC about her hours in the clinic. "A two-year-old had been hit. His little tummy just kept heaving until he died. It is shelling with impunity and merciless disregard." Her voice was calm and steady as Conroy's footage beamed all over the world. "I could feel the intensity of the shelling increasing not long after," Conroy said. "At that point, Marie and I just looked at each other, and it was, like, How do we survive?"

Colvin emailed Ryan: "All well here. It is the worst day of shelling in the days I have been here I did interviews for BBC Hub and for Channel 4. ITN is asking, not really sure of the etiquette, as it were. Is doing an interview for everyone just guaranteed to piss everyone off?... Two cars of the activists who tool around Baba Amr getting video both hit today, one destroyed." Ryan tried to Skype with Colvin, then emailed her. "Can you Skype me please? I am alarmed."

Soon after that, two French journalists appeared. "We can't leave now that the Eurotrash is here," Colvin told Conroy, and she emailed Ryan: "I want to move at 5:30 in the morning I refuse to be beaten by the French." Ryan emailed back, "I don't think their arrival makes you and Paul any safer. Leave tomorrow night."

At 6:00 a.m., they were jolted from their sleeping bags as an outer wall shook. "It sounded like the Battle of Stalingrad. We were directly targeted," Conroy said. "Then another shell landed on the building. Everyone started screaming, 'We have to get the hell out!' If you had gone out carrying a flag, none of it would have made a difference. After the third shell, I reached for my camera. I was trying to move for the door. Marie had run to get her shoes. The next blast blew through the door. It hit our translator and snapped his arm. I felt the hot steel in my leg. I shouted, 'I'm hit!' It went in one side and out another. I could see the hole through my leg. I knew I had to get out. And as I did, I fell over. I was next to Marie. I could see her black jacket and her jeans in the rubble. I listened to her chest. She was gone."

For five days, with little medication and racked with pain, Conroy was taken care of by Free Syrian Army commanders. Meanwhile, the *Sunday Times* went into overdrive: Mission to save journalists fails. Syria's cycle of hate traps wounded *Sunday Times* photographer. "We did not know how we were going to get out," Conroy told me. Finally, he was strapped onto the back of a motorcycle and taken through the dark tunnel.

"I really don't have a good feeling about this trip," Colvin had said the night before she left for Syria. There was a last dinner in

Beirut—Colvin wanted Lebanese food—and she came in wearing the boots she always wore. "Where am I going to get long johns?" she asked. With her was her friend Farnaz Fassihi, of the *Wall Street Journal*. "Marie was the trailblazer," she said. "That night I said, 'Marie, don't go.' We all knew how dangerous it was. All of the activists had told us." Colvin hesitated, then said, "No, I have to go. I must see what is going on."

One year earlier, Colvin had been caught in a tear-gas explosion in Cairo while running in a crowd with Fassihi's partner, a *Newsweek* reporter. It was a perfect moment for Colvin, watching the force of a new world order sweep through Tahrir Square as acid clouds mixed with the crowd's screams. "Are you all right?" the reporter called back. "You bet. I have one good eye, and it's on you!" Colvin yelled, laughing as she ran.

THE BALLAD OF
RICHARD JEWELL

FEBRUARY 1997

"The weird thing was that when they were searching my apartment I was, like, 'Take everything. Take the carpet. I am law enforcement. I am just like you. Guys, take whatever you are going to take, because it is going to prove that I didn't do anything.' And a couple of them were looking at me like I was crazy."

The search warrant was short and succinct, dated August 3, 9:41 a.m. FBI special agent Diader Rosario was instructed to produce "hair samples (twenty-five pulled and twenty-five combed hairs from the head)" of Richard Allensworth Jewell. That Saturday, Atlanta was humid; the temperature would rise to eighty-five degrees. There were thirty-four Olympic events scheduled, including women's team handball, but Richard Jewell was in his mother's apartment playing Defender on a computer set up in the spare bedroom. Jewell hadn't slept at all the night before, or the night before that. He could hear the noise from the throng of reporters massed on the hill outside the small apartment in the suburbs. All morning long, he had been focused on the screen, try-ing to score off "the little guy who goes back and forth shooting the aliens," but at 12:30 the sound of the telephone disturbed his concentration. Very few people had his new number, by necessity unlisted. Since the FBI had singled him out as the Olympic Park bombing suspect three days earlier, Jewell had received approxi-mately one thousand calls a day—someone had posted his moth-er's home number on the Internet.

"I'll be right over," his lawyer Watson Bryant told him. "They want your hair, they want your palm prints, and they want some-thing called a voice exemplar—the goddamn bastards." The cur-tains were drawn in the pastel apartment filled with his mother's crafts and samplers; a home without a dog is just a house, one read. By this time Bryant had a system. He would call Jewell from his car phone so that the door could be unlatched and Bryant could avoid the questions from the phalanx of reporters on the hill.

Turning into the parking lot in a white Explorer, Bryant could see sound trucks parked up and down Buford Highway. The mid-dle-class neighborhood of apartment complexes and shopping centers was near the DeKalb Peachtree Airport, where local mil-lionaires kept their private planes. The moment Bryant got out of his car, the reporters began to shout: "Hey, Watson, do they have the murderer?" "Are they arresting Jewell?" Bryant moved quickly toward the staircase to the Jewells' apartment. He wore a baseball cap, khaki shorts, and a frayed Brooks Brothers polo shirt. He was forty-five years old, with strong features and thinning hair, a southern preppy from a country-club family. Bryant had a stern demeanor lightened by a contrarian's sense of the absurd. He was often distracted—from time to time he would miss his exits on the highway—and he had the regional tendency of defining himself by explaining what he was not. "I am not a Democrat, because they want your money. I am not a Republican, because they take your rights away," he told me soon after I met him. Bryant can talk your ear off about the Bill of Rights, ending with a flourish: "I think everyone ought to have the right to be stupid. I am a Libertarian."

At the time Richard Jewell was named as a suspect by the FBI, Watson Bryant made a modest living by doing real estate closings in the suburbs, but Jewell and his lawyer had formed an unusual friendship a decade earlier, when Jewell worked as a mailroom clerk at a federal disaster-relief agency where Bryant practiced law. Jewell was then a stocky kid without a father, who had trained as an auto mechanic but dreamed of being a policeman; Bryant had always had a soft spot for oddballs and strays, a personality quirk that annoyed his then wife no end.

The serendipity of this friendship, an alliance particularly southern in its eccentricity, would bring Watson Bryant to the immense task of attempting to save Richard Jewell from the murky quagmire of a national terrorism case. The simple fact was that Bryant had no qualifications for the job. He had no legal staff except for his assistant, Nadya Light, no contacts in the press, and no history in Washington. He was the opposite of media-savvy; he rarely read the papers and never watched the nightly news, preferring the Discovery Channel's shows on dog psychology. Now that Richard Jewell was his client, he had entered a zone of worldwide media hysteria fraught with potential peril. Jewell suspected that his pickup truck had been flown in a C-130 transport plane to the FBI unit at Quantico in Virginia, and Bryant worried that his friend would be arrested any minute. Worse, Bryant knew that he had nothing going for him, no levers anywhere. His only asset was his personality; he had the bravado and profane hyperbole of a southern rich boy, but he was in way over his head.

For hours that Saturday, Bryant and Jewell sat and waited for the FBI. From time to time Jewell would put binoculars under the drawn curtain in his mother's bedroom to peer at the reporters on the hill. Bryant was nervous that Jewell's mother, Bobi, would return from babysitting and see her son having hairs pulled out of his head. Bryant stalked around the apartment complaining about the FBI. "The sons of bitches did not show up until 3:00 p.m.," he later recalled, and when they did, there were five of them. The FBI medic was tall and muscular and wore rubber gloves. He asked Jewell to sit at a small round table in the living room, where his mother puts her holiday-theme displays. Bryant stood by the sofa next to a portrait of Jewell in his Habersham County deputy's uniform. He watched the FBI procedure carefully. The medic, who had huge hands, used tiny drugstore tweezers. "He eyeballed his scalp and took his hair in sections. First he ran a comb through it, and then he took these hairs and plucked them out one by one."

Jewell "went stone-cold," but Bryant could not contain his temper. "I am his lawyer. I know you can have this, I know you have a search warrant, but I tell you this: *If you were doing this to me, you would have to fight me. You would have to beat the shit out of me,*" Bryant recalled telling the case agent Ed Bazar. Bazar, Bryant later said, was apologetic. "He seemed almost embarrassed to be there." As he counted out the hairs, he placed them in an envelope. The irony of the situation was not lost on Bryant. He was a lawyer, an officer of the court, but he had a disdain for authority, and he was representing a former deputy who read the Georgia law code for fun in his spare time.

It took ten minutes to pluck Jewell's thick auburn hair. Then the FBI agents led him into the kitchen and took his palm prints on the table. "That took thirty minutes, and they got ink all over the table," Bryant said. Then Bazar told Bryant they wanted Jewell to sit on the sofa and say into the telephone, "There is a bomb in Centennial Park. You have thirty minutes." That was the message given by the 911 caller on the night of the bombing. He was to repeat the message twelve times. Bryant saw the possibility of phony evidence and of his client's going to jail. "I said, 'I am not sure about this. Maybe you can do this, maybe you can't, but you are not doing this today.'"

All afternoon, Jewell was strangely quiet. He had a sophisticated knowledge of police work and believed, he later said, "They must have had some evidence if they wanted my hair. . . . I knew their game was intimidation. That is why they brought five agents instead of two." He felt "violated and humiliated," he told me, but he was passive, even docile, through Bryant's outburst. He thought of the bombing victims—Alice Hawthorne, the forty-four-year-old mother from Albany, Georgia, at the park with her stepdaughter; Melih Uzunyol, the Turkish cameraman who died of a heart attack; the more than one hundred people taken to area hospitals, some of whom were his friends. "I kept thinking, These guys think I did this. These guys were accusing me of murder. This was the biggest case in the nation and the world. If they could pin it on me, they were going to put me in the electric chair."

I met Richard Jewell three months later, on October 28, a few hours before a press conference called by his lawyers to allow Jewell to speak publicly for the first time since the FBI had cleared him. Jewell's lawyers also intended to announce that they would file damage suits against NBC and the *Atlanta Journal-Constitution.* It was a Monday, and that weekend the local U.S. attorney had delivered a letter to one of the lawyers stating Jewell was no longer a suspect. "Goddamn it," Bryant had told me on the phone, "the sons of bitches did not even have the decency to address it to Richard Jewell."

I had been instructed to come early to the offices of Wood & Grant, the flashy plaintiff lawyers Bryant had pulled in to help him with Jewell's civil suits. When I arrived, I was alone in the office with Sharon Anderson, the redheaded assistant answering the phones. "Wood & Grant . . . Wood & Grant . . . Wood & Grant"—the calls overwhelmed her. Lin Wood and Wayne Grant were rushing from CNN to the local NBC and ABC affiliates, working the shows. "Everyone has theories of who the real bomber is," Sharon said. "I just write it all down and give it to the boys."

When Lin Wood arrived, he was still in full makeup. Movie-star handsome with green eyes and styled hair, Wood has the heated oratory of a trial lawyer. "It's a war! Why in this bevy of stories does not anyone point out the fact that Richard was a hero one day and a demon the next? They have destroyed this man's life!"

Watson Bryant had worked with Wood and Grant years before in a local law firm. He admired Wayne Grant for his methodical sense of detail; Grant, a New Yorker, had once forced the city of Atlanta to pay large damages to a man injured while illegally digging for antique bottles in a park. But Lin Wood's suppressed rage was a marvel to Bryant. "He is so tough he could make people cry in depositions when we were kids," Bryant told me. Wood possessed the smooth style of a member of the Atlanta establishment, but he had a hardscrabble past. He was a boy from "the wrong side of the tracks" in Macon who at age seventeen discovered his mother's body after his father had murdered her. His father went to jail, and Wood wound up as a lawyer. He went through college and law school on scholarships and with part-time jobs. I could hear Wood on Sharon's telephone: "He's more than innocent. He's a goddamn hero. . . . Everyone is going to pay who wronged Richard Jewell. Besides NBC and the *AJC*, we are going to look into suing CNN and Jay Leno."

Through the large picture window, I had a clear view of the remains of the Centennial Olympic Park, where the bomb had exploded on the night of July 26. Where the sound-and-light tower had once been, there was now a flattened dirt field. It was possible to see the Greek commemorative sculpture that Richard Jewell used to describe for tourists at the AT&T pavilion, where he worked as a security guard.

Suddenly, Jewell was in the room. "Hi. I'm Richard. I'm a little late. I don't want you to think I am rude. I am not like that." He had an open face, a bland pleasantness, an eagerness to please. "Can I get you a Coke?" he asked me. "How about some coffee?" Jewell wore a blue-and-white-striped shirt and chinos. He occupied physical space like a teenager; he sprawled, he lumbered, he pawed through

Sharon's candy bowl. On TV his face had a porcine blankness; he appeared suspicious. In person, Jewell has a hard time disguising his emotions.

We were alone in the conference room; I noticed that Jewell avoided looking out the window toward the park. He shifted his glance nervously away from the view. He often awakens in the middle of the night, drenched in sweat, thinking of the events in the park in the early morning hours of July 27. "It took me days before I could even come in here," he said anxiously.

When Jewell noticed a local ABC reporter outside near Sharon's desk, his face darkened. "I don't want to be around reporters right now. I guess I am a little nervous. What is he doing here?" The atmosphere was now filled with tension; the reporter was escorted out.

Moments later, we gathered in the hallway. Wood was steely: "We are going in two cars. Richard, you drive with me. Your mother will go with Wayne. As we walk down the hall right now, if the ABC people are outside, I will tap you on the shoulder and I will say, 'How are you doing?' You will say, 'Fine.' Is that understood?" "Okay, Lin. I understand," Jewell said quietly, head bowed.

As Jewell walked down the hall, an ABC cameraman photographed him looking grim. Seconds after the elevator doors closed, Jewell exploded: "What are they doing here, Lin? Did you invite them? They are animals. Why didn't you get them out of here?"

"ABC has been good to you. How do I get them out of the office on the day of your press conference?"

"That is what security is for!" Jewell said, quivering with rage. "Where is Watson?" he asked in the garage. "I told you: he's at a real-estate closing. He will meet you at the press conference," Wood said. Jewell moved to his mother's side, as solicitous as a child. "Are you all right, Mother?" he asked. "It is all I am going to be able to do not to do something!" she said angrily.

When we arrived at the Marriott hotel on I-75, there was another discussion in the parking lot, about who would walk with whom in front of the cameras. Jewell turned to his close friend Dave Dutchess: "Are you all right, man?" Dutchess, a truck driver who worked with Jewell years ago, has long hair and a tattoo of a panther on his forearm. "Richard and I are like brothers," he told me. "I would die for him." As the cameras closed in on them, the group fled to a private room in the Marriott. The auditorium was filled with reporters. "Showtime! Showtime!" the cameramen yelled when Jewell, his mother, and all the lawyers took the stage.

"I hope and pray that no one else is ever subjected to the pain and the ordeal that I have gone through," Jewell said, his voice breaking. "The authorities should keep in mind the rights of the citizens. I thank God it is ended and that you now know what I have known all along: I am an innocent man."

After the press conference, Bobi and Richard Jewell remained in a private room. The bookers from *Good Morning America* and the *Today Show* pressed Jewell to step before their cameras, and when Watson Bryant told them no, Monica, the *GMA* booker, began to cry, "I'll lose my job." Then Yael, the *Today* show booker, cornered Nadya Light: "Is Richard doing something with *GMA*?"

Upstairs, Jewell and his mother were being filmed by a CBS camera crew for a *60 Minutes* news update. "Well, Bobi, did you get your Tupperware back?" Mike Wallace asked by phone from New York. "Richard, you need to lose some more weight." Despite

Wallace's festive spirit, the atmosphere was curiously flat. Bryant urged Jewell to talk to a *USA Today* reporter. Jewell balked: "They can all go suck wind."

In the car on the way back to Wood & Grant, Bobi was angry. All of her possessions had come back from the FBI marked up with ink. "Every piece of Tupperware I own is ruined, thank you very much. They wrote numbers all over it, and I have tried everything to clean it—Comet and Brillo—but nothing works."

Back at the office, she sat on the sofa and listened as Bryant negotiated with Yael for a flight to New York—Delta, first-class, 9:30 p.m. Jewell was scheduled to appear on three shows in New York, visit the American Museum of Natural History, and then fly to Washington, D.C., for *Larry King Live.* "I would like to go home, put on my outfit, and walk in the woods," Bobi said. "Richard, we are leaving."

"Yes, ma'am," Richard said.

One hour later, a telephone call came in to the offices of Wood & Grant. The lawyers had the call on speaker, and it blared through the room. "Goddamn it, Lin. When will this be over?" In the background, you could hear Bobi sobbing. "What in the world?" Wood asked. Jewell explained that a sound truck from ABC had been waiting in the parking lot when the Jewells got home. There had been words and threats, and Dave Dutchess had taken his stun gun off his motorcycle and waved it at the ABC van. The cameraman yelled, "Stop harassing us!" Dave yelled back "You are harassing us! Now get your ass out of here!"

Wood shouted into the speakerphone: "Do not meddle! You

cannot jeopardize where you have gotten to and what you want to do! All you have to do is put up with this for one more day and the damn thing is over. Bobi, there is nothing you can do about it; you have to stay cool." Bobi cried back, "They are going to destroy me!"

The moment they hung up, Wood turned to Bryant. "New York is canceled. No Katie Couric. No *Good Morning America*. They are losing it. You better call Yael." "No," Bryant said, "they have lost it. All of the above: their patience, their temper and heart."

That evening a very testy Katie Couric tracked Bryant down at Nadya Light's apartment, where we had gone to watch the news. "I want you to know that I canceled interviewing Barbra Streisand in L.A. for Richard Jewell. Don't think he is always going to be a news story. No one will care about him in three days," she said, according to Bryant. "Look, Katie, I am sorry. But Richard is in no condition to talk to the press. He is worn out," Bryant told her.

Later, Jewell would tell me that that day, which should have been one of his most satisfying, was actually his worst. His notoriety had tainted the triumph; everything positive had become negative. "I was in despair," he said. As he had for most of the previous eighty-eight days, he spent the night confined in the Buford Highway apartment, a prisoner of his circumstances, with his mother, Dave Dutchess, and Dave's fiancée, Beatty, eating Domino's Pizza and watching himself lead the newscasts on NBC, CBS, and ABC.

"This case has everything—the FBI, the press, the violation of the Bill of Rights, from the First to the Sixth Amendment," Watson Bryant told me in one of our first conversations. It has become common to characterize the FBI's investigation of Richard Jewell as the epitome of false accusation. The phrase "the Jewell syndrome," a rush to judgment, has entered the language of newsrooms and First Amendment forums. On the night of Jewell's press conference, a commentator on CNN's *Crossfire* compared Jewell's situation to "Kafka in Prague." The case became an investigative catastrophe, which laid bare long-simmering resentments of many FBI career professionals regarding the micromanagement style and imperious attitude of Louis Freeh and his inner circle of former New York prosecutors, who have worked together since their days at the U.S. Attorney's Office in the Southern District. Within the bureau, the beleaguered director now has a new nickname: J. Edgar Hoover with children. Like Freeh, those near him have also acquired a nickname: Louie's yes-men. Two of Freeh's closest associates, FBI general counsel Howard Shapiro and former deputy director Larry Potts, have been severely criticized, respectively, for advising the White House of confidential FBI material and for an alleged cover-up of the mishandling of the 1992 standoff at Ruby Ridge, where FBI agents killed the wife and son of Randy Weaver, a white supremacist.

In November and December, the Office of Professional Responsibility conducted an exhaustive investigation into the Jewell affair. Responding to an attempt by headquarters and certain officials to distance themselves, according to FBI sources, several agents, including a senior FBI supervisor in Atlanta, have provided the OPR with signed statements insisting that Freeh himself was responsible for "oversight" during the crisis. These agents "shocked the investigators" because they reiterated, when asked who was in charge of the overall command of the investigation, that it was the director himself.

What happened to Richard Jewell raises an important question central to Freeh's future tenure: in the midst of a media frenzy, does the FBI have any responsibility to protect the privacy of an innocent man? Over the last year, this concept was broached with Bob Bucknam, Louis Freeh's chief of staff. During the long Pizza Connection trial in the 1980s, it was Bucknam who handed Freeh files at the prosecutor's table. According to highly placed sources in the bureau, Bucknam's answer was immediate: the FBI has no responsibility to correct information in the public domain.

Richard Jewell had a reverence for authority that blinded him to the paradox of his situation. He idealized the investigative skills of the FBI and could not understand that he had become ensnared in a web fraught with the weaknesses of a self-protective bureaucracy. Pennsylvania senator Arlen Specter has invited Jewell to Washington to testify at congressional hearings on the FBI's conduct in the Atlanta bombing. Ironically, the bungling of the investigation might lead to the reshuffling of personalities at the top of the bureau and threaten Freeh's reputation. In October, according to the *Washington Post,* Freeh sent an unusual memo to all twenty-five thousand FBI personnel: He would not be abandoning his post amid reports of problems with the Jewell case and Filegate, and of a growing dissatisfaction inside the bureau. "I am proud to be the FBI director," Freeh wrote.

From the beginning, Jewell was perceived in the public imagination as a hapless dummy, a plodding misfit, a Forrest Gump. On one of the first days he worked as a security guard at the AT&T pavilion, he noticed that his coworkers were covering the steps inside the sound tower with graffiti. On one step Jewell scrawled with a flourish two bromides: If you didn't go past me, you are not sup-posed to be here and life is tough. Tougher when you are stupid. Soon after he was targeted as a suspect in the Olympics bombing, the FBI confiscated the step. Analysts appeared to believe that the graffiti contained a clue to his character. "They told the lawyers the statement was an obvious taunt," Jewell said. In fact, the second line was an expression he had cribbed from one of his favorite ac-tors, John Wayne.

"To understand Richard Jewell, you have to be aware that he is a cop. He talks like a cop and thinks like a cop," his criminal lawyer, Jack Martin, told me. The tone of Jewell's voice drops no-ticeably when he says the word "officer," and his conversation is filled with observations about traffic patterns, security devices, and car wrecks. Even the vocabulary he uses to describe the eighty-eight days he was a suspect is out of the lexicon of police work, and he continues to talk about his situation then in the present tense: "This is an out-and-out ambush, and I am a hostage."

Jewell has a need to accommodate. He can be startlingly opaque. On the afternoon of July 30, Jewell answered the door of his mother's apartment to Don Johnson and Diader Rosario from the FBI. "We need your help making a training film," they told him. "I never questioned it," he told me. The next day Rosario appeared again with a search warrant. "The weird thing was that when they were searching my apartment I was, like, 'Take everything. Take the carpet. I am law enforcement. I am just like you. Guys, take what-ever you are going to take, because it is going to prove that I didn't do anything.' And a couple of them were looking at me like I was crazy."

Leaving the apartment on one occasion, he told the agents, "I am wearing a bright shirt so y'all can see me easier." He recalled feeling anger when he read descriptions of himself as a child-man, a mama's boy, and "a wannabe policeman," but he said, "If I was in the place of everybody else and I saw a thirty-four-year-old guy living with his mother, I would have reservations about that, too. I would think, Why is he doing that?"

Atlanta magazine reported that there was no record of a Jewell family in Danville, Virginia, where Richard Jewell was born. *Atlanta* referred to an article in the *Danville Register & Bee* that asked, "Did Richard Jewell ever sleep here?" "This is a part of my life. Richard and I do not like to speak about," Bobi Jewell told me one night at dinner. Richard was born in Danville, but his name was Richard White; his father was Bobi's first husband, Robert Earl White, who worked for Chevrolet. According to Bobi, Richard's father, who died recently, was "irresponsible and a ladies' man." When Richard was four, the marriage broke up. Bobi found work as an insurance-agency claims coordinator and soon met John Jewell, an executive in the same business. Shortly after John Jewell married Bobi, he adopted Richard.

From the time Richard was a child, he and his mother were a unit. Bobi, a woman of intelligence and disciplined work habits, is both tender and tough on the subject of her son. She still calls Richard "my boy," but she has a peppery disposition. Richard was brought up in a strict Baptist home. "If I didn't say 'Yes, ma'am' or 'No, ma'am' and get it out quick enough, I would be on the ground," he said. When he was six, the family moved to Atlanta. Richard was the boy who helped the teachers and worked as a school crossing guard, but he had few friends in high school. "I was a wannabe athlete, but I wasn't good enough," he said. He ran the movie projector in the library. A military-history buff, he liked to talk about Napoleon and the Vietnam War and read books on both world wars.

Jewell's ambition was to work on cars, so he enrolled in a technical school in southern Georgia. On his third day there, Bobi discovered that her husband had packed a suitcase. "He left a note saying that he was a failure and no good for us," Jewell said. Almost immediately, Richard moved back home and took a job repairing cars. "My mom and I tried to take care of each other," he said. "I think I handled it pretty much better than she did." Richard took the brunt of his father's abandonment; Bobi pulled even closer to her son. "She hated all men for about three years after that, and she became overly protective of me. She looked at it that I was going to do the same thing that my dad did. I was eighteen or nineteen. I was working. She never liked my dates, but I never held that against her. We have always been able to lean on each other."

Richard managed a local TCBY yogurt shop and once stopped a burglary in progress. At the age of twenty-two, he was hired as a clerk at the Small Business Administration, and he impressed Watson Bryant and the other lawyers in the office with his personable nature. They called him Radar because of his efficiency. "You could say, 'I'm hungry,' and suddenly this kid would be by your side with a Snickers bar," Bryant recalled. When Jewell's contract with the SBA ran out, he moved on to be a Marriott house detective. In 1990 he was hired as a jailer in the Habersham County Sheriff's Office, and in 1991 he became a deputy. As part of his training, he was sent to the Northeast Georgia Police Academy, where he finished in the upper 25 percent of his class. He finally had an identity; he was a law-enforcement officer.

Jewell was unlucky in love. He presented one woman with an engagement ring, and later, in Habersham County, he would give another a large wooden key with a sign that read, this is the key to unlock your heart, but both relationships came apart. In northern Georgia, Jewell worked nights and became wedded to his job. By his own description, he was methodical. "I am the kind of person who plans everything. I like to go from A to B to C to D. This going from A to D and arguing over everything—I say no." Habersham County, a scenic part of the piney woods in Georgia's Bible Belt, was for Jewell like "leaving the 1990s and going into the 1970s in terms of law enforcement." Many rich Atlantans have country houses in the mountains, but the small towns of Demorest and Charlottesville are relatively undeveloped, reminding one of Jewell's lawyers of the scenery in the movie *Deliverance*. "If you get lost up there, you might find a guy with a bow and arrow," the lawyer said.

Recently, Jewell and I took the ninety-minute drive from Atlanta to Habersham County, which has acres of apple orchards. The leaves were turning, and the roads were mostly deserted. In the towns, however, were stores, apple stands, and even a good Chinese restaurant. As Jewell's blue pickup truck turned into the parking lot of a shopping center, several people came out to greet him.

Jewell had lived in a small yellow house up a steep rocky driveway. On the day we visited, the current resident's Halloween decorations were still up, as were faded white satin ribbons hanging from many trees, remnants of a campaign to clear Richard Jewell organized by area friends. Jewell had lived fifty yards from the Chattahoochee River near a kayak-and-canoe tourist concession on a main road—not in a "cabin in the woods," as several reports stated after the bombing. He worked the night shift, and when he would arrive home at dawn, he told me, he could look up and "see a sky filled with stars."

He was not a loner; he made friends with several local families. He would often leave a box of Dunkin' Donuts on friends' porches at 4:00 a.m. During the O. J. Simpson trial, he and the other deputies would meet in the turnaround on Highway 985 in the middle of the night and review the day's events and the bungling by the Los Angeles Police Department. Jewell would later be annoyed that the FBI confiscated his copy of former prosecutor Vincent Bugliosi's account of the trial. Jewell dated a local girl, Sheree Chastain, and had a close relationship with her family.

Jewell had a complex history working at the Habersham County Sheriff's Office. When he was still a jailer, he arrested a couple making too much noise in a hot tub at an apartment building where he did part-time security work. He was arrested for impersonating an officer and, after pleading guilty to a lesser charge, was placed on probation on the condition that he seek psychological counseling.

By his own estimation, Jewell's strength as a cop was "working car wrecks." He had his mother's diligence; he worked fourteen hours a day and organized a safety fair. Later in 1995 he wrecked his patrol car and was demoted to working in the jail. Rick Moore, a local deputy, advised him to accept the job, but Jewell despised the jailhouse atmosphere. He told me, "It was a small room filled with cigarette smoke. I couldn't take it." He resigned, and in a short time he moved to a police job at Piedmont College, a liberal-arts school with approximately one thousand students on the main road in Demorest. The college police had jurisdiction only on campus and in an area extending out five hundred feet. Jewell chased cars speeding down the highway and had arguments over turf with other officers. He was instrumental in several arrests, including that of a suspected burglar he discovered hiding at the top of a tree. For his work on a volunteer rescue squad, he was named citizen of the year.

According to Brad Mattear, a former resident director, Piedmont was a school of "PKs"—preachers' kids. It was 80 percent Baptist, with a strict no-drinking rule. The college had many rebellious students, according to Mattear, kids who were "away from home for the first time and wanted to party and drink." Mattear knew Jewell well and recalled his good manners and playful nature. "It was always 'Yes, sir' and 'Yes, ma'am.'" Jewell would tell students, "I know y'all are going to drink. Don't do it on campus."

Jewell felt confined by his boundaries and could be heavy-handed when it came to writing out reports on minor infractions. Once when we were driving by the campus, he pointed to a small brick dormitory. "That was where all the partying would go on," he told me. Jewell would raid dorm rooms and report drinking violations. "I did not hesitate to tell the parents—in no uncertain terms—what their kids were up to," he said.

He soon made enemies at the school. "Three or four times a week," Mattear said, Piedmont students were in the office of Ray Cleere, the president of the college, complaining about Jewell and other Piedmont police. After Jewell was admonished for a number of controversial arrests, he resigned.

———

Jewell had an out: His mother was going to have an operation on her foot. He would go home to Atlanta for the Olympics and look for a new job. He called his mother: "Is it all right with you if I stay with you while you have your surgery?" He hoped he might get a job with the Atlanta police or, failing that, work security at the Olympics. "I thought, Working at the Centennial Olympic Park will look really good on my résumé."

At the age of thirty-three, back in his mother's apartment, he was at first treated like a wayward teenager. Bobi was sharp with him about his slovenly habits, his weight, and his driving. Bobi had carved out a life for herself; she arrived at work by eight each morning and had many friends. Trim, with short-cropped hair, Bobi Jewell is the kind of woman who labels her clothes and spices and spends much of her spare time baking cakes and babysitting for extra money. She carries on telephone friendships with claim adjusters at other companies. It was somewhat unsettling for her, she told me, to have Richard at home after she had grown used to living with only her dog, Brandi, and her cat, Boots. Bobi was annoyed that he had wrecked a patrol car, and worried about his safety. "Every time he leaves the apartment, I'll say, 'Richard . . .' And he'll say, 'Yes, ma'am. I know. The person that I am going to see will be there when I get there,'" she said. On one occasion Bobi talked about Richard's return to Atlanta. "What is wrong with trying to revamp your life?" she asked me. Her eyes filled with tears. "Why does everyone in the media think it is so strange?"

On Friday, July 26, Bobi Jewell was home waiting for her niece to arrive from Virginia for the Olympic softball competition the following week. In preparation, she had stocked her apartment with food. It was a clear Georgia evening, not as hot as had been expected. As usual, Richard left for the park at 4:45 p.m. and arrived at the AT&T pavilion about 5:30. His stomach was bothering him; he was convinced that he had eaten a bad hamburger the day before. Lin Wood and Wayne Grant had arranged to take their children to Centennial Park that night. The park, in downtown Atlanta, stretches over twenty-one acres. There were air-conditioned tents, concerts on the stage, and hot-dog and souvenir stands. Downtown Atlanta was usually deserted in the oppressively hot, humid summer, but this year thousands of tourists filled the sidewalks, or sat on benches in the shade of some crape-myrtle trees, or cooled off by a fountain. Tour buses clogged the main arteries, and everyone complained that it took hours to get anywhere; stories were traded about athletes' getting to their competitions late because of the poor planning of the Atlanta Committee for the Olympic Games.

As always, Jewell was working the twelve-hour night shift near the sound-and-light tower by the stage. He was pleased because one of his favorite groups—Jack Mack and the Heart Attack—was going to perform at 12:45. Jewell had a routine: He would check in and fill the ice chest he kept by a bench at his station. Jewell liked to offer water and Cokes to pregnant women or policemen who stopped to rest.

After he arrived at the park, his stomach cramps grew worse and he had a bout of diarrhea. At approximately 10:00 p.m. he took a break to go to the bathroom. The closest one was by the stage, but the security staff was not allowed to use it. "I really have to go," Jewell says he told the stage manager. "And he said, 'Well, okay this time.'"

When Jewell came out, he noticed that it was "real calm" and there wasn't much wind blowing. At that time of night, the crowd from Bud World became a little more raucous. Jewell was annoyed when he saw a group of drunks near his bench and beer cans littering the area beside the fence nearby. As he went to report the trash and the group that was carousing, he spotted a large olive-green military-style backpack, known as an Alice pack, under the bench. There had been a similar bag found the week before. Jewell later told an FBI agent that he was annoyed that one of the drunks had tried to get into the lens of a camera crew. Jewell had told them to cut it out. "They were running off at the mouth," Jewell would later tell Larry Landers of the Georgia Bureau of Investigation (GBI).

"I was light about the package at first," he told me, "kidding around with Tom Davis from the GBI: 'Well, are you going to open it?' At that point, it was not a concern. I was thinking to myself, Well, I am sure one of these people left it on the ground. When Davis came back and said, 'Nobody said it was theirs,' that is when the little hairs on the back of my head began to stand up. I thought, Uh-oh. This is not good.

"I never really had time to be frightened. My law-enforcement background paid off here. What went through my head was like a computer screen of this list I had to do. I had to call my supervisor. I have to tell people in the tower that something was going on. I have to be firm with them, stay calm, and be professional."

Almost immediately, Jewell and Tom Davis cleared a twenty-five-foot-square area around the backpack; Jewell made two trips into the tower to warn the technicians. "I want y'all out now. This is serious."

Two blocks away on Marietta Street, approximately three hundred editors, copywriters, and reporters from Cox newspapers around the country had taken over the extra desks in the new eighth-floor newsroom at the *Atlanta Journal-Constitution* to prepare the special Olympics edition they put out each afternoon. The paper had gone "Olympics-crazy," according to one reporter. The editor, Ron Martin, and the managing editor, John Walter—"Wal-Mart," as they were called—had let it be known that no expense would be spared. Ann Hardie, who normally covers science, had been sent around the world to master the fine points of beach volleyball; Bill Rankin, officially on the federal-court beat, was assigned table tennis. The paper intended to set new standards in its hometown during the games, but in addition there was a hint of redemption in the air.

Since Cox newspaper executives had forced the resignation of the distinguished editor Bill Kovach in 1988, the paper had suffered a severe loss of reputation. "We all felt just kind of beaten down," one reporter said. Kovach had been brought to Atlanta from the *New York Times* to elevate the *AJC* into being the definitive paper of the New South, but eventually he irritated the local powers. Atlanta was inbred, a city of deals, and he resigned in a blaze of press outrage.

Within the profession, the *AJC* had become something of a joke. More and more, its emphasis was on what John Walter called "chunklets"—short bits in a soft-news style known as eye-candy. The paper published features on couples massage and how mushrooms grow in the rain. Walter had fired off several terse memos to ensure that there would be no more jumps of news stories to back pages and no more unsourced news stories, except on rare occasions. "I don't see any reason why you can't report hard news in a short form," one editor told me.

The *AJC* style of reporting in declarative sentences had a name, too: the voice of God. It was omniscient, because it allowed no references to unattributed sources. Subjects such as AIDS, which often required confidentiality, could not be covered properly in the paper, in the opinion of several reporters. *The AJC* picked up news stories with unnamed sources from the *New York Times*, however, and reporters groused about the hypocrisy of the double standard.

On Saturday morning, July 27, Bob Johnson, the night metro editor, left the newsroom at 1:00 a.m. The sidewalks were still crowded; Johnson sat on a wall outside waiting for an *AJC* shuttle bus to pick him up. About 1:25 he heard a strange noise. "It sounded like an aerial bomb at a fireworks show," he said. He recalled thinking, Damn, that is sort of foolish. Then he heard screams and saw people running. Johnson rushed back upstairs to the almost deserted sixth-floor newsroom. Lyda Longa, a night police reporter, was still there. Johnson sent her down to the park and turned on the news, but nothing had moved across the wires. Just after 2:00 a.m., Longa called from the park. She told Johnson that one person had been killed and dozens were down—it was absolute chaos. Johnson could hear the sirens and the screams through the telephone; he began to type into his computer. "We were trying to get a bullet into the street edition," Johnson recalled. In the crisis, it took only minutes for reporters to return to the newsroom; several had been at the park when the bomb went off. Rochelle Bozman, an Olympics editor, appeared and took over for Johnson. Soon John Walter was there, as was Bert Roughton, who would assist him in supervising the *AJC* coverage of the bombing.

———

At the park, Jewell spoke with the first FBI agents to arrive on the scene. The smell and the noise, he remembered, were overwhelming, and sensations blurred together. "It was hard to describe the sound," he said. "It was like what you hear in the movies. It was, like, kaboom. I had seen an explosion in police training. We had ear protection when it went off. It smelled like a flash-bang grenade. The sky was not filled with black smoke, but grayish-white. All the shrapnel that was inside the package kept flying around, and some of the people got hit from the bench and some with metal."

Bobi Jewell had just gone to sleep when the telephone rang. It was Richard. "Mom, they had a bomb go off down here, but I am okay regardless of what the TV says." He could hardly speak; he seemed paralyzed. Jewell did not mention to his mother that he had found the knapsack and alerted Tom Davis. Bobi was perplexed. "I thought, What does he mean?" All night long she stayed on the foldout sofa watching the news reports. She was frightened by the ambulances, the noise, the bodies in the park.

Soon veteran homicide detectives in the Atlanta police arrived at the bomb site. One sergeant was trying to make his way through the crowd when an Olympics official stopped him. "Tell these cops to get the hell out of here," he said, according to a captain in the homicide division. "Well, you get the fuck out of here. Who are you?" the sergeant demanded. Agents from the Atlanta FBI office and the Bureau of Alcohol, Tobacco, and Firearms were in a shouting match over jurisdiction. "We are handling this!" one said. "No, this is ours!" an FBI agent snapped.

In the command center at FBI headquarters in northeastern

Atlanta, there was complete pandemonium. The Olympics were a national convention for law enforcement. Some thirty thousand security personnel were on hand. Over the next few days, there would be an internal debate: Who was going to be in charge of the bombing investigation? In Atlanta at that time were three veteran investigators with executive experience: Tom Fuentes, who is credited with helping to bring John Gotti to heel; Barry Mawn, who has worked extensively in organized-crime probes; and Robin Montgomery, the head of the critical-incident unit at Quantico, who at Ruby Ridge in 1992 questioned the disastrous "rules of engagement" that led to tragedy.

In the early-morning hours, FBI agents picked up several suspects, including one referred to as "the drunk in the bar." According to FBI sources, Louis Freeh himself got on the telephone to Barry Mawn. Freeh, a former FBI agent, was personally monitoring the initial investigation by means of a series of conference calls from the command post at FBI headquarters. He focused on "the drunk in the bar," who had been making threats the night before, and within hours the information was leaked that the FBI had a suspect. From Atlanta, Barry Mawn contacted his superiors in Washington. "This suspect is not the bomber," he reportedly said, according to a former high-level FBI executive. Freeh allegedly lost his temper and belittled Mawn's professional abilities. He is said to have told Mawn that he "had handled this all wrong." The words one hears characterizing Freeh's telephone calls to the agents on duty in Atlanta are "abusive," "condescending," and "dismissive." A story went around the command center that Freeh was already saying, "We have our man," according to a source in the bureau.

Freeh made a decision: However experienced Montgomery,

Fuentes, and Mawn were, this investigation would be run by Division 5 of the FBI, the National Security Division, a former counterintelligence unit that has been looking for a purpose since the Cold War ended. Trained in observation, division members rarely made a criminal case—their strength was intimidation and manipulation rather than the deliberate gathering of evidence to be presented in court. The FBI promptly declared the bombing a terrorism case and placed it under the authority of Bob Bryant, head of the division. David Tubbs of Division 5 was sent to Atlanta to be the spokesman and to augment Woody Johnson, the Atlanta special agent in charge (SAC), who had been trained in hostage rescue and who was awkward in press briefings. Tubbs was not as experienced in criminal cases as Mawn or Montgomery, who returned to Newark and Quantico, respectively, "to get out of the line of fire," according to numerous FBI sources. But Bryant and Freeh were reportedly micromanaging the SACs and, later, the case agents Don Johnson and Diader Rosario.

On the morning of the bombing, Watson Bryant's alarm went off at six o'clock. He was going to the Olympic kayak competition on the Ocoee River with Andy Currie, a friend from his Vanderbilt University days. He learned of the bombing on the radio as he was getting ready to go to Currie's house. "Whoever has done this should be skinned alive," he told Currie. He spent the day in the country, and on Sunday he went out to run errands. When he got home, there was a message on his answering machine: "Watson, this is Richard Jewell. You may have heard that I found the bomb and people are calling me a hero. Somebody told me I might get a book contract."

It had been years since Bryant had spoken to Jewell, but he did not immediately return the call; he was busy finishing up some contracts so that he could take a few days off to enjoy the Olympics.

In addition, Bryant was annoyed with Jewell. After Bryant had befriended him in their days at the Small Business Administration, Jewell had borrowed his new, $250 radar detector and never returned it. He had promised to pay him $100 for it, but he never had. In the meantime, Bryant's life had changed; he had set up an office as a solo practitioner. Bryant despised corporate politics and had no gift for them. His penchant for taking on pro bono work for friends annoyed his wife, however. Bryant believed that Richard Jewell had attached himself to him years earlier because he lacked a father, but nevertheless Jewell could get on his nerves. By the summer of 1996, Bryant was preoccupied; his marriage had come apart two years earlier, and he was trying to sort out his life.

When he finally returned Jewell's phone call, he said, "Well, damn it, where's my $100?" Jewell laughed uneasily and told him about discovering the green backpack that contained the bomb. "Didn't you see me on the news?" Bryant reminded him that he rarely watched TV. "I am proud of you, Richard," he said. "About this book contract, I think it's far-fetched, but don't sign anything unless I see it first."

In the *Newsweek* cover story detailing the bombing, published Monday, July 29, there was no mention of Richard Jewell. It said only that "a security guard" had alerted Tom Davis of the GBI. that no one had claimed the backpack under his bench. By the time *Newsweek* was on the stands, however, Jewell had been interviewed on CNN. The AT&T publicity department had booked him on TV and told him to wear the shirt with the AT&T logo. Jewell reluctantly agreed. "The idea of going on TV made me nervous," he told me. "I was not the hero. There were so many others who saved lives."

In Demorest, Ray Cleere, the president of Piedmont College, was home on Saturday, July 27, watching CNN. Cleere had at one time been Mississippi's commissioner of higher education, but he was now posted at the rural Baptist mountain school. He was said to feel that he had suffered a loss of status in the boondocks, where he was out of the academic mainstream. He called Dick Martin, his chief of campus police. Shouldn't they call the FBI and tell them about Richard Jewell? he asked. Cleere had had a strong disagreement with Jewell when one of the students was caught smoking pot. Jewell wanted to arrest him; Cleere said no. Cleere, Brad Mattear recalled, "worried constantly about the image of the college." According to Mattear, "Cleere loved the limelight. He wanted public attention"—the very trait he reportedly ascribed to Richard Jewell.

Dick Martin, who was fond of Jewell, suggested a compromise, according to Lin Wood: He would call a friend in the GBI. Cleere then called the FBI hotline in Washington himself. Wood says Cleere later complained that no one had seemed to want to listen to what he had to say about Richard Jewell. But his telephone call would trigger a complex set of circumstances in Habersham County, where FBI investigators fanned out over the hills, attempting to uncover evidence that could lead to Jewell's arrest. "The FBI took his word, and what it actually did was get them both in a bunch of trouble," Mattear said. (Cleere has declined to comment.)

For Richard Jewell, Tuesday, July 30, would become a haze in which his life was turned upside down. "The hours of the day ran so fast it is hard to remember what all happened," he told me. He started the day early at the Atlanta studio of the *Today* show. He was tired; the evening before he had had his friend Tim Attaway, a GBI agent, over for dinner. He had made lasagna and had drawn Attaway a diagram of the sound-and-light tower. Jewell had talked into the night about the bombing; only later would he learn that Attaway was wearing a wire.

Despite the late evening, Jewell was excited at the thought of meeting Katie Couric and being interviewed about finding the Alice pack in the park. His mother asked him to try to get Tom Brokaw's autograph. "He was a man my mom respected a great deal," he said.

When he got back to the apartment, he was surprised to see a cluster of reporters in the parking lot. "Do you think you are a suspect?" one asked. Jewell laughed. "I know they'll investigate anyone who was at the park that night," he said. "That includes you-all, too." Jewell did not turn on the TV, but he noticed that the group outside the door continued to grow. At four that afternoon, Jewell received a phone call from Anthony Davis, the head of the security company Jewell worked for at AT&T. "Have you seen the news?" Davis asked. "They are saying you are a suspect." Jewell said, "They are talking to everybody." According to Jewell, Davis said, "They are zeroing in on you. To keep the publicity down, don't go to work."

Within minutes, Don Johnson and Diader Rosario knocked on Jewell's door. They exuded sincerity, Jewell recalled. "They told me they wanted me to come with them to headquarters to help them make a training film to be used at Quantico," he said. Johnson played to Jewell's pride. Despite the reporters in the parking lot and the call from Anthony Davis, Jewell had no doubt that they were telling the truth. He drove the short distance to FBI headquarters in Buckhead in his own truck, but he noticed that four cars were following him. "The press is on us," Jewell told Johnson when they arrived. "No, those are our guys," Johnson told him. This tactic would continue through the next eighty-eight days and be severely criticized: Why would you have an armada of surveillance vehicles stacked up on a suspected bomber?

It was then that Jewell started to wonder why he was at the FBI, but he followed Johnson and Rosario inside. Rosario was known for his skills as a negotiator; he had once helped calm a riot of Cuban prisoners in Atlanta. Johnson, however, had a reputation for overreaching. In Albany, New York, in 1987, he had pursued an investigation of then mayor Thomas Whalen. According to Whalen, the local U.S. attorney found no evidence to support Johnson's assertions and issued a letter to Whalen exonerating him completely, but Whalen believed it cost him an appointment as a federal judge.

As Jewell sat in a small office, he wondered why the cameraman recording the interview was staring at him so intently. After an hour, Johnson was called out of the room. When he returned, he said to Jewell, "Let's pretend that none of this happened. You are going to come in and start over, and by the way, we want you to fill out this waiver of rights."

"At that moment a million things were going through my head," Jewell told me. "You don't give anyone a waiver of rights unless they are being investigated. I said, 'I need to contact my attorney,' and then all of a sudden it was an instant change. 'What do you need to contact your attorney for? You didn't do anything.

We thought you were a hero. Is there something you want to tell us about?'" Jewell grew increasingly apprehensive and later recalled thinking, *These guys think I did this.*

When the agents took a break, Jewell asked to use the phone. "I called Watson four times. I called his brother. I told his parents that I had to get hold of Watson—it was urgent. I was, like, 'I have to speak to him right now.' What was going on was that Washington was on the phone with Atlanta. The people in Washington were giving them questions." Jewell said he knew this because the videotapes in the cameras were two hours long and "Johnson and Rosario would leave every thirty minutes, like they had to speak on the phone." The OPR report, however, would assert that no one at headquarters knew about the videotaping or the training-film ruse. Lying to get a statement out of a suspect is, in fact, not illegal, but clearly Johnson and Rosario were not making decisions on their own. Even the procedure of having a fleet of cars follow a suspect was an intimidation tactic used by the FBI. Later, according to Jewell, Johnson and Rosario would both tell him privately that they believed he was innocent, but that the investigation was being run by the "highest levels in Washington."

Within the bureau, the belief is that during one of the telephone calls Freeh instructed Johnson and Rosario to read Jewell his Miranda rights. Freeh is said to have learned of Johnson's history from a member of his security detail who had worked in Atlanta. He told Freeh that "Johnson had a reputation for being obnoxious and a problem." In addition, a week after Jewell's interview, Freeh reportedly received a call from Janet Reno, who had learned about the ruse from Kent Alexander, the local U.S. attorney, and Deputy Attorney General Jamie Gorelick. Freeh wondered aloud how it was that, of all the agents in Atlanta, Johnson had been selected to work on the Jewell case. Like Jewell, Johnson had wound up in Atlanta because of his overzealous behavior—according to an FBI source, the Whalen episode had resulted in a "loss-of-effectiveness transfer," an FBI euphemism. (Johnson declined to respond.)

On that same Tuesday, Watson Bryant and Nadya Light closed the office early and went to Centennial Park. Light, thirty-five, a Russian immigrant, had never met Radar, Bryant's old friend, and wanted to buy him a celebratory meal. Killing time until Jewell came on duty, they went into the House of Blues and then bought some hot sauce. Walking toward his car, Bryant saw newsboys hawking the afternoon edition of the *Atlanta Journal-Constitution*. "It was like out of a cartoon. They were all yelling!" he recalled. "I caught the headline out of the corner of my eye." The headline read: "FBI Suspects 'Hero' Guard May Have Planted Bomb."

Bryant borrowed fifty cents from Light to buy the paper and began to read: "'Richard Jewell, 33 . . . fits the profile of the lone bomber.' I could not believe it."

At that moment, Bryant's brother, Bruce, who was on his way to the diving competition, got a call from Jewell. "Where is Watson?" As Bruce Bryant walked past a Speedo billboard with a TV screen, he saw Richard Jewell's face filling the screen. "Oh, my God," he said to his wife. At the same moment, Watson was in his car a block away on Northside Drive when he, too, noticed the Speedo screen. He could not get back to his house—the streets were blocked off for the cycling competition. From his car he called FBI headquarters and demanded to speak to Jewell. "He is not here," the operator said. From his home phone, he picked up his messages and heard Jewell's low, urgent tones. "He didn't leave a number," Bryant told Light. "Call Star 69," she said. The number came back: 679-9000, the number for FBI headquarters, which he had just dialed. Within minutes, Bryant had Jewell on the phone. Jewell told him he was making a training film. "You idiot! You are a suspect. Get your ass out of there now!" Bryant told him.

Before the *Atlanta Journal-Constitution* broke the story of Richard Jewell, there had been a debate in the newsroom over whether to name him. One block away, CNN's Art Harris and Henry Schuster had alerted the network's president that Jewell was targeted, but they held the story, because they understood its potential magnitude. At the *AJC*, Kathy Scruggs, a police reporter, who had allegedly gotten a tip from a close friend in the FBI, got a confirmation from someone in the Atlanta police. According to the managing editor, John Walter, the first edition of the paper that Tuesday had a brief profile of Jewell. It was dropped in later editions as Walter questioned whether the paper had enough facts to support the scoop. Because of the voice-of-God style, the paper ended up making a flat-out statement: "Richard Jewell . . . fits the profile of the lone bomber."

When I asked John Walter about the lone-bomber sentence, he said, "I ultimately edited it. . . . One of the tests we put to the material is, is it a verifiable fact?" One editor added, "The whole story is voice-of-God. . . . Because we see this event taking place, the need to attribute it to sources—FBI or law enforcement—is less than if there is no public acknowledgment." John Walter indicated that he had not seen a lone-bomber profile. I asked him, "Whose profile of a lone bomber does Richard Jewell fit? Where is the 'says who' in this sentence?" Walter said that he felt comfortable with the assertion.

The page-one story had a double byline: Kathy Scruggs and Ron Martz. Walter had told these two early on that they would be the reporters assigned to any Olympic catastrophe. Martz, who had covered the Gulf War, had been assigned the security beat for the Olympics; Scruggs routinely covered local crime. Scruggs had good contacts in the Atlanta police, and she was tough. She was characterized as "a police groupie" by one former staff member. "Kathy has a hard edge that some people find offensive," one of her editors told me, but he praised her skills. Police reporters are often "dictation pads" for local law enforcement; recently the *American Journalism Review* sharply criticized the *AJC* for the scanty confirmation and lack of skepticism in its coverage of Jewell.

The newsroom atmosphere resembled that at FBI headquarters; there was a frenzy to be first. Kent Walker, a newsroom intern, published a story in the same edition, with a glaring mistake in the headline: bomb suspect had sought limelight, press interviews. Since Ray Cleere's tip to the FBI, the "hero bomber" theory had been circulating among Atlanta law-enforcement officers. Maria Elena Fernandez, a reporter, was sent to Habersham County on July 29. By coincidence, William Rathburn, the head of security for the Olympics, had been at the Los Angeles Olympics in 1984 when a fake bomb was found on a bus—left by a policeman who sought attention.

On the surface, the story had an irresistible newsroom logic: Jewell was clearly looking for recognition. Bert Roughton, the city editor, had answered the telephone when a representative from AT&T called to ask if the paper would like a Jewell interview. According to Walter, Roughton himself typed a sentence in the Scruggs-and-Martz piece: "He [Jewell] also has approached newspapers, including the *Atlanta Journal-Constitution,* seeking publicity for his actions." But he hadn't. Walter explained, "There was nothing wrong with that sentence. That's journalistically proper. It is not common practice, to my knowledge, to ask someone you are interviewing . . . 'Are you here of your own free will?'" Jewell had not contacted the paper—a fact that would have been easy enough to check. Walter became snappish when I described the sentence as "a mistake." "It was not a mistake," he said angrily. Scruggs and Martz quoted Piedmont College president Ray Cleere as backup. According to Cleere, Jewell had been "a little erratic" and "almost too excitable."

There was no doubt raised by the *AJC* about the value of Cleere's information or the fragility of the FBI's potential case. On Tuesday morning, July 30, Christina Headrick, a young intern on the paper, was sent to Buford Highway to stake out Richard Jewell's apartment. She phoned in that there were men doing surveillance. By deadline, John Walter had made a decision: He would tear up the afternoon Olympics edition and lead with Jewell.

Several states away, Colonel Robert Ressler was watching CNN when the *AJC* extra edition was shown. Ressler, who was retired from the behavioral-science unit of the FBI, had, along with John Douglas, developed the concept of criminal-personality profiling. He was the coauthor of the *Crime Classification Manual,* which is used by the FBI. He had interviewed Ted Bundy, Jeffrey Dahmer, and John Wayne Gacy, and as he watched the TV report, he was mystified. "They were talking about an FBI profile of a hero bomber, and I thought, What FBI profile? It rather surprised me." According to Ressler, the definition of "hero homicide"—a person looking for recognition without an intent to kill—perhaps emerged as "hero bomber." "There is no such classification as the hero bomber," he told me recently. "This was a myth." Later he said, "It occurred to me that there was no database of any bomber who lived with his mother, was a security guard and unmarried. How many hero bombers had we ever encountered? Only one that I know of, in Los Angeles, and his bomb did not go off." Ressler knew that something was off; profiles are developed from a complex set of evidence and facts derived only in part from a crime scene. The bomb had been deadly, which was not consistent with the "hero complex." Furthermore, he wondered, where did they get the information to put the profile together that fast? He asked himself, What came first here, the chicken or the egg? Was the so-called profile actually developed from the circumstances, or was it invented for Richard Jewell?

When Jewell returned home from FBI headquarters just before 8:00 p.m., NBC was showing special Olympic coverage. He sat on the sofa and watched Tom Brokaw say, "They probably have enough to arrest him right now, probably enough to prosecute him, but you always want to have enough to convict him as well. There are still holes in this case."

Jewell knew that Brokaw was his mother's favorite newsman; he looked at her and noticed "the color and the blood flow out of her face when she heard that." Bobi turned to him and asked, "What is he talking about?" Jewell later recalled, "Brokaw was talking about her son as a murderer. . . . She started crying, and what am I going to say to her? 'Mom, Watson is going to fix this'? What do you say? She doesn't hear anything anyway—she was in hysterics." At that point, Jewell said, he broke down as well.

The day Watson Bryant inadvertently became the lead lawyer for Richard Jewell, he was an attorney whom almost no one in the Atlanta legal establishment had ever heard of. "Who the hell is Watson Bryant?" a caption in the daily legal sheet, the *Fulton County Daily Report*, would read after he had appeared on the *Today* show. Bryant understood Jewell's vulnerability and decided on a strategy: He would treat him as a member of his own family. In Atlanta, the Bryants were a clan: Watson's father, Goble Bryant, had been a West Point tackle, on the 1949 college all-star team; his grandfather had invented a process for putting handles on paper bags. Watson had partied through Vanderbilt University and had barely gotten accepted to law school at the University of South Carolina. He had a close relationship with his brother, Bruce, and their sister, Barbara Ann, and if he lacked staff at his office, he knew he could count on his family to pick up the slack. Bruce enlisted Jewell to help coach his junior football team; Watson had a picnic for Richard and Bobi at his parents' house at the Atlanta Country Club.

When Bryant arrived at the Jewells' apartment that night, he pushed his way through the crowd standing outside in the spongy Atlanta humidity. Microphones were shoved in his face. "What is happening, Watson?" Bobi asked him. Bryant asked Jewell to speak to him alone. "I want to know if you can tell me, without any hesitation at all, if you had anything to do with the bombing," he said. "I didn't," Jewell told him. "I said, 'I am going to ask you again.' He would not look me in the eye. I said, 'Don't give me this "sir" shit.' I said, 'Richard, these people want to kill you. I cannot help you unless you tell me the absolute, unequivocal truth.' I was in his face. He said he did not have anything to do with it." Jewell was bewildered and numb, said Bryant, who left at 10:30 p.m. At midnight, Jewell called him to say, "They are massing outside the apartment, Watson."

The next morning, Bryant went from talk show to talk show, starting with NBC. With the notable exception of the *New York Times,* virtually every newspaper in the country had picked up the *AJC* story and run it as front-page news. There were ten thousand reporters in Atlanta; the *Los Angeles Times* would later call the squad bearing down on the Jewells "a massive strike force . . . Tora! Tora! Tora!" Bryant was in a daze, but he held his own. "Is it true that Jewell was at some time ordered to seek psychological counseling?" Bryant Gumbel asked him. "I know a lot of people that ought to have psychological counseling," Watson Bryant replied.

By 10:00 a.m. he was back at the Jewells' apartment, studying a search warrant that had been delivered that day. The FBI, Jewell recalled, said that he could not be inside the apartment during the search. Bryant called FBI headquarters: "What the hell is this? Why can't he be there?" Within an hour, at least forty members of the FBI had arrived, with dogs. "There was a physical-evidence team. There was a scientific team. There was a team for the bomb-squad people, and then the ATF. . . . They all had different-color shirts. Light blue for bombs, dark blue for evidence protection, red and yellow." Bryant could not believe what he was seeing. "This is like damn Six Flags over Georgia," he told them.

"I kept saying to Watson, 'I didn't do this.' And he said, 'Hey, kid, I believe you—we are doing what we can.'" Jewell was a gun collector. Bryant was sharp with him: "You get all those guns out of your closets and put them on your bed. We don't want any trouble."

For seven hours, Jewell sat outside on the staircase in what has become one of the most famous images of last summer. Bryant had to take his daughter, Meredith, to the Olympic equestrian competition, a once-in-a-lifetime opportunity for her. As he left, he said, "Don't do anything stupid. Just shut up and let them do what they have to do." Hours passed as Jewell sat in the heat. "Finally I decided I would ask them if I could go in and use the rest room. They said, 'We got the order a couple of hours ago you could come in; you just can't get in our way.'" Jewell was told he had to wear rubber socks and gloves in order not to contaminate the site. The Jewell apartment is small—two bedrooms with a bathroom in between, a living room, an alcove dining room that has been turned into a den. As Jewell sat on the sofa, he thought he heard a crash in his bedroom. "I thought my CD player was on the floor, and I said, 'What are you-all tearing up?' and they said, 'You can't go in there right now; we are searching.' I said, 'I want to know what you-all just broke.'" One search warrant listed some two hundred items the FBI could confiscate, including "magazines, books . . . and photographs which would include descriptive information such as telephone numbers, addresses, affiliations and contact points of individuals involved in a conspiracy to manufacture, transport and . . . detonate . . . the explosive device used in the bombing at the Olympic Centennial Park on July 27, 1996."

"They had all my pictures, all the stuff that was in the drawers. My personal things. How would you like to know that twelve different guys had been in your underwear, laid it out on the floor, probably walked on it and then folded it back up like nothing ever happened and put it in your drawer? So then Mom got to go and watch it on TV: 'Live from the Jewell house, the search continues. . . . We are expecting an arrest any minute.'"

When Bobi Jewell returned home, the apartment appeared neat, until she walked into her kitchen. She looked down at her counters, where all her condiments, dog biscuits, spices, and crackers had been taken out of their Tupperware containers and placed in Ziploc bags. She began to cry. And then she went into the bedroom and "immediately started washing clothes," Jewell said.

Driving home from the equestrian events, Bryant heard the live coverage of the search on the radio. "Why are you helping this guy if he's guilty?" Meredith asked.

The next morning, Bryant received a copy of the FBI inventory of articles confiscated in the apartment. On the list he was stunned to see "one hollowed-out hand grenade, ball-shaped" and "one hollowed-out hand grenade, pinecone-shaped." "What the hell is this?" he asked Jewell. "They were paperweights," Jewell said. "I bought them at a military store." "Oh, shit," Bryant said.

For the first few days, the Jewells lived on ham omelettes; a neighbor had brought them half a ham from the Honey Baked Ham Company on Buford Highway. Bobi Jewell had a vacation scheduled, so she remained at home, lying on the bed and "listening to the ball game if it was on." For two weeks, she cleaned out her bureau drawers. Richard would spend the day watching CNN or movies such as *Backdraft* and *Midnight Run*. "I would look out the window and see about 150 to 200 press people. Then it would drop to five or six on the hill. They had one person sitting up there at all times with their binoculars." Richard believed they were being monitored. "They heard everything that was going on. They were over there with high-intensity zoom lenses. They had people over there who could read lips. They had a sound dish. They could hear everything that we said. They had a person writing down everything we said. I saw them."

Once, Bobi's cat jumped on the window ledge under the curtain and the photographers began frenetically shooting pictures, believing that one of the Jewells was in the window. Sound trucks and boom microphones prevented the neighbors from getting near the apartment. Three FBI agents were usually sitting near the tiny swimming pool; each time Jewell or his mother left the house, a cavalcade of unmarked cars would follow. Richard soon began to write a speech describing the horror he felt at being falsely accused. He ate grilled-cheese sandwiches, huge pans of lasagna, and can after can of Campbell's tomato soup.

"If my mom and I had something we wanted to talk about that we didn't want anyone to hear, we wrote it on pieces of paper. When she left to go to work the next day, she would take it with her, tear it up, and put it in the trash! That is how I kept my mother informed about what was going on with the case." The notes were specific: "What the Justice Department was saying, what my attorneys were hearing through the grapevine that I could tell my mom that was not privileged. It was mainly stuff like 'Keep the faith' and 'Can I borrow ten dollars for gas in the truck?'"

Jewell described how, when his mother would walk out the door, "They would holler obscenities at her. They would yell, 'Did he do it? Did he blow those people up?' They would yell, 'You should both die.'" According to Jewell, "The cameramen were just trying to get us aggravated so they could get it on-camera. You don't know how hard it is when they are saying stuff about my mother and me. . . . All she was trying to do was walk her dog. And she cannot do that without hearing that yelling. When someone did that to my mother, I would want to be up on the hill calling the police, because I would want them arrested. I was going to say, 'Mom, tell me which one said that!' And I was going to walk up to that person and introduce myself and say, 'Hi, my name is Richard Jewell. What is yours? Who do you work for? Who is your supervisor?' And I was going to go home and call 911 to get a warrant."

By disposition, Jewell is a night person, but he would get up early when his mother went back to work and make her breakfast. By 11:00 a.m. he would be playing Mortal Kombat II and listening to 96 Rock on the radio, where one of his friends is a disc jockey. Four days into his period of captivity, he called the DeKalb County police. He recalled telling a Mr. Brown, "'This is Richard Jewell. I am sure you are aware of my situation over on Buford Highway.' He said, 'Yes, Richard, I know.' I said, 'I just want to tell you my situation. Number one: I did not do this. Number two: I am here and I am not leaving the apartment for any reason at all.' I said that all the press was doing right now was aggravating my mother and disturbing my neighbors, and I would really appreciate it if the neighbors could return to a normal life."

On Saturday, August 3, as Bryant stared at the FBI agent plucking Jewell's hair, he had already made a decision. "It was, like, screw it. I had had it." The next day was the closing ceremony of the Olympics; Bryant imagined that that would be the day the government might choose to arrest Jewell. "Who is the best criminal lawyer in Georgia?" he asked a state lawyers' association. Within a day, he had brought in Jack Martin, an expert on the federal death penalty and a Harvard law school graduate with close ties to the local U.S. attorney, Kent Alexander. "Let me tell you something about myself," Jewell told him in their first meeting. "I hate criminal lawyers." "Well, Richard," Martin said, "I don't much like cops, but sometimes I need one, and this is a time you sure need a criminal lawyer."

That weekend, watching the Olympic basketball finals, Bryant had an idea: He wanted to be prepared with his own polygraph test of Jewell if the FBI arrested him. From the game, Bryant called a close friend who was a former federal prosecutor. "Try Richard Rackleff," he said. "We worked together on the Walter Moody bombing case." Rackleff had recently set up a private practice, and he agreed to test Jewell the next day. On Sunday morning, Bryant was up early, unable to sleep. He drove around town, making calls from his cell phone. He dialed 679-9000—the FBI. "This is Watson Bryant. I am going to pick up Richard Jewell. I just want you to know that. I don't have a white Bronco. I don't have a wig, and I don't have cash in my car. We are just going to my office."

Watson had coordinated an elaborate plan with his brother to dodge reporters; he would use a decoy and snake through a parking garage. Rackleff had been instructed to park blocks from Bryant's office, because his car could be identified easily, since he was well known in Atlanta law enforcement.

When Rackleff sat down with Richard Jewell in the conference room, he later told me, he sensed almost immediately that Jewell was innocent. Rackleff had tested many bombers before, including Walter Moody, who was convicted of killing a federal judge. "They are strange ducks—they leave their attorneys cold," Rackleff said. Although no one knew Rackleff was in the building, more than one hundred reporters gathered outside to get a look at Jewell. Inside, Jack Martin, Bryant, Nadya Light, and Jewell spent twelve hours in Bryant's office. Rackleff asked Jewell a series of questions, but the test was inconclusive. "Richard is tormented. He is exploding on the inside," Rackleff said. While he was testing him, CNN's Art Harris was visible through the window of Bryant's office, but he could not see inside. Bryant was thoroughly deflated, close to despair. "You have got to try to buck Richard up," Rackleff told him. "Who is going to buck me up?" Bryant asked.

"We are not in missile range of arresting Richard Jewell, but we want him to take our own polygraph," Kent Alexander told Bryant and Jack Martin in their first meeting on the case. In the meantime, Rackleff had tested Jewell again, and he had passed with "no deception," the highest rating. By this time, it was clear that there was no damning evidence against Jewell discovered at the apartment or in his old house in Habersham County.

Alexander was only thirty-eight, but he had been groomed for politics. His father was a senior partner in a good Atlanta law firm, and he had worked as an intern for Senator Sam Nunn. Bryant worried about Alexander's lack of experience, but Alexander told colleagues that he was disturbed by the lack of substantial evidence against Jewell. He was trying to operate with decency, but he was cautious and had to check every detail with Washington.

Bryant, however, didn't trust Alexander; he had had a bad experience with Alexander's predecessor. In 1990, Bryant had almost been put out of business in a tussle with the then U.S. attorney. The local Small Business Administration accused a bank Bryant represented of improper use of funds; the bank blamed Bryant, who was brought before a grand jury and over the next two years almost lost his practice. He spent $50,000 defending himself, and Nadya Light had to take another job, but eventually the case was settled with Bryant's agreeing not to do business with the SBA for eighteen months. Bryant had always felt that he had been manhandled by the office. "I learned everything I needed to know about dealing with this office in 1990," Bryant recalled telling Alexander. "No polygraph for Richard."

At the meeting, Alexander told Bryant and Martin, "This is all off the record. This is a request that is strictly confidential." Weeks later, Louis Freeh came to town to address a breakfast of former FBI agents. Almost immediately, the polygraph request was reported on CNN. "Kent, I thought we had an agreement," Bryant told him. "I cannot control Washington," Alexander said.

When two of the bomb-blast victims sued Richard Jewell, Bryant brought in Wood and Grant to handle the civil litigation. Martin opposed the move. He believed in the cone of silence: "Circle the wagons and don't speak." He said that Wood and Grant had a different perspective: *Attack, attack, and if you give any quarter, it is a sign of weakness.* Martin had been reassured in private by Kent

Alexander that Jewell was not in any immediate danger of being arrested, but the team disagreed about press tactics. Martin worked through the Atlanta-establishment back channels; Lin Wood was a rhetoric man. He favored "one big newsbreak a week." "You know who wrote the book *Masters of Deceit*? J. Edgar Hoover! And that was about the Communist Party in America. So now they have gone from masters of investigation to masters of deceit!" he would routinely tell reporters who called.

Three days after Wood and Grant surfaced as the two new civil lawyers, a Ford van with a tinted bubble-shaped window appeared on the top level of the Macy's parking garage that faced the conference-room windows of their offices. According to Wood, the van did not move for ten days. "We used to sit there and wave at it." Then the lawyers placed a camera in the window, and the next day the vehicle was gone. "For sure that van had laser sound-detecting equipment," Wood said.

Jewell was annoyed that press descriptions of him always emphasized his "overzealousness"; he considers himself a man of details. Often, when he's watching movies at home, he freeze-frames in order to study props in scenes. The second weekend he was considered a suspect, he told me, "I walked in and I noticed white powder all over the telephone table in the conference room." It was a Saturday morning, and Jewell had been with his lawyers until late the night before. He told me he was convinced that the FBI "had lifted a ceiling tile," and that the white powder was "dust that came down." Bryant and Jewell made light of it and did not sweep their phones, believing that any tap the FBI would use would be of a laser or satellite variety and impossible to trace. "In the beginning of every conversation, Watson would curse for about a minute and tell them what lowlifes they were. And then he would say, 'By the way, this is Richard's lawyer. Y'all can cut your tape players off,'" Jewell said. "I would call them dirty scumbags," said Bryant. But the local U.S. attorney, Kent Alexander, insisted that their phones were not tapped. "There are no wiretap warrants," he said.

The FBI did turn up one bit of potentially troublesome evidence in the Jewells' apartment—fragments of a fence that had been blown up in the explosion. After a telephone conversation with Watson Bryant, Kathy Scruggs quoted him saying, "Yes, he did have a sample of the blown-up bomb." Bryant accused her of egregiously misquoting him. He remembered saying to her, "Yes, Richard had souvenirs of the bombing." Scruggs had not taped their conversation. "She cut the 'ing' off of 'bomb,'" Bryant later told me, but Scruggs strongly denies this. The day the story broke, Bryant criticized Scruggs on local radio. That afternoon she appeared at his office to attempt to clear up the misunderstanding. "I don't like your reporting," Bryant recalled telling her. "I'm human, too," she said. The next day, Ron Martz inserted a quote from Bryant in an unrelated news story: "Oh, man, it's not even a scrap of the bomb—it's a piece of damned fence, for God's sake." But the quote would have little impact. Scruggs's version had been picked up; gathering force, it was eventually related by Bill Press on *Crossfire* on the evening of October 28: "The guy was seen with a homemade bomb at his home a few days before." (The next day CNN would be forced to apologize for the mistake.)

By this time Bryant had grown enraged by the media coverage. The *New York Post* had called Jewell "a Village Rambo" and "a fat, failed former sheriff's deputy." Jay Leno had said that Jewell "had a scary resemblance to the guy who whacked Nancy Kerrigan," and asked, "What is it about the Olympic Games that brings out big fat stupid guys?" The *AJC*'s star columnist, Dave Kindred, had compared Jewell to serial murderer Wayne Williams: "Like this one, that suspect was drawn to the blue lights and sirens of police work. Like this one, he became famous in the aftermath of murder."

Television journalism was also a revelation to Bryant; he felt he had "landed on Mars," and spent hours channel-surfing. On CNN, one criminologist said "it was possible" that Jewell had a hero complex. Bryant told his brother, Bruce, "I know I am going to sue someone. I just don't know who." Bruce Bryant searched for Jewell's name on the Internet three weeks into his ordeal and found ten thousand stories. The tone many of the journalists took was accusatory and predetermined, with a few rare exceptions, such as that of CBS correspondent Jim Stewart. "Don't jump to any conclusion yet," he said sharply in a broadcast at the height of the frenzy.

In his first week as Jewell's lawyer, Bryant went to the CNN studio to be interviewed by Larry King. After the broadcast, he was asked to stop in at the office of CNN president Tom Johnson. "They wanted to know what I thought of their reporting so far." Art Harris was in the room. "I turned around and I said to Art Harris, 'Who the hell are you and the rest of the media to make fun of how Richard Jewell and his mother live? Who are you to make fun of working people who live in a $470-a-month apartment? Is there something wrong with that? Who are you to say that he is a weirdo because he lives with his mother?'"

According to Jack Martin, the FBI spent weeks on one erroneous early theory—that Richard Jewell was an enraged homosexual cop-hater who had been aided in the bombing by his lover. Jewell had purportedly planted the bomb; the lover then made the 911 phone call warning that it would go off in Centennial Park. The rationale behind this idea was that Jewell was "mad at the cops and wanted to kill other cops," Martin told me.

The rumor began at Piedmont College, perhaps invented by several of the students Jewell had turned in for smoking pot, but it had a chilling consequence. In mid-August, three agents appeared at the Curtis Mathes video store in Cornelia, where Chris Simmons, a senior at Piedmont, worked part-time. Simmons, a friend of Jewell's, who was engaged to be married, was a B student, but he displayed the same porcine blankness as Jewell and spoke in a slow drawl. He had a deep distrust of the government and carried a card in his pocket that read: Christopher Dwayne Simmons—campaign support for conservative candidates.

The agents questioned Simmons in the store for one and a half hours. "They asked me if I was a homosexual. They asked me if I had accessed the Internet. . . . They later wanted to wire me. They said, 'If he is really a hero, we will find out, and if not, he has killed someone and injured a lot of people.'" Simmons was short with the agents and denied everything. They accused him of lying and said they could take him to Atlanta. The agents told someone Simmons had once worked with that Simmons might be involved in the bombing. "They kept wording questions differently. They kept saying: Do you think Richard Jewell could have done this if he believed that he could get people out in time and nobody would get hurt?" Simmons later called one of the FBI agents and said, "I hear you don't believe my story." He recalled their conversation: "'I think you are sugarcoating your answers,' he said. I said, 'Next time I talk with you, it will be with a lawyer.' And he asked me if I was threatening him. Then he hung up on me." Ultimately, Simmons volunteered to take a polygraph, which he says he passed. "I was a nervous wreck," he said. "I had only seen this on TV."

What was not known outside a small circle of investigators was how deadly the Centennial Park bomb really was. It was well constructed, with a piece of metal shaped like a V, and inside, it had canisters filled with nails and screws. Jack Martin, who had spent time in Vietnam, compared its construction to that of a claymore mine, a sophisticated and lethal device. The bomb weighed more than forty pounds. It was "a shaped charge," FBI deputy director Weldon Kennedy would announce in December. It could blast out fragments from three separate canisters, but only one of the canisters exploded on July 27. Someone had moved the Alice pack slightly before the bomb detonated, causing most of the shrapnel to shoot into the sky. The composition of the bomb did not suggest the work of an amateur, Kathy Scruggs would ironically later report, after interviewing an ATF chemist.

As the weeks went by, Richard Jewell withdrew into a state of psychological limbo; he began to try to analyze what the agents might think of his behavior within the small apartment. "I would be watching a spy show on TV or something like a John Wayne movie. Someone would be talking about blowing something up, and I would think to myself, My God, that is going to sound really bad if they think I am listening to that." He worried that "they would think I was some kind of a nut," and often, when he could not sleep, he would find himself consciously switching to exercise videos and soap operas.

Over Labor Day weekend, he drove up to Habersham County for a picnic with his ex-girlfriend's family, the Chastains. As usual, three FBI cars followed him, but he had gotten adept at picking out the unmarked vehicles. As Jewell drove into town, he noticed that white ribbons hung from hundreds of trees; the Chastains had organized a campaign in his behalf. On the way home, Jewell drove with his friend Dave Dutchess. For the first time, he did not see an FBI car following him, but he noticed an airplane flying low overhead. He drove another twenty miles, and the plane was still on him. "I said, 'Dave, do you think the FBI would be following us in an airplane? It wouldn't be that hard to do, if they put some kind of beeper on the car.'" The plane followed them through Gainesville all the way to Atlanta—an hour's drive. "Just to make sure, we got off on an exit ramp and went about five miles back north. And I got out and took a picture. They followed us all the way back to the apartment! And they circled the apartment for about fifteen minutes, until the FBI car showed back up. I got very emotional. My cheeks got beet red. And Mom came home and said, 'What is going on? What is the matter?' It just destroyed the whole day."

On September 2, Dave Dutchess and his fiancée, Beatty, were driving to their house in Tennessee. It was raining hard, and they noticed they were being followed by several FBI cars. The storm grew worse, and they stopped at a hotel for the night. The next day, while getting coffee at a McDonald's, they were surrounded by FBI agents. "We just want to talk to you. We are trying to be discreet." One agent, Dutchess recalled, spoke into his radio: "We have the suspect in hand." As they walked back toward their car, Dutchess said to Beatty, "They think I am his accomplice. I heard on the news they were looking for his accomplice!"

After the interview, which lasted several hours, Dutchess spoke to Watson Bryant. "What did they ask you that concerns you?" Bryant asked him. "Well, I decided that I had to tell them the truth. Me and one of my friends used to set off pipe bombs for fun," Dutchess told him. "What?" Bryant exclaimed, incredulous. "Yeah, I told them we liked to throw pipe bombs down gopher holes when we lived out in West Virginia."

"Did Richard know this friend?" Bryant asked apprehensively. "Hell, no. He never met him," Dutchess said, but Bryant knew that this could prolong the FBI's investigation perhaps by months. "I hung up and I was thinking, I cannot believe that I even know anyone who throws pipe bombs into gopher holes."

As part of their strategy, Wood and Grant decided to mount a strong counterattack against the government. Wayne Grant had come up with the idea: Bobi Jewell should hold a press conference during the Democratic convention and make a direct plea to Bill Clinton. The day before she was to appear, Grant rehearsed her. It was difficult to work with Bobi; she was exhausted and could not stop crying. Confined under siege for almost a month, she could not see an end to it, since every day brought a new humiliation. The resident manager had threatened to take away their lease, and the manager's son was out selling pictures he took of them. A close friend from church was dying, Bobi said, and Richard could not go to see him, because of the swarm of FBI agents and reporters who followed him everywhere. All of it came out in a rush in the conference room with Wayne Grant: Bobi had even had to give Bryant and Nadya Light the Olympic basketball tickets she had won as colleague of the year, and every night she and her son were stuck together, staring at each other across the kitchen table. They were often irritable, and Richard sometimes lost his temper. "Mother, just shut up," he would tell her when she nagged him about the case. Then, Bobi later recalled, she would go into her bedroom and lie on the four-poster bed hoping that the photographers who rented an apartment across the way for $1,000 a day had no way of knowing what was going on.

Grant kept careful notes on the session. Bobi was terrified about appearing in front of cameras. She sobbed and told him, "If I go on TV Monday, I'll be embarrassed. It will be, like, whenever I go anywhere, people will be looking at me: 'Did he do it or didn't he do it?'"

"If you talked to the person who is in charge of the investigation, what would you say?" Grant asked her calmly. Bobi's voice was halting, but she was firm: "He is innocent. Clear his name and let us get back to a life that is normal."

A few weeks later, Wayne Grant went to a party for a Bar Mitzvah, and a guest cornered him. She asked him if he had told Bobi Jewell to cry at the end of her press conference, and then added coldly, "Nice touch."

———

The lawyers' strategy worked: After Bobi's press conference, the Jewells were deluged with interview requests. Bryant often received one hundred phone calls a day. Bobi soon developed a system: Letters from Oprah Winfrey, Sally Jessy Raphael, and TV producers were stacked on the console in the living room; flowers and baskets of Godiva chocolates and cheese and crackers from the networks were sent to the offices of Wood & Grant and then on to a children's hospital.

At the U.S. Attorney's Office, it had become increasingly clear to Kent Alexander that something had to be done about Richard Jewell. Janet Reno had seen Bobi Jewell on TV and was moved by her sincerity. Privately, Reno and Deputy Attorney General Jamie Gorelick were said to be concerned about the heavy-handed tactics of the FBI. "The case had become a total embarrassment," a Justice Department official told me, but Alexander was in a complicated situation. He was working closely with the FBI, and there was no sign that the bureau was ready to let go, despite growing consternation among the local agents that the Washington command center had mishandled the case. And there was another problem: Alexander did not trust Lin Wood.

By late September, there was a tremendous strain within the team Bryant had hastily assembled. The other lawyers accused Jack Martin of cutting private deals with his friend Kent Alexander, pulling focus, and not being tough enough. For his part, Alexander, according to Martin, admired Bryant even though he believed he was a loose cannon, but he was fed up with Lin Wood.

"Alexander would say something fairly candid to me, and I

would report it to the attorneys, and the next day he would see it on TV," said Jack Martin. "Alexander had checked out Lin, and he knew that he was a take-no-prisoners guy." The lawyers often argued among themselves. Wood insisted on a full-blowout press-attack strategy. Bryant had mastered his sound bite: "The FBI is a five-hundred-pound gorilla who will kick the shit out of anyone." Martin wanted the lawyers to ease up on the hyperbole: "I would say, 'We do not need to do this.' And Lin would say, 'Let's go public with this.' He was manic about it." In one argument, Wood told him, "Goddamn it, Martin, you're like my ex-wives. There isn't anything you can say I won't object to."

There was an atmosphere of extreme apprehension between Bryant and Jewell as they drove to FBI headquarters on the afternoon of October 6. They were on their way to what would seemingly be a session with conclusional overtones, but Jewell was worried: What if this meeting was a trick? It was difficult to believe that the bureau was really ending its two-month-long investigation into his life. For weeks, Jack Martin and Bryant had been going back and forth with Kent Alexander. Finally, Jewell had agreed to an unusual suggestion: If he submitted to a lengthy voluntary interview with the bureau, and if Division 5 was satisfied, then perhaps the Justice Department could issue a letter publicly stating that he was no longer a suspect. Jewell tried to imagine the questions he would be asked. "I wanted to look at everything from their angle," he told me, "trying to assess it and reassess it in my head."

Kent Alexander had set a firm ground rule: Only one lawyer representing Jewell could be in the room. It had been agreed that

Jack Martin, the criminal specialist, would be the man, which en-raged Lin Wood. "You could really see how these guys did not like each other," Jewell said.

"I am not comfortable with the one-lawyer agreement," Wood told John Davis, Kent Alexander's second in command, when they were assembled. "We have an agreement. If you attempt to renego-tiate it, I will have egg on my face," Davis said, adding, "You are not a man of your word." With that, Wood recalled, he rose from his chair and started screaming, "You are not going to say that to me, you son of a bitch!" Kent Alexander interrupted, saying, "This is deteriorating. We aim to stop this. Let's just regroup."

When Jewell, Davis, and Martin finally sat down for the inter-view, Larry Landers, a special agent with the GBI, and FBI special agent Bill Lewis had lists of questions with blank space for answers in front of them. On the wall of the windowless room, there were extensive aerial photographs of the park and, as a prop, an actual park bench was later brought in. Martin believed that the agents intended to resolve areas in the affidavits and other questions: Had Richard ever accessed Candyman's Candyland for information on the *Anarchists' Cookbook*? Had Richard picked up any pieces of pipe when the park was under construction? Had he told anyone, "Take my picture now, because I am going to be famous"? None of this had happened, Jewell said. All he could remember telling someone was that he was off to Atlanta and "going to be in that mess down there," meaning the traffic jams. They pressed him about seemingly inconsistent statements he had made on the morning of the bomb-ing: Why had he told Agent Poor everything was normal when he checked the perimeter of the fence? Jewell explained that he had been walking the "inside of the fence." He once again explained that he had wanted to work the sound-and-light tower so that he could watch the entertainment; he had arranged for his mother to hear Kenny Rogers four days before the explosion.

The area, he told Landers, was "a sweet site" and a great place to look at girls. During a break, Martin asked about all his references to women. Jewell said he wanted them to know he wasn't gay. On several occasions, Landers became annoyed: Why couldn't Jewell pin down the times? Had he seen the drunks on the bench between 10:30 and 11:00 or between 11:00 and 11:30? Why hadn't he looked at his watch? Jewell later recalled, "I said, 'I don't go through my life looking at my watch. I don't care about time. When the bomb went off, I did not look at my watch.' They were wanting to know what time I went to the bathroom and stuff like that. When you have the runs, you are not really concerned about what time it is. You are concerned with getting to the bathroom."

On the day after the FBI meeting, Jack Martin dictated a twenty-seven-page account of everything that had been said during the six-hour interview. In the last moments, Davis said, "He wanted to give Richard the opportunity once and for all to say that he didn't do it." Jewell, Martin wrote, "unequivocally and fortunately said that he had nothing to do with the bomb and didn't know anything about the bomb and if he did he would be the first to deliver the bastard to their door." When Martin walked out, he thought to himself, This really was a formality. They had nothing.

In November a rumor swept through the newsroom of the *AJC* that Cox newspaper executives were rethinking their news policies. According to one reporter, "The sloppiness of the Jewell reporting and the lack of sources was the last straw." A reporter named Carrie Teegardin was assigned to write a piece examining how the media spotlight was turned on Richard Jewell. In large part, her article wound up being an examination of the role of the *AJC*. After Wood and Grant threatened to sue, the article was killed. "We didn't get through the editing of it," John Walter said. "The Jewells' attorney began saying, 'We're thinking lawsuit' . . . and that made us more cautious." Meanwhile, Lin Wood and Wayne Grant were busy holding meetings with lawyers from NBC and Piedmont College. At NBC, Tom Brokaw's carelessness reportedly cost the network more than $500,000 to settle Jewell's claims, although Jewell's lawyers would not confirm a figure. "Brokaw Goofed and NBC Paid," the *New York Daily News* would later headline. In talks with Ray Cleere, the figure of $450,000 by way of settlement was first suggested, then withdrawn when Piedmont College learned that it had insurance. "This will cost them millions now," Lin Wood believes.

On one occasion I asked Richard Jewell if he had any theories about who might have placed the bomb. Jewell said he had popped "two or three theories off the top of my head" on the night he was interviewed by the FBI. "I have gone over that night hundreds of times in my head. You try to think, What type of person would do that? I know it is someone who wanted to hurt people. It is someone who is sick. I hope they find him so he can get the help he needs. Because I am totally torn up about what happened. Every day I think about it, and I will think about it for the rest of my life."

Jewell often speaks with Bryant three times a day. As Jewell searches for a new job, he hangs around Bryant's office, and he recently studied handwriting analysis at the police academy. He has been offered several security jobs with Georgia companies, but he is hoping he will be hired as a Cobb County deputy. In the meantime, Bryant, Wood, and Grant have become sought-after speakers on the First Amendment.

At FBI headquarters in late October, Bobi Jewell broke down and cried as she identified their possessions—the Disney tapes, the Tupperware, Richard's AT&T uniforms, address books. It was a tableau of ordinary middle-class life, laid out on brown paper on a long conference-room table. "I just don't fucking believe this," Watson Bryant said angrily as he packed Bobi's videos into packing crates. "The agents tried to shake my hand," Bobi told me. "I wouldn't touch them." It took ten hours to remove their possessions, Bobi recalled, and four minutes to return them.

The FBI is working on a new and elaborate theory of who did place the bomb in Centennial Park. There is an informed opinion that the backpack discovered a week earlier had in fact been a test run to check FBI procedures, and that the bomber—perhaps a member of a militia group—was quite experienced and had struck before. After a torrent of criticism in the press, Louis Freeh announced that the FBI had arrested Harold Nicholson, an alleged spy for Russia, and he used the opportunity to appear on the *Today Show* and *Good Morning America,* hyping his role in what was a minor arrest, according to one former FBI agent.

In Australia in November, Bill Clinton was asked about his campaign contributions from Indonesia. "One of the things I would urge you to do, remembering what happened to Mr. Jewell in Atlanta, remembering what has happened to so many of the accusations . . . that have been made against me that turned out to be totally baseless, I just think that we ought to . . . get the facts out." When Jewell learned of his comment, he pulled up the transcript from the Internet and became angry: "The president is just using me, like everyone else."

What rights does a private citizen have against the government? The legal precedent for suing the FBI, *Bivens* v. *Six Unknown Agents*, focuses on the behavior of individual agents. Wood believes that Jewell has a strong case against Johnson and Rosario. When Wood learned of Colonel Ressler, he hired him as a possible trial expert. In December, the FBI announced that it would pay up to $500,000 to anyone who could lead it to the Olympic Park bomber.

As Jewell and I drove back from Habersham County in November, he went over the early-morning hours of July 27: "I remember all of the people who were my responsibility. I remember the guys' faces who were flying through the air. I remember people screaming. The sirens going off. I don't think I will ever forget any of that. You just kind of wish sometimes. You think, Could I have done something else? . . . What if we only had five more minutes? Then maybe nobody would have been hurt. But you are what-if-ing. I have been over it a thousand times. I think we could not have done it any better. I think that is something I will always be wondering."

He said he was not sure if he would ever get a job in law enforcement again, particularly since he had been held up as a cartoon figure. On the day of Jewell's exoneration, Jay Leno apologized for having called him a Unadoofus, and said, "If Jewell wins his lawsuit with NBC, he will be my new boss." He later said that this was "the greatest week in trailer-park history." The Atlanta radio station 96

Rock had put billboards of Jewell all over town; "Freebird," they said, a reference to the Lynyrd Skynyrd song. Jewell would later file suit against the station, but the billboard's message was clear. Jewell knows that for many people in America there will perhaps always be a subtle doubt: What if, after all, Richard Jewell really did do it? What if the government let him go simply because it could not make its case? Then he becomes not the innocent Richard Jewell, but the Richard Jewell who may be innocent. "You don't get back what you were originally," he told me. "I don't think I will ever get that back. The first three days, I was supposedly their hero—the person who saves lives. They don't refer to me that way anymore. Now I am the Olympic Park bombing suspect. That's the guy they thought did it."

THE TARGET

APRIL 2013

"They cannot stop me. I will get my education, if it is home, school, or any place."

One day in November 2007, on an editing console in the Dawn television news bureau in Peshawar, Pakistan, the bright brown eyes of a young girl popped from the computer screen. Just three hours to the northeast, in the Swat Valley, the mountain town of Mingora was under siege. Walking by the desk of the bureau chief, a reporter named Syed Irfan Ashraf stopped to take a look at the edit, which was being translated into English for that night's news, and heard the girl's voice. "I'm very frightened," she said crisply. "Earlier, the situation was quite peaceful in Swat, but now it has worsened. Nowadays explosions are increasing. We can't sleep. Our siblings are terrified, and we cannot come to school." She spoke an Urdu of startling refinement for a rural child. "Who is that girl?" Ashraf asked the bureau chief. The answer came in Pashto, the local language: "*Takra jenai,*" which means "a shining young lady." He added, "I think her name is Malala."

The bureau chief had driven to Mingora to interview a local

activist, the owner of the Khushal Girls High School & College. On the roads, Taliban soldiers in black turbans pulled drivers out of cars at checkpoints, searching for DVDs, alcohol, and anything else in violation of Shari'a, or strict Islamic law. In a lane near the market, a low wall protected the two-story private school. Inside, the bureau chief visited a fourth-grade class, where several girls shot up their hands when asked if they wanted to be interviewed. Seeing girls speak out in public was very unusual, even in the Swat Valley, a cultivated, 3,500-square-mile Shangri-la with 1.5 million inhabitants. That night, the brown-eyed girl's sound bite led the news.

Later that evening the bureau chief ran into the school's owner, Ziauddin Yousafzai, who said, "The girl who spoke on your broadcast. That Malala is my daughter." The highly educated Yousafzai clearly understood that in the rigid class system of Pakistan he was an invisible member of the rural underclass, unseen by the elite of Lahore and Karachi. For his family, a moment on national news was huge. Like his daughter, Ziauddin spoke excellent English. Ashraf, who had been a professor at the University of Peshawar, could not get the image of Malala's piercing gaze out of his mind. "She was an ordinary girl, but on-camera extraordinary," he said. His beat at Dawn television included covering the bombings that were devastating remote villages all through Swat, and he determined to meet Malala and her father the next time he was on assignment in Mingora.

Last autumn, I contacted Ashraf at a computer lab in Carbondale, Illinois, where he is studying for a doctorate in media studies at Southern Illinois University. On October 9, he had seen in a news flash the horrifying image of Malala Yousafzai lying bandaged on a stretcher, after having been shot by an unknown extremist on her school bus. For the next three days, Ashraf did not leave his cubicle as the world grieved for this teenager who had stood up to the Taliban. Then he wrote an anguished column in *Dawn*, Pakistan's most widely read English-language newspaper, which seemed like a profound mea culpa. Ashraf was savage regarding his role in Malala's tragedy. "Hype is created with the help of the media while the people wait for the dénouement," he wrote. He decried "the media's role in dragging bright young people into dirty wars with horrible consequences for the innocent." On the telephone he told me, "I was in shock. I could not call anyone." He described his mute agony watching the TV coverage. "It is criminal what I did," he said in an apoplectic tone. "I lured in a child of eleven."

Ashraf had watched the news as Malala was later rushed to a hospital in Birmingham, England, where army trauma victims are treated. She was mysteriously separated from her family for ten days. Many wondered why no relative had been allowed to travel with her. In Pakistan, thousands held candlelight vigils and carried posters that read: WE ARE ALL MALALA. Before she was flown to Birmingham, General Ashfaq Kayani, the Pakistan army chief and former head of the all-powerful Inter-services Intelligence agency (ISI), had gone to the hospital in Peshawar where she struggled for life on a ventilator. The question arose: Why would the most powerful man in Pakistan's military rush to the provincial capital? Other girls had been assaulted, and the government had hardly reacted.

A country of conspiracy theorists, Pakistan has a long history of

Kabuki theater masking the ISI's and the army's possible involvement in silencing anyone who attempts to expose the military's links with extremists. At least fifty-one journalists have been killed there since 1992.

The attack on Malala exposed not only the dark side of an army unable to provide security but also the abysmal quality of education in Pakistan. Only 2.3 percent of its gross domestic product is allocated to education. Pakistan spends seven times more on its military. According to a recent UN study, 5.1 million children are out of school—the second-highest number in the world—and two-thirds of them are female.

"We have a national lie. Why do we have to tell the truth to the world?" says Husain Haqqani, Pakistan's former ambassador to the United States. "The national lie is that the Swat Valley has been liberated from the bad Taliban. Young Malala and her father mess up that narrative."

Suddenly a fifteen-year-old who traded copies of *The Twilight Saga* with her friends was being talked about as a possible future prime minister, if she could just recover from the bullet wound she had sustained while sitting on her school bus after taking an exam on the Holy Koran.

I told Ashraf I wanted to understand how a girl from a remote village had become a cosmic force for change as well as a focus for a number of complex agendas. He said, "We had to get the story out. No one was paying attention to what was happening in Mingora. We took a very brave eleven-year-old and created her to get the attention of the world. We made her a commodity. Then she and her father had to step into the roles we gave them." At first I thought he must be exaggerating.

THE GIFTED CHILD

The capital of Khyber-Pakhtunkhwa Province, Peshawar in 2007 was a boomtown for local journalists. At the Pearl Continental Hotel, reporters jockeyed for the services of a freelance professor or writer who might want to earn $200 a day to guide them safely into the Federally Administered Tribal Areas (FATA), a poor, mountainous region along the Pakistan-Afghanistan border, and long a refuge for the Taliban and other jihadists from around the world. Editors who had interviewed Osama bin Laden a decade earlier could command $500 for a three-hour session with a reporter from the West. In 2006, *Dawn* had begun hiring for the launch of its national TV channel in an effort to grab a market share of Pakistan's recently deregulated airwaves. The explosion of cable networks set off a hiring frenzy for instant experts who could do a decent two-minute stand-up on the terrorist chiefs, the al-Qaeda-related Haqqani network, and the dozens of Taliban groups that passed between Afghanistan and Pakistan. To interview the Taliban commanders and tribal chiefs, foreign reporters darkened their hair, grew beards, and went with a Pashtun fixer who could use his contacts to ensure their safety.

You entered another world when you drove from Peshawar into the mountains. NO FOREIGNERS ALLOWED PAST THIS POINT, warned signs along the entrances to FATA. Pakistan's history of intrigue, coups, and assassinations had long paralyzed its dealings with the frontier.

In the lower Swat Valley was the town of Mingora, a remote getaway for much of Islamabad, Pakistan's capital. Many of Pakistan's most popular Pashtun singers, dancers, and musicians came from the area, and in summer, tourists from around the world would arrive in Mingora for its Sufi music and dance festivals. The area was close to a UNESCO site of ancient Gandhara Buddhist art and ruins. In recent years, however, the Taliban had changed all that; the Pearl Continental Hotel was now empty except for a few reporters and their fixers.

On a cement wall at a corner on Haji Baba Road, the red sign of the Khushal school carried the school crest—a blue-and-white shield with Muhammad's words in Arabic: O my lord, equip me with more knowledge—as well as the Pashto phrase "learning is light." Inside, beneath a portrait of Sir Isaac Newton, some of the girls would remove their headscarves and throw their backpacks on benches. Zahra Jilani, a young American working at a local NGO, recalled walking into the school for the first time: "I heard all this laughter, and girls running in the halls." She told Malala and her class on one visit, "Girls, you must speak up for what you believe." Malala asked her, "What is it like in America? Tell us!" The question was hardly casual. Malala had spent years observing her teachers shrouding themselves in burkas to shop at the bazaar, as if they were living under the Taliban in the 1990s. In Islamabad many young women went to work without even scarves.

Down the alley from the school, Malala lived in a concrete house with a garden. Small rooms opened off a central hall, and Malala kept her royal-blue school uniform on a hook near her bed. At night, her father often read the poetry of Rumi to her and her two younger brothers. Yousafzai was himself a poet, and recitation had played a large part in his education. "I have the right of education. I have the right to play. I have the right to sing. I have the right to speak up," Malala would later tell CNN. As a young teenager, she was reading Paulo Coelho's *The Alchemist* and watching her favorite show, *My Dream Boy Will Come to Marry Me*, on Star Plus TV—until the Taliban cut all cable to the valley.

The Khushal school was an oasis of enlightenment, a tiny dot in a surrounding theater of war, where classes were taught in English. The city of 180,000 had two hundred schools for girls. The curriculum at the Khushal included English, Pashto, Urdu, physics, biology, math, and Islamic studies, imposed by General Mohammad Zia-ul-Haq, the religious fanatic who seized power in a 1977 coup and later declared Islamic law.

Mingora has long been dominated by tribal culture dictated by the vast number of Pashtun inhabitants, whose religion and tradition braided together. For outsiders, one of the most difficult aspects of the culture to understand was Pashtunwali, a personal code that stamps every aspect of Pashtun life, including morality, hospitality, independence, and revenge. Pakistan's Pashtuns were closely connected to Afghanistan's, making the frontier a staging area for the military and the ISI well before the Soviets invaded Afghanistan, in 1979. In recent times, the Pashtuns have been divided between extremists and prodemocracy nationalists who push for greater autonomy. It was commonly known that the army's and ISI's links to jihadist groups such as the Taliban ran far deeper than was ever acknowledged. There were frequent explosions in the area, and power could be cut for days. The Taliban became a well-established presence in Swat. A decade earlier it had taken over the Mingora airport.

Arriving in Mingora in 2007, Ashraf quickly grasped the danger in the surrounding hills. "The most important district official refused to come on-camera," he said. "'Appearing on TV is not Islamic,' he told me. This was the government representative." The musicians who had made the city a tourist draw were now putting ads in the newspapers pledging to lead pious lives. Swat was a microcosm of the shifting loyalties in a dusty war for control of Pakistan among the military, the Islamists, and the progressives.

Everyone in Swat understood the significance of the name of Yousafzai's school. As a young man, Yousafzai had learned to be a passionate nationalist in part by reciting the verse of Khushal Khan Khattak, the seventeenth-century Pashtun warrior-poet known for his courage against the conquering Moguls. The man to see in Mingora, Yousafzai served on the city's Qaumi Jirga, or assembly of elders, and fought a constant battle with the army and the local authorities over the woeful conditions in the city—power outages, unclean water, unsanitary clinics, inadequate education facilities. Funds for textbooks took months to arrive and were often stolen by bureaucrats. The vast gulf between Pakistan's cities and its rural areas was a travesty; FATA and Swat were ruled by Draconian laws based on tribal practice and a code that dated back to the colonial era. Yousafzai wrapped himself in optimism, convinced that he could make a difference in the city by applying the principles of peaceful dissent promoted by the twentieth-century Pashtun leader Abdul Ghaffar (Badshah) Khan, known as "the Frontier Gandhi," who also fought for the establishment of an autonomous nation—Pashtunistan.

"I used to warn him, 'Ziauddin, be careful. There are people out to get you.' He never listened," said the author Aqeel Yousafzai, a war reporter based in Peshawar. Ziauddin named Malala after Malalai, the Afghan Joan of Arc, who died in battle, carrying ammunition to the freedom fighters at war with the British in 1880.

As a teenager, Ziauddin had experienced the changes when Swat became the training ground for jihadists on their way to fight in Afghanistan. His favorite teacher tried to persuade him to join the crusade. "I had nightmares all through those years," he said recently. "I loved my teacher, but he tried to brainwash me." Education saved him, and he determined to spend his life trying to improve schools for children, especially girls. A man with a desperate mission, he would drive every few weeks to Peshawar to alert the media to the increasing danger in his area, and he sent reporters there emails describing the failure of the army to keep order and the anarchy created by a new Taliban squad on the edge of Mingora. The Taliban presence in Swat, he told the writer Shaheen Buneri, "was not possible without the tacit support of the government and Pakistan's intelligence agencies. Both view militant organizations as strategic assets."

"Are you an actress or a circus performer?" the tutor to the young Prince of Swat asked *Life* photographer Margaret Bourke-White when she visited the principality in 1947. No one in Swat, Bourke-White noted in her book *Halfway to Freedom,* had ever seen a woman in slacks. For years Swat was a British princely state, under the rule of an appointed regent, the Wali of Swat. The bearded wali, whom Bourke-White photographed, ruled his feudal land of five hundred thousand subjects with a few telephones connecting his fortresses. But his son, the prince, was determined to bring the outside world into Swat.

The wali had been known for his English suits and his rose garden. In 1961, Queen Elizabeth II visited the enchanted Brigadoon and praised it as "the Switzerland of the British Empire." Each morning the new wali toured his principality—about the size of Delaware—to see how he could help his subjects. Passionate about education, the wali built tuition-free colleges, which every child could attend. Swat became a province of Pakistan in 1969, and its universities turned out many freethinkers, including Ziauddin Yousafzai, who was the president of the Pashtun Student Federation.

"Right from the beginning, Malala was my pet," Yousafzai told me. "She was always in the school and always very curious."

"They went everywhere together. Ziauddin loves all children too much. And no one more than Malala," said Maryam Khalique, the principal of Khushal school, who lived next door to the family. Ziauddin teased his young sons by calling them "those naughty little boys," but his daughter was special. For the first years of Malala's life, the family lived in a two-room apartment in the school. She had the run of all the classrooms. "She would sit in the classes when she was only three, listening, her eyes sparkling," Khalique said. "A little girl taking in the lessons of the older children."

Malala's mother was traditional and chose to remain in purdah, but in private she backed Malala's independence, friends say. Later, in front of reporters, Malala would listen quietly when her father was chided for not allowing her mother the freedom he encouraged in his students. Ziauddin once asked Zebu Jilani, a granddaughter of the last wali and founder of the Swat Relief Initiative, who lives in Princeton, New Jersey, to speak to his Jirga. "Five hundred men and I, the only woman? And an American woman at that?" she asked him. Ziauddin obliged her by taking his wife, completely covered. As a child, Malala could go anywhere as long as she was escorted by a male relative, usually her father. She would even sit by his side when he met in the house with the Jirga.

"He encouraged Malala to speak freely and learn everything she could," one teacher told me. She wrote long compositions in perfect penmanship. By the fifth grade she was winning debating contests. Urdu poetry was part of the curriculum, and Faiz Ahmed Faiz, the revolutionary poet and former editor of the *Pakistan Times,* was a favorite writer: "We shall witness [the day] that has been promised when . . . the enormous mountains of tyranny blow away like cotton." Khalique had one strict rule for her students: no shortwave radio from the two channels that broadcast Maulana Fazlullah, the shock jock who had declared himself the leader of the Swat Taliban.

THE RISING TERROR

"We need to fight against America! We need to stop the NATO forces. They are infidels!" In the autumn of 2007, the big get for Peshawar's TV journalists was the hard-line radio mullah who was terrorizing the Swat Valley. Fazlullah's emblematic white horse grazed outside his compound. One of Ashraf's first assignments for Dawn TV was to get Fazlullah on-camera. Why, Ashraf wondered, would anyone take seriously a fat killer who had dropped out of his madrassa and for a time run the local chairlift? In the villages, Taliban squads with Kalashnikovs stood by cots covered with gold jewelry that Fazlullah's followers had been exhorted to donate for his cause. "Turn off your TV," he told his listeners. "Shows like *Dallas* are the instruments of the Great Satan." Ziauddin said of him, "He was not a sane person. He was against polio vaccinations.

He burned TVs and cassettes. A crazy madman. And one has to speak out against that." At first, "Maulana Radio" was considered a joke, a Talib cartoon with gaps between his teeth. Shortwave and battery-operated radio was crucial in rural Pakistan, where few could read and there was hardly any electricity. Fazlullah hijacked two FM channels for his twice-daily broadcasts, and he threatened to kill anyone who tried to compete on the area's forty stations. For Swatis, Fazlullah's harangues became a favorite entertainment. Pakistan's think tanks warned of "Talibanization" in rural areas, but mullahs such as Fazlullah were perceived as Robin Hoods, who promised to fight the endless corruption and decrepit infrastructure of the frontier.

There was only one public, dial-up computer in Mingora. Every day Ashraf struggled to get online, trudging through Green Square, where Fazlullah's thugs would dump the bodies of apostates they had flogged. Crowds would gather at Fazlullah's mosque to witness the floggings. "The government says we shouldn't do things like this public punishment, but we don't follow their orders. We follow the orders of Allah!" Fazlullah screamed into his PA system. *New Yorker* writer Nicholas Schmidle, as a young visiting scholar, was able to penetrate the area with a fixer. He saw men on roofs with rocket launchers, scanning the rice paddies and poplar fields for anyone who opposed them. "Are you ready for an Islamic system? Are you prepared to make the sacrifices?" Fazlullah would yell. "*Allahu Akbar!* [Allah is the greatest!]," the crowd responded, raising their fists in the air.

It could take Ashraf four hours to transmit twenty-eight seconds of film when the computer was able to connect, but there were days with no power. By the summer of 2007, women had been told not to leave their houses. There were rumors that a revered dancer had been found dead in the town square. "I had the story more or less to myself," Ashraf said, but no one paid much attention. A news editor in Islamabad said, "Why is no one else reporting this?"

By November 2007 they were. Islamabad's Red Mosque was in ruins, badly damaged in July, when the government sent troops to clean out hundreds of extremists. The mosque was a few blocks from the ISI headquarters, a symbol to many of how complex the political alliances were. Soon Fazlullah declared an all-out war on Swat. The first target was a girls' school in a town twenty minutes from the Khushal school. The explosions occurred at night, when there were no children in school, for Pashtuns believe that children must never be harmed in an act of revenge.

In December 2007 former prime minister Benazir Bhutto returned to Pakistan to seek reelection, and millions turned out to greet her. In one of her last interviews Bhutto said that al-Qaeda could be "marching on Islamabad in two to four years." In late December she was assassinated by terrorists, and the country erupted. There were more than five hundred attacks in a two-year period, aimed at politicians, reporters, hotels, mosques, and civilians.

Soon terror chiefs were living openly in Lahore. In Mingora, girls whose schools had been destroyed now attended the Khushal school. Government schools were not an option. The monthly budget of two dollars per student that Pakistan allots "could not cover the community schools in the poorest areas, not even in the refugee camps," said the author Fatima Bhutto, a niece of Benazir Bhutto. "Teachers were political appointees chosen for their loyalty to the ruling party." Rarely shielded from seeing the injured and the dead, Malala learned to navigate in a war zone, taking on her father's determination to change the lives of Swatis.

All that year, terror came to Mingora. By December 2008, helicopters and tanks scoured the area, but ten thousand army troops could not take out Fazlullah's three thousand guerrillas. One-third of the city fled. "The rich have moved out of Swat, while the poor have no place but to stay here," Malala later wrote. She dreaded Fridays, "when suicide attackers think that killing has special meaning." Reporters struggled to persuade people to talk on the record, and Ziauddin always would. "There was never any sign of fear," my colleague Pir Zubair Shah, who then worked for the *New York Times,* recalled. Shah, who is from a prominent Pashtun family, knew where to get a true sense of what was transpiring. "I would come to see Ziauddin, and Malala would serve us tea," he said.

THE RIGHT GIRL

"Would you consider hiring on for a month or so to work with the video journalist Adam Ellick?" *New York Times* documentary producer David Rummel emailed Ashraf in December, after meeting him in Peshawar. Ellick had reported from Prague, Indonesia, and Afghanistan, and was now producing short videos that took viewers inside a compelling personal story. Flying into Islamabad from Kabul, Ellick had the bushy beard of a Talib, but he had little if any experience in Pakistan. He could appear oblivious to tribal codes and brisk to Ashraf when the reporter went through the elaborate greetings dictated by Pashtunwali. "I was used to being called 'sir' by my students," Ashraf told me, "and suddenly someone younger would say to me, 'Focus on your work. When we work, we work. Why are you shaking hands all the time?'"

Working with Ellick was a big break for Ashraf. In graduate school, Ashraf had written his thesis on how Pakistan was perceived in the *New York Times*. For hours, the two would sit together as Ellick coached him on editing and interviewing techniques. It was a dangerous time for reporters in Pakistan. Working on the links between Taliban extremists and the army, *New York Times* reporter Carlotta Gall was attacked in her hotel room in Quetta by ISI agents, who took her computer, notebooks, and cell phone. Pir Shah was held by Talib commanders for three days in FATA. Aqeel Yousafzai was almost killed in a Taliban camp outside Peshawar. Brutally beaten, he lost half his teeth before he was rescued. As conditions in FATA grew worse, Dawn's bureau chief had Ashraf focus completely on Mingora.

The tipping point there came in January 2009 when a dancer named Shabana was murdered, her bullet-ridden body left on display in Green Square. Malala saw it all. "They cannot stop me," she would later say on-camera. "I will get my education, if it is home, school, or any place. This is our request to all the world. Save our schools. Save our world. Save our Pakistan. Save our Swat." The English teacher at the school, before announcing that he was leaving, asked Ashraf, "How can I teach these children Keats and Shelley when such things are happening three blocks from our school?" Over the next six months, a million refugees would flee. Then Fazlullah decreed that, as of January 15, all of the girls' schools in Swat would be closed.

Ashraf saw this as a call to action. "I went to Adam Ellick and I convinced him this is what we should launch as part of the video forum. Education is the most important issue to me, not militancy. I met him in Islamabad, and he said, 'Go for it.' Adam asked, 'Who could be the protagonist who could carry this story?'" Ashraf suggested Malala. "When Adam said yes, I went to Ziauddin and said, 'We can launch this issue in a global forum.'" Did it occur to him, I asked, that Malala could be in danger? "Of course not," he said. "She was a child. Who would shoot a child? The Pashtun tradition is that all children are spared from harm."

As a fixer, Ashraf had often been fearful of putting foreign reporters in danger. Now he no longer considered himself just a reporter, but a partisan. Along with his closest friend, the BBC's Abdul Hai Kakar, he was part of a secret resistance operation with Ziauddin and several others. "We would write and report from Fazlullah's camp half the day and try to stop him the other half of the day," Ashraf said. He compared their situation to that of the French Resistance. "I was undercover fifteen days of the month. I would tell everyone in Mingora I was leaving for Peshawar, but I would stay, trying to gather information about what was going on." He and Kakar developed good relations with Fazlullah's deputies and frequently interviewed the cocky mullah himself, who hoped to use the reporters for propaganda. "Fazlullah, your ambitions will do you in," Kakar warned him. "They will riot in Islamabad if you try to stop the schools." By then Malala and her cousins had been forbidden to leave their house, a four-minute walk from school.

"I'm looking for a girl who could bring the human side to this catastrophe. We would hide her identity," Kakar told Ashraf. "An

Anne Frank?" Ashraf answered, going on to explain the power of the girl in Amsterdam who became an icon through her diary. Meanwhile, Kakar and Ashraf got many queries from French and English news organizations, asking if they knew fixers who could get into the region.

In New York, Dave Rummel saw how powerful a story on the closing of the Swat schools could be. He knew Pakistan well, however, so he was concerned about safety in an area controlled by the Taliban. From Islamabad, Ellick emailed Ashraf:

> We need a main character family to follow on both the final days of school (Jan 14–15) and again on the possible new days of school (Jan 31–Feb 2). We want it to play out like film, where we don't know the ending. That is narrative journalism. And most of all, the family and daughters should be expressive and have strong personalities and emotions on the issue. They must care! . . . Remember, as we discussed several times on Monday, safety first. Don't take any risks. . . . If you have fear, that is OK. Simply stop reporting.

Ashraf read the email many times and kept coming back to the term "narrative journalism." He told me, "I had no idea what it meant." But he had exactly the family in mind he believed would cooperate.

Narrative journalism is almost unknown in India and Pakistan, where stories are told mostly through facts and critical analysis. The intimate narrative—its requirements of real-life emotions and private moments—could be considered a violation in a very traditional area, and for a Pashtun, schooled in hospitality, it would be incomprehensible that such a sensitive line would be crossed. The complexities of personality are considered the work of novelists.

"If this is okay with Ziauddin, let's do it," Ellick told him. Ashraf said, "I had to convince Ziauddin. I told him it was important for both of us—and for our cause." Ziauddin rushed to Peshawar with Malala to discuss the idea, since it was too dangerous for foreign reporters to enter Mingora. Ashraf would be the coproducer and make every decision in Mingora.

Ashraf told me, "Ziauddin was very reluctant. He thought it was going to be about all of the schools in Mingora. I kept telling him in Pashto, 'Don't worry about the security.' This was criminal on my part." At their meeting, Ellick pressed Ziauddin about the danger involved, but no one had to tell a Pashtun about danger. "I will give up my life for Swat," he told Ashraf on-camera. "Fortunately or unfortunately, Malala answered questions very quickly," Ziauddin later said. At one point, Malala answered in perfect English, "The Taliban are trying to close our schools."

"I was opposed," said Ziauddin. "I did not want to impose my liberalism on my daughter, but a close friend said, 'This documentary will do more for Swat than you could do in a hundred years.' I could not imagine the bad consequences." Later, under an assumed name, Malala would give a speech, "How the Taliban Is Trying to Stop Education," that was reported in the Urdu press. Inside the *Times* there was tremendous concern about the risk. "All of the editors were pulled in," said Rummel. They finally agreed that—given the urgency of the situation—Ziauddin's role as an activist made the risk one they could take.

_____

What Ashraf didn't know was that Ziauddin had already decided on his own to reach out to the international media. "Would you consider allowing one of your students to blog about this order [to close the schools]?" Abdul Kakar had asked him a few weeks earlier. "The BBC needs to broadcast this to the world." No parent whom Ziauddin approached was willing to take part, however. "Would you consider allowing my daughter?" Ziauddin finally asked. "She's young, but she can do it." To protect her identity, Kakar chose the name Gul Makai, the heroine of a Pashto folktale. Her conversations with Kakar would be brief—only a few minutes, just time enough for him to take down a paragraph or two.

Kakar always called her on a special line that would be difficult to trace. "I would start off with her in Pashto. 'Are you ready? Let's start.'" Then they would switch to Urdu. Later, there would be accusations that Kakar had coached her. "They ran unedited," he told me.

On January 3, Malala posted, "On my way from school to home, I heard a man saying 'I will kill you.' I hastened my pace and after a while I looked back [to see] if the man was still coming behind me. But to my utter relief he was talking on his mobile." There would be thirty-five entries in all, the last on March 4. Malala was cautious, but in one entry, she criticized the army: "It seems that it is only when dozens of schools have been destroyed and hundreds [of] others closed down that the army thinks about protecting them. Had they conducted their operations here properly, this situation would not have arisen." In one entry she almost tipped her hand: "My mother liked my pen name Gul Makai and said to my father 'why not change her name to Gul Makai?' I also like the name, because my real name means 'grief stricken.' My father said that some days ago someone brought the printout of this diary, saying how wonderful it was. My father said that he smiled but could not even say it was written by his daughter."

THE LAST DAY OF SCHOOL

Ashraf drove to Mingora in the middle of the night with his cameraman. He had twenty-four hours to get into and out of the city. "To be seen with a camera was an invitation to be killed," he told me. Coming over the mountains in the darkness, Ashraf heard the muezzins' call to prayer. "I had a sense of disaster," he said. Just before dawn, as he approached the city, Ashraf called Yousafzai. "It is too early," Ziauddin said. "I was not expecting you." He told Ashraf that Malala's uncle was staying with them, and he was strongly opposed to having journalists present on this last day of school. There was no mention of Malala's blog. Ashraf was completely unaware of the calls she had made with Kakar. "I told no one," Kakar later said.

It was clear to Ashraf, however, that something had happened to frighten Yousafzai. "He was clearly upset. He did not want me there." From a friend's house, just before dawn, Ashraf called Ellick. "Adam said, 'Shoot everything from the moment Malala gets up and has her breakfast to every moment of her last day at school.' Nothing was to be left out." Ashraf told him, "Ziauddin is reluctant." Ellick said, "But he has promised us." Ashraf was suddenly caught in a dilemma: upset his close friend or fail. "I didn't know what to do," he said. "I decided I must try to convince him directly."

Terrified that he might be stopped by soldiers, he hurried to Yousafzai's house. "What are you doing here?" Yousafzai said, clearly angry that Ashraf was putting his family in danger. "It was criminal on my part," Ashraf said later. "I talked to him about the danger we were in, and that this was the moment he could alert the world. I explained that we needed to stay with Malala all day, shooting her, and Ziauddin said, 'What!'" It was clear he had never understood that Malala would be the star of the video. "I was in a panic," Ashraf told me. "He said, 'I thought it would be only about all the other schools.' I said, 'No, to make this important, we need to follow Malala and you the entire day.'"

Ashraf now believes that the code of Pashtunwali made it impossible for Yousafzai to refuse. A worried father, he was also driven by *nanawatai,* the obligation to give shelter. When Malala woke up, Ashraf and the cameraman were in her bedroom, setting up for a shot. Outside the window was the sound of shelling. "Malala did not understand what we were doing there," Ashraf said. "She was shy. I had to say to her, 'Malala, imagine this is your last day of school.' It was her last day, but we had to work with her. Trying to brush her teeth, she kept looking at us. I said, 'Be natural. Don't look at the camera. Pretend we are not here.' It took her hours to understand. We helped to mold her into a part—a part she very much believed."

Ashraf's voice broke as he described to me the rush of adrenaline that came over him as they struggled to get every shot. Half the classes at the school were empty, and there were nearby explosions all day. For hours, the camera stayed on Malala and her father, who sat in his office calling parents who had pulled their children out. "Pay us some of your dues," he said.

"Ziauddin was adamant. He did not want us taking pictures of the girls at school. Soon he said, 'Enough. You must leave.'" But after Ziauddin left the school, Ashraf continued to film in the courtyard, where one scene would jump out at viewers. Wearing headscarves, eight girls line up, and one with a veiled face reads her essay directly into the camera, demanding, "Why the peace and innocent people of the valley are targeted?" Ashraf recalled with emotion, "I arranged that. I grouped them in the courtyard and said, 'Girls, tell me how you feel about your school.'" What guided him, he said, was his trust in Islam: "Children are never attacked. They are sacred."

Watching "Class Dismissed," the thirteen-minute video, a viewer is struck by the raw power of Malala, timidly determined to express her deeply held beliefs, which would be very simple if she lived in the middle-class world of Lahore, or Karachi, or New York. At one point she declares, "I want to become a doctor. It's my own dream. But my father told me that 'you have to become a politician.' But I don't like politics." Ashraf would later have to deal with a question that plagues all journalists: What are the consequences of exposure? He would also have to ask himself a corollary question: What would have been the implications of deciding not to expose the horrors of Mingora? Ashraf still blames himself for teasing her strong beliefs out of a child who would be seen as an exemplary agent for change in one world and as a danger that had to be stopped in another.

All through February, Malala continued to blog. She reported on the peace negotiations as the army capitulated and signed off on turning Swat over to strict Islamic law. Britain and some other countries immediately protested; the United States did not. The Taliban seemed to be appeased, but they continued to kidnap government officials and assassinate reporters.

"In a valley where people do not even hear the voice of a girl, a girl comes forward and speaks a language that the local people cannot even think of. She writes diaries for the BBC, she speaks up in front of diplomats, on television, and her class follows," said Jehangir Khattak, the former news editor of Peshawar's *Frontier Post*. "Ziauddin allowed his daughter to rise in a society where she was seeing dead bodies every day. She didn't hear about the threat—she lived it. In a closed society, she did not mince words."

GOING PUBLIC

"You are right now in a car going into a city where you are a wanted man," Ellick says off-camera in a second *New York Times* web video, "A Schoolgirl's Odyssey," which is twenty minutes long. Six months had passed since the Taliban moved into Swat. The Yousafzais had fled, along with 1.5 million other refugees from the area. As many as one million moved into camps, where often the only relief organizations providing food were religious Islamic groups with ties to the Taliban, who delivered it with invective about foreign enemies. "There was no sign of the army or the police," Ziauddin told Ellick. Malala and her mother went to stay with relatives. Ziauddin, in Peshawar, moved in with three close friends from the Jirga. For months Mingora was under siege. And still the army could not—or would not—put the resources into annihilating the Taliban. That spring of 2009, Mingora became a ghost town as the Taliban advanced on nearby Buner, only one hundred miles from the capital. Finally the army sent more troops, backed by helicopters and rockets, to the area.

In the video, Malala and her father return to the school and find total devastation. Discovering a message left in a student's composition book, Malala says, "They have written something." Then she reads, "I am proud to be a Pakistani and a soldier of the Pakistani army." Looking angrily at the camera, she says, "He doesn't know the spelling of 'soldier.'" They find a letter intended for Ziauddin: "We have lost so much dear and precious lives of our soldiers. And this is all due to your negligence." Looking at a hole blasted in one wall, Malala says, "The Taliban destroyed us."

Later in the video, Malala and her father meet the late Richard Holbrooke, America's special envoy, in Pakistan to inspect the refugee camps. Holbrooke seems surprised by the tone the girl takes with him. "If you can help us in our education, please help us," Malala tells him. "Your country faces a lot of problems," Holbrooke replies. Later, Urdu bloggers would use this footage against her as proof that she was "a Zionist agent" and "a CIA spy."

"I was sick when I saw the video for the first time," Ashraf told me. "In New York, the editors had added footage of Taliban floggings." Now convinced that Malala was a possible target, he emailed Ellick that he was alarmed. "I was thinking we were making a commodity out of this small and graceful shining little girl. This conflict should not have been fought by Malala—it should have been fought by my army, my military, my police. This should not have been Malala's job. That was a camouflage! This was an excuse for us to focus on Malala—not on the forces behind Malala, who were doing little to help the people of Mingora."

Fazlullah had fled to Afghanistan, but his troops remained in the hills. Interviewing in the refugee camps, Pir Shah and *New York Times* bureau chief Jane Perlez heard reports that the army was kidnapping and killing anyone thought to be an extremist. Footage of suspected army assassinations came to them and ran in the *Times*. Soon Perlez's visa was not renewed, and Shah, threatened by the ISI, left Pakistan.

Malala now spoke much more openly. In August, she appeared on Geo TV star anchor Hamid Mir's news show. She talked about the two years her city had been under constant shelling. "What would you like to be?" Mir asked her. "I would like to be a politician. Our country is full of crisis. Our politicians are lazy. I would like to remove the prevalent laziness and serve the nation."

As Pakistan imploded, Ellick filed story after story from Karachi and Islamabad. "At dinners and over tea, I would tell my urban middle-upper-class friends about what I had witnessed in Swat—and about Malala," he posted on Facebook. "I could not get anyone to care. They looked at me like I had a contagious disease—as if I was describing an atrocity in a village in Surinam." In 2010, one year after making his film, he returned there during a period of devastating floods. "I found hundreds and hundreds of kids that were furious at the fact that their schools had not been rebuilt and they openly said to me, 'You know our government is corrupt.'"

It had become an open secret that Malala was the blogger known as Gul Makai. "I am going to apply Malala for the International Children's Peace Prize," Ziauddin told Kakar, referring to the annual awards of the KidsRights Foundation, in Amsterdam. Later, Kakar told him, "Do not chase after fame. Malala is already known and could go abroad to study." He explained, "I was worried they [reporters] would ask Malala a question: 'What would you do if the Taliban comes?' She would not know what to say. This question is not about education. Instead she would tell them, 'Listen to me, the Taliban is very bad.'"

As Malala increased her TV appearances, Pakistan's relationship with the United States deteriorated severely. In 2011, CIA agent Raymond Davis was arrested and later released in Lahore, Osama bin Laden was assassinated, Pakistan cut NATO supply lines after an accidental bombing killed soldiers on the border, and drone strikes resulted in a large number of civilian casualties.

When Malala appeared on the talk show *A Morning with Farah*, she was dressed modestly in a pastel tunic and headscarf. Farah Hussain, glamorous in a black shalwar kameez and high heels, could hardly disguise her condescension. "Your Urdu is so perfect," she told Malala, and then brought up the Taliban. Malala said, "If a Talib is coming, I will pull off my sandal and slap him on his face." For a country girl of fourteen, she was approaching a dangerous line.

Ziauddin and Malala often received threats, and rocks were thrown over the walls of the school and their house. The government offered protection, but Ziauddin turned it down, saying, "We cannot have normalcy in our classes if there are guns." Malala used the consolation-prize money she had received from her own government to buy a school bus. In June the threats continued: "Malala is an obscenity." "You are befriending the kaffir [infidels]."

In May, the local newspaper, *Zama Swat*, reported the killings of numerous prisoners under mysterious circumstances while they were in police custody. For months, the menace from the army had gone unreported—the looting of forests by army patrols, assassinations without trials, local people roughed up at check-points.

With the end of the school year, the Sufi dance festival resumed and field flowers covered the hills. Each year Yousafzai arranged a school picnic at the waterfall in Marghazar, thirty minutes away. Days later someone dropped a note over the wall: "You are giving our girls loose morals and spreading vulgarity by taking the girls to the picnic spot where they run around without purdah."

In June the owner of the Swat Continental Hotel, in Mingora, an outspoken critic of the army's failure to root out the extremists, was gunned down in the street. Then Zahid Khan, the head of the hotel association, was attacked on the way home from his mosque. "I wanted an inquiry," he told me. "Why were these Taliban not attacking anyone in the army? No one was arrested." The Jirga re-acted by announcing that its members would not take part in the Independence Day celebration on August 14, when the military would demonstrate its presence in Swat. Immediately they were summoned to the base to have tea with the brigadier, which one member saw as a chilling threat. They decided not to accept the invitation, but Yousafzai persuaded them to negotiate. He later told a friend, "The meeting was a success. I cannot take on the Pakistani army."

"Ziauddin, you are on a list to be killed," Aqeel Yousafzai told him in September. "You must stop allowing Malala to speak out in public. Or leave the country." Close friends had already advised Ziauddin to leave and get a scholarship somewhere for Malala. "I came early in the morning," Aqeel told me. "Malala was asleep. Ziauddin awakened her, and she came and joined us. 'Your uncle Aqeel thinks we are in a lot of danger,' he said. 'He thinks you should leave.' Malala looked at me and said, 'My uncle is a very good man, but what he is suggesting does not fit with the code of bravery.'"

"They want to silence every critic," said former presidential media adviser Faranahz Ispahani, the wife of former ambassador Husain Haqqani, who was once the target of a trumped-up smear. "So how do they do it? They silence dissident voices, whether it is Benazir Bhutto, [Punjab governor] Salman Taseer, or Malala. With my husband, they called him a traitor. Ziauddin would not shut up, so they put a bullet into his daughter. They did not expect that all of us Pakistanis have reached a point where pluralistic progressive Pakistan is standing up and saying, 'No more.'"

THE ATTACK

On October 9 last year, Ziauddin was at the press club, speaking out against the local government, which was trying to impose control over private schools. "Hold my phone," he told his friend Ahmed Shah. Shah saw the number of the Khushal school on an incoming call, and Ziauddin indicated for him to answer it. The caller said, "Someone has attacked the bus. Come quickly." Shah told me, "We rushed to the clinic. Yousafzai said, 'It could be that someone has come after Malala.' The first sight of her there was blood coming out of her mouth. She was weeping. Then she passed out."

One officer described the shooter as a teenager with shaking hands, but the story changed constantly. A few moments after the bus left the school, the girls started singing. Someone in the road who looked friendly waved for the bus to stop, then asked, "Which one of you is Malala?" No one saw a gun in his hand. They looked toward their friend. Then the assassin put a bullet in Malala's head, and perhaps his unsteadiness saved her life. The bullet only grazed her skull, but it damaged the soft tissue underneath, which controls the face and neck. Two other girls were also badly injured.

"Look at this map," Aqeel Yousafzai told me in New York as he drew a diagram. "The checkpoint was a four-minute walk away. The driver screamed for help. No one came. Twenty minutes passed. No one came. Finally they had to rush from the school with the police. Why? Many people believe the military is responsible. The feeling is Malala and her father had to be silenced."

The Tehrik-I-Taleban Party, Fazlullah's umbrella group, took credit for the attack. By defying Pashtun tradition, Malala was "a clear sinner" who had violated Shari'a and "a spy who divulged secrets of the mujahideen and Taliban through BBC and in return received awards and rewards from the Zionists." They accused her of wearing makeup in interviews. In a seven-page statement, they announced that Ziauddin would be next. Reports in the press mentioned Yousafzai's desire for asylum.

Within hours of Malala's attack, Ashraf received a phone call from Ellick: "Are we responsible?" Later, Ashraf recalled, Ellick consoled him, saying, "We did nothing wrong. If you feel you must write about it, you should. It could be a catharsis." Ellick also emailed Ziauddin expressing his own sense of guilt, Yousafzai said. On WGBH, Boston's public-television station, discussing the ethics of putting a child on-camera, Ellick said, "I'm part of a system that continuously gave them awards . . . which emboldened her . . . and made her more public, more brash, more outspoken."

All over Pakistan, editorials demanded the obvious: Were the military's ties to extremists more important than human rights? Shouldn't the government guarantee a proper education for girls? Within twenty-four hours, General Kayani was in Peshawar.

Soon a curious counternarrative began to grow in the Urdu press. Malala's picture with Richard Holbrooke was widely distributed. Yousafzai, who had always spoken openly with reporters, was suddenly incommunicado. In Mingora, posters were distributed with the headline: "Who Is the Bigger Enemy, the U.S. or the Taliban?" The bullet in Malala's cranium had become a political instrument. At the hospital one doctor said, "We do not know if we can save her, but we think that if she lives she will be completely paralyzed." Ziauddin said, "My God, who could do this to a child?" He was in shock as the Peshawar hospital filled with dignitaries, including Interior Minister Rehman Malik. When Ziauddin finally appeared before the press, Malik was by his side. Ziauddin said he would not be seeking asylum, and he thanked General Kayani.

"I was not thinking about what general or what president. I was in a great trauma," Ziauddin said. He was now dependent on the very establishment he had spent years criticizing. When he was finally allowed to fly to Birmingham, the hospital there arranged for a press conference. But Yousafzai took no questions.

In the last decade, thirty-six thousand people have been killed in Pakistan, and the situation seems to worsen every week. In Birmingham, Ziauddin Yousafzai monitors the news from Pakistan as Malala recovers from two more delicate operations to replace part of her skull with a titanium plate. She plans to write a memoir. For Vital Voices, the women's organization that has raised $150,000 for the Malala Fund, she announced in a widely distributed video,

"I want to serve. I want to serve the people. I want every child to be educated. For that reason we have organized the Malala Fund." Publishers have offered more than $2 million for the rights to her book. "I will not allow Malala's story to be used for someone's agenda. I love Pakistan, and I loved my land before it was Pakistan," Ziauddin said.

Hamid Mir, who almost lost his life when he discovered a bomb under his car before it exploded, said, "Malala called me. She spoke very softly. She said I must not lose courage. I must fight." She also called Geo TV reporter Mahboob Ali in Mingora, the day Fazlullah's forces blew up a nearby mosque, where twenty-two were killed. "Please do not let them put anyone in danger," she said. "I don't want my name to cause harm." Meanwhile, in Mingora, the government renamed a school after Malala. Within a short time it was attacked.

In a phone conversation Ali had a day before Malala's video was launched, he said that Ziauddin seemed resigned to a life that was no longer his to control. He told Ali, "You are a person who can go from one place to another in our town. And I cannot now. Sometimes I become very desperate. I feel I should go back to Pakistan and be in my own village and my own state." Later he added, "This is a fourth life for me. I did not choose it. This is a great country with great values, but when you are taken from your own land, you even miss the bad people of your area."

In January, the Jirga demanded a full judicial commission to investigate "the mayhem that has occurred in Swat and is still happening"—an obvious reference to the military involvement, insiders say.

Not long after I spoke briefly with Yousafzai on the phone, it was announced that he was going to work as a global-education consultant for the Pakistan High Commission in Birmingham. Malala will remain in England, recovering from the damage caused to her speech and hearing. Her left jaw and facial nerves have been reconstructed. A cochlear implant will lessen the deafness in her left ear. Pakistan recently announced that, by the end of 2015, girls' education will be a compulsory legal right.

In February, Malala was nominated for the Nobel Peace Prize. If she recovers, she has been primed to campaign, as Benazir Bhutto once did, against all religious extremism. "That little girl stood up and was not deterred," said Faranahz Ispahani. "She paid a terrible price, but the price she paid may have awoken the world in a way that nothing else has."

AFTER THE GOLD RUSH

SEPTEMBER 1990

"This is in no way a comeback.
Because I never went anywhere."

"We have an old custom here at Mar-a-Lago," Donald Trump was saying one night at dinner in his 118-room winter palace in Palm Beach. "Our custom is to go around the table after dinner and introduce ourselves to each other." Trump had seemed fidgety that night, understandably eager to move the dinner party along so that he could go to bed.

"Old custom? He's only had Mrs. Post's house a few months. Really! I'm going home," one Palm Beach resident whispered to his date.

"Oh, stay," she said. "It will be so amusing."

It was spring, four years ago. Donald and Ivana Trump were seated at opposite ends of their long Sheraton table in Mrs. Marjorie Merriweather Post's former dining room. They were posed in imperial style, as if they were a king and queen. They were at the height of their ride, and it was plenty glorious. Trump was seen on the news shows offering his services to negotiate with the Russians.

There was talk that he might make a run for president. Ivana had had so much publicity that she now offered interviewers a press kit of flattering clips. Anything seemed possible, the Trumps had grown to such stature in the golden city of New York.

It was balmy that night in Palm Beach; Ivana wore a strapless dress. The air was redolent with the fragrance of oleander and bougainvillea, mingled with the slight smell of mildew that clung to the old house. To his credit, Trump had no interest in mastering the Palm Beach style of navy blazers and linen trousers. Often he wore a business suit to his table; his only concession to local custom was to wear a pink tie or pale shoes. To her credit, Ivana still served the dinners her husband preferred, so on that warm night the guests ate beef with potatoes. Mrs. Post's faux-Tiepolo ceiling remained in the dining room, but an immense silver bowl now rested in the center of the table, filled with plastic fruit. As always, it was business with the Trumps, for that was their common purpose, the bond between them. In recent years, they never seemed to touch each other or exchange intimate remarks in public. They had become less like man and wife and more like two ambassadors from different countries, each with a separate agenda.

The Trumps had bought Mar-a-Lago only a few months earlier, but already they had become Palm Beach curiosities. Across the road was the Bath and Tennis Club, "the B and T," as the locals called it, and it was said that the Trumps had yet to be invited to join. "Utter bullshit! They kiss my ass in Palm Beach," Trump told me recently. "Those phonies! That club called me and asked me if they could have my consent to use part of my beach to expand the space for their cabanas! I said, 'Of course!' Do you think if I wanted to be a member they would have turned me down? I wouldn't join that club, because they don't take blacks and Jews."

As if Mar-a-Lago and the *Trump Princess* yacht were James Gatz's West Egg estate, invitations were much prized, for the local snobs loved to dine out on tales of the Trumps. And now this! Embarrassing their guests by having them make speeches, as if they were at a sales convention!

When it was Ivana's turn to introduce herself that night, she rose quickly. "I am married to the most *wonderful* husband. He is so generous and smart. We are so lucky to have this life." She was desperately playing to him, but Donald said nothing in return. He seemed tired of hearing Ivana's endless praise; her subservient quality appeared to be getting to him. Perhaps he was spoiling for something to excite him, like a fight. Maybe all the public posturing was beginning to get boring, too. "Well, I'm done," he said before dessert, tossing his napkin on the table and vanishing from the room.

Palm Beach had been Ivana Trump's idea. Long ago, Donald had screamed at her, "I want nothing social that you aspire to. If that is what makes you happy, get another husband!" But she had no intention of doing that, for Ivana, like Donald, was living out a fantasy. She had seen that in the Trump life everything and everybody appeared to come with a price, or a marker for future use. Ivana had learned to look through Donald with glazed eyes when he said to close friends, as he had in the early years of their marriage, "I would never buy Ivana any decent jewels or pictures. Why give her negotiable assets?" She had gotten out of Eastern Europe by being tough and highly disciplined, and she had compounded her skills through her husband, the master manipulator. She had learned the lingua franca in a world where everyone seemed to be using everyone else in a relentless drive for power. How was she to know that there was another way to live? Besides, she often told her friends, however cruel Donald could be, she was very much in love with him.

This night Ivana had managed to wedge in the publisher of the local social paper, "the Shiny Sheet." As usual, Donald's weekend guests were paybacks, for he trusted few people. He had invited one of his construction executives, the mayor of West Palm Beach, and the former governor of New York, Hugh Carey, who in his days running the state as "Society Carey," boosted by huge Trump donations, had been crucial to Trump's early success.

For years, Ivana appeared to have studied the public behavior of the royals. Her friends now called this "Ivana's imperial-couple syndrome," and they teased her about it, for they knew that Ivana, like Donald, was inventing and reinventing herself all the time. When she had first come to New York, she wore elaborate helmet hairdos and bouffant satin dresses, very Hollywood; her image of rich American women probably came from the movies she had seen as a child. Ivana had now spent years passing through the fine rooms of New York, but she had never seemed to learn the real way of the truly rich, the art of understatement. Instead, she had become regal, filling her houses with the kind of ormolu found in palaces in Eastern Europe. She had taken to waving to friends with tiny hand motions, as if to conserve her energy. At her own charity receptions, she insisted that she and Donald form a receiving line, and she would stand in pinpoint heels, never sinking into the deep grass—such was her control.

This spring night, a squad of servants had been outside to greet the guests, as if they had arrived at Cliveden between the wars. Most of the staff, however, were not a permanent part of Mar-a-Lago; they were local caterers and car parks, hired for the evening. In addition to the dining-room ceiling, Ivana had left Mrs. Post's shabby fringed sofas and Moroccan suites totally in place, giving the impression that she was trying on Mrs. Post's persona, too. One of the few signs of the new owners' taste was the dozens of silver frames on the many end tables. The frames did not contain family pictures, but magazine covers. Each cover featured the face of Donald Trump.

When the Trump plane landed in Palm Beach, two cars were usually waiting, the first a Rolls-Royce for the adults, the second a station wagon for the children, the nannies, and a bodyguard. Occasionally, state troopers were on hand to speed the Trump motorcade along. This took a certain amount of planning and coordination, but the effort was crucial for what Ivana was trying to achieve. "In fifty years Donald and I will be considered old money like the Vanderbilts," she once told the writer Dominick Dunne.

This past April, when his empire was in danger of collapse, Trump isolated himself in a small apartment on a lower floor of Trump Tower. He would lie on his bed, staring at the ceiling, talking into the night on the telephone. The Trumps had separated. Ivana remained upstairs in the family triplex with its beige onyx floors and low-ceilinged living room painted with murals in the style of Michelangelo. The murals had occasioned one of their frequent fights: Ivana wanted cherubs, Donald preferred warriors. The warriors won. "If this were on the ceiling of the Sistine Chapel, it would be very much in place in terms of quality," Trump once said of the work. That April, Ivana began to tell her friends that she was worried about Donald's state of mind.

She had been completely humiliated by Donald through his public association with Marla Maples. "How can you say you love us? You don't love us! You don't even love yourself. You just love your money," twelve-year-old Donald junior told his father, according to friends of Ivana's. "What kind of son have I created?" Trump's mother, Mary, is said to have asked Ivana.

However unlikely it seemed, Ivana was now considered a tabloid heroine, and her popularity seemed in inverse proportion to the fickle city's new dislike of her husband. "Ivana is now a media goddess on par with Princess Di, Madonna, and Elizabeth Taylor," Liz Smith reported. Months earlier, Ivana had undergone cosmetic reconstruction with a California doctor. She emerged unrecognizable to her friends and perhaps her children, as fresh and innocent of face as Heidi of Edelweiss Farms. Although she had negotiated four separate marital-property agreements over the last fourteen years, she was suing her husband for half his assets. Trump was trying to be philosophical. "When a man leaves a woman, especially when it was perceived that he has left for a piece of ass—a good one!—there are 50 percent of the population who will love the woman who was left," he told me.

Ivana had hired a public-relations man to help her in her new role. "This is all very calculated," one of her advisers told me. "Ivana is very shrewd. She's playing it to the hilt."

Many floors beneath the Trumps, Japanese tourists roamed the Trump Tower lobby with their cameras. Inevitably, they took pictures of the display of Trump's familiar portrait from the cover of his book *Trump: The Art of the Deal*, which was propped on an easel outside the Trump Tower real-estate office. The Japanese still took Donald Trump to be the very image of power and money, and seemed to believe, as Trump once had, that this red-marble-and-brass monument was the center of the world.

For days, Trump rarely left his building. Hamburgers and French fries were sent up to him from the nearby New York Delicatessen. His body ballooned, his hair curled down his neck. "You remind me of Howard Hughes," a friend told him. "Thanks," Trump replied, "I admire him." On the telephone he sounded ebullient, without a care, as confident as the image he projected in his lobby portrait.

Like John Connally, the former governor of Texas, Trump had millions of dollars signed away in personal guarantees. The personal debt on the Trump Shuttle alone was $135 million. Bear Stearns had been guaranteed $56 million for Trump's Alexander's and American Airlines positions. The Taj Mahal casino had a complicated set of provisions that made Trump responsible for $35 million. Trump had personally guaranteed $125 million for the Plaza Hotel. In West Palm Beach, Trump Plaza was so empty it was nicknamed "the Trump See-Through." That building alone carried $14 million worth of personal debt. Trump's mansions in Greenwich and Palm Beach, as well as the yacht, had been promised to the banks for $40 million in outstanding loans. The *Wall Street Journal* estimated that Trump's guarantees could exceed $600 million. In one astonishing decade, Donald Trump had become the Brazil of Manhattan.

"Anybody who is anybody sits between the columns. The food is the worst, but you'll see everybody here," Donald Trump told me at the "21" Club. Donald had already cut a swath in this preserve of the New York establishment; we were immediately seated between the columns in the old upstairs room, then decorated with black paneling and red Naugahyde banquettes. It was the autumn of 1980, a fine season in New York. The Yankees were in the pennant race; a movie star was running for president and using the term "deregulation" in his campaign. Donald was new then, thirty-four years old and very brash, just beginning to make copy and loving it. He was already fodder for the dailies and the weeklies, but he was desperate for national attention. "Did you see that the *New York Times* said I looked like Robert Redford?" he asked me.

Trump hasn't changed much physically in the last ten years. Then, as now, he was all cheeks and jaw, with a tendency to look soft in the middle. He retains the blond hair, youthful swagger, and elastic face that give him the quality of the cartoon tough Baby Huey. Trump is a head swiveler, always looking around to see who else is in the room. As a boy, he was equally restless. "Donald was the child who would throw the cake at the birthday parties," his brother Robert once told me. "If I built the bricks up, Donald would come along and glue them all together, and that would be the end of my bricks."

He was already married to Ivana, a former model and athlete from Czechoslovakia. One night in 1976, Trump had been at the bar in Maxwell's Plum. Maxwell's Plum is gone now, but the very name evokes the era of frantic singles underneath the Art Nouveau ceiling. It was the place where flight attendants hoped to find bankers, and models looked for dates. Donald met his model, Ivana Zelnickova, visiting from Montreal. She liked to tell the story of how she had gone skiing with Donald, pretending to be a learner like him, and then humiliated him by whizzing past him down the slopes.

They were married in New York during Easter of 1977. Mayor Beame attended the wedding at Marble Collegiate Church. Donald had already made his alliance with Roy Cohn, who would become his lawyer and mentor. Shortly before the wedding, Donald reportedly told Ivana, "You have to sign this agreement." "What is this?" she asked. "Just a document that will protect my family money." Cohn gallantly offered to find Ivana a lawyer. "We don't have these documents in Czechoslovakia," Ivana reportedly said, but she told friends that she was terrified of Cohn and his power over Donald. The first agreement gave Ivana $20,000 a year. Two years later, Trump had made his own fortune. "You better redo the agreement, Donald," Cohn reportedly told him. "Otherwise you're going to look hard and greedy." Ivana resisted. "You don't like it, stick to the old agreement," Trump is said to have replied.

Donald was determined to have a large family. "I want five children, like in my own family, because with five, then I will know that one will be guaranteed to turn out like me," Donald told a close friend. He was willing to be generous with Ivana, and a story went around that he was giving her a cash bonus of $250,000 for each child.

The Trumps and their baby, Donald junior, lived in a Fifth Avenue apartment decorated with beige velvet sectional sofas and a bone-and-goatskin table from the Italian furniture store Casa Bella. They had a collection of Steuben glass animals which they displayed on glass shelves in the front hall. The shelves were outlined with a string of tiny white lights usually seen on a Christmas tree.

Donald was trying to make time in the world of aesthetes and little black cocktail dresses. He had just completed the Grand Hyatt, on East Forty-second Street, and was considered a comer. He had put together the Fifth Avenue parcel that would become Trump Tower and had enraged the city establishment with his demolition of the cherished Art Deco friezes that had decorated the Bonwit Teller building. Even then, Trump's style was to turn on his audience.

"What do you think? Do you think blowing up the sculptures has hurt me?" he asked me that day at "21."

"Yes."

"Who cares?" he said. "Let's say that I had given that junk to the Met. They would have just put them in their basement. I'll never have the goodwill of the Establishment, the tastemakers of New York. Do you think, if I failed, these guys in New York would be unhappy? They would be thrilled! Because they have never tried anything on the scale that I am trying things in this city. I don't care about their goodwill."

Donald was like an overgrown kid, all rough edges and inflated ego. He had brought the broad style of Brooklyn and Queens into Manhattan, flouting what he considered effete conventions, such as landmark preservation. His suits were badly cut, with wide cuffs on his trousers; he was a shade away from cigars. "I don't put on any airs," he told me. He tooled around New York in a silver Cadillac with "DJT" plates and tinted windows and had a former city cop for his driver.

Donald and I were not alone at lunch that day. He had invited Stanley Friedman to join us. Friedman was a partner of Roy Cohn's and, like Cohn, a legend in the city. He was part of the

Bronx political machine, and would soon be appointed the Bronx County leader. Later, Friedman would go to jail for his role in the city parking-meter scandal. Trump and Friedman spent most of our lunch swapping stories about Roy Cohn. "Roy could fix anyone in the city," Friedman told me. "He's a genius." "He's a lousy lawyer, but he's a genius," Trump said.

At one point, Preston Robert Tisch, known to all as Bob, came into the upstairs room at "21." Bob Tisch and his brother, Laurence, now the head of CBS, had made their fortune in New York and Florida real estate and hotels. Bob Tisch, like his brother, was a city booster, a man of goodwill and manners, a benefactor of hospitals and universities.

"I beat Bob Tisch on the convention-center site," Donald said loudly when Tisch stopped by our table. "But we're friends now, good friends, isn't that right, Bob? Isn't that right?"

Bob Tisch's smile remained on his face, but there was a sudden strain in his tone, as if a child had misbehaved. "Oh, yes, Donald," he said, "good friends. Very good friends."

Late on summer Friday afternoons, the city of noise takes on an eerie quiet. In June I was with one of Donald Trump's more combative lawyers. "We certainly won't win in the popular press," he told me, "but we will win. You'll see." I thought of Trump a few blocks away, isolated in Trump Tower, fighting for his financial life.

The phone rang several times. "Yeah, yeah? Is that so?" the lawyer said, and then laughed at the sheer—as he phrased it—"brass balls" of his client, standing up to the numbers guys who were representing Chase Manhattan and Bankers Trust, whom he was into for hundreds of millions of dollars. "Donald's very up. This is the kind of challenge Donald likes," the lawyer told me. "It's weird. You would never know anything is wrong." "Don't believe anything you read in the papers," Trump had told his publisher Joni Evans. "When they hear the good news about me, what are they going to do?" Random House was rushing to publish his new book, *Trump: Surviving at the Top*, with a first printing of five hundred thousand.

In the Trump Tower conference room that week, one lawyer had reportedly told Trump the obvious: The Plaza Hotel might never bring the $400 million he had paid for it. Trump stayed cool. "Get me the Sultan of Brunei on the telephone," he said. "I have a personal guarantee that the Sultan of Brunei will take me out of the Plaza at an immense profit."

The bankers and lawyers in the conference room looked at Trump with a combination of awe and disbelief. Whatever their cynical instincts, Trump, the Music Man of real estate, could set off in them the power of imagination, for his real skill has always been his ability to convince others of his possibilities. The line between a con man and an entrepreneur is often fuzzy. "They say the Plaza is worth $400 million? Trump says it's worth $800 million. Who the hell knows what it is worth? I can tell you one thing: It is worth a lot more than I paid for it," Trump told me. "When *Forbes* puts low values on all my properties, they say I am only worth $500 million! Well, that's $500 million more than I started with."

"Do people really think I am in trouble?" Trump asked me recently.

"Yes," I said, "they think you're finished."

It was an afternoon in July, when the dust seemed to be settling, and we were in the middle of a two-hour phone conversation. The conversation itself was a negotiation. Trump attempted to put me on the defensive. I had written about him ten years before. Trump had talked about a close friend of his who was the son of a famous New York real-estate developer. "I told him to get out from under his father's thumb," Trump told me then. "That was off the record," Trump told me now. I looked up my old notes. "Wrong, Donald," I said. "What was off the record was when you attacked your other friend and said he was an alcoholic." Without missing a beat, Trump said, "I believe you." Then Trump laughed. "Some things never change."

"Just wait five years," Trump told me. "This is really a no-brainer. Just like the Merv Griffin deal. When I took him to the cleaners, the press wanted me to lose. They said, 'Holy shit! Trump got taken!' Let me tell you something. It's good for me to be thought of as poor right now. You wouldn't believe some of the deals I am making! I guess I have a perverse personality. . . . I've really enjoyed the last few weeks," he said, as if he had been rejuvenated at a spa.

Deals had always been his only art. He was reportedly getting unbelievable deals now from the contractors he had hired to build his casinos and the fiberglass elephants that decorate the Boardwalk in front of the Taj Mahal, for they were desperate, unsure that they would ever get paid for months of work. Trump was famous for his skill at squeezing every last bit out of his transactions. He was known to be making shocking deals now that he never could have made two months before. "Trump won't do a deal unless there's something extra—a kind of moral larceny—in it," one of his rivals once said of him. "Things had gotten too easy for me," Trump told me. "I made a lot of money and I made it too easily, to the point of boredom. Anything I did worked! I took on Bally, I made $32 million. After a while it was too easy."

The fear of boredom has always loomed large in Trump's life. He has a short attention span. He even gave the appearance of having grown bored with his wife. He told me he had grown weary of his deals, his companies, "New York phonies," "Palm Beach phonies," most social people, "negative" writers, and "negatives" in general. "You keep hitting and hitting and hitting, and after a while it doesn't mean as much to you," Trump told me. "Hey, when you first knew me, I basically had done nothing! So I had built a building or two, big deal."

That morning, Trump had been yet again on the front page of the *New York Daily News*, because *Forbes* had dropped him off the list of the world's richest men, placing his net worth at $500 million, down from $1.7 billion in 1989. "They put me on the front page for this bullshit reason!" Trump said. "If they put me on the cover of the *Daily News*, they sell more papers! They put me on the cover of the *Daily News* today with wars breaking out! You know why? Malcolm Forbes got thrown out of the Plaza by me! You know the story about me and Malcolm Forbes, when I kicked him out of the Plaza Hotel? No? Well, I did. You'll read all about it in my new book. And I didn't throw him out because he didn't pay his bill. So I've been expecting this attack from *Forbes*. The same writer who wrote about this also wrote that Merv kicked my ass! The same writer is under investigation. You heard about that, didn't you?" (A *Forbes* writer is under investigation—for alleged use of outdated police credentials. He did not write that Trump was taken by Merv Griffin.) "What happened to me is what is happening in every company in America right now. There is not a company in America that isn't restructuring! Didn't you see the *Wall Street Journal* this morning about Revlon? What is going on at Revlon is what has happened to Donald Trump. But no one makes Revlon a front-page story. My problems didn't even merit a *column* in the *Wall Street Journal.*" (Revlon was selling $182 million worth of stock to raise cash, but that was hardly the same as Trump's crisis.)

Trump spoke in a hypnotic, unending torrent of words. Often he appeared to free-associate. He referred to himself in the third person: "Trump says . . . Trump believes." His phrases skibbled around and doubled back on themselves like fireworks in a summer sky. He reminded me of a carnival barker trying to fill his tent. "I'm more popular now than I was two months ago. There are two publics as far as I'm concerned. The real public and then there's the New York society horseshit. The real public has always liked Donald Trump. The real public feels that Donald Trump is going through Trump-bashing. When I go out now, forget about it. I'm mobbed. It's bedlam," Trump told me.

Trump is often belligerent, as if to pep things up. On the telephone with me, he attacked a local writer as "a disgrace" and savaged a financier's wife I knew as "a giant, a three in the looks department." After the Resorts International deal, at a New Year's Eve party at the Aspen home of Barbara Walters and Merv Adelson, Trump was asked to make a wish for the coming year. "I wish I had another Merv Griffin to bat around," he said.

Before the opening of the Taj Mahal, Marvin Roffman, a financial analyst from Philadelphia, correctly stated that the Taj was in for a rough ride. For that, Roffman believes, Trump had him fired. "Is that why you attacked him?" I asked Trump. "I'd do it again. Here's a guy that used to call me, begging me to buy stock through him, with the implication that if I'd buy stock he'd give me positive comments." "Are you accusing him of fraud?" I asked. "I'm accusing him of being not very good at what he does." Congressman John Dingell of Michigan asked the SEC to investigate the circumstances of Roffman's firing. When I asked Roffman about Trump's charges he said, "That's the most unbelievable garbage I've ever heard in my entire life." Roffman's attorney James Schwartzman called Trump's allegations "the desperate act of a desperate man." Roffman is now suing Trump for defamation of character.

"Donald is a believer in the big-lie theory," his lawyer had told me. "If you say something again and again, people will believe you."

"One of my lawyers said that?" Trump said when I asked him about it. "I think if one of my lawyers said that, I'd like to know who it is, because I'd fire his ass. I'd like to find out who the scumbag is!"

One of Trump's first major deals in New York was to acquire a large tract of land on West Thirty-fourth Street being offered by the bankrupt Penn Central Railroad. Trump submitted a plan for a convention center to city officials. "He told us he'd forgo his $4.4 million fee if we would name the new convention center after his father," former deputy mayor Peter Solomon said. "Someone finally read the contract. He wasn't entitled to anywhere near the money he was claiming. It was unbelievable. He almost got us to name the convention center after his father in return for something he never really had to give away."

Trump's first major real-estate coup in New York was the acquisition of the Commodore Hotel, which would become the Grand

Hyatt. This deal, secured with a controversial tax abatement from the city, made Trump's reputation. His partner at the time was the well-respected Pritzker family of Chicago, who owned the Hyatt chain. Their contract was specific: Trump and Jay Pritzker agreed that if there were any sticking points they would have a ten-day period to arbitrate their differences. At one point, they had a minor disagreement. "Jay Pritzker was leaving for a trip to Nepal, where he was to be incommunicado," a lawyer for the Pritzker family told me. "Donald waited until Jay was in the airplane before he called him. Naturally, Jay couldn't call him back. He was on a mountain in Nepal. Later, Donald kept saying, 'I tried to call you. I gave you the ten days. But you were in Nepal.' It was outrageous. Pritzker was his partner, not his enemy! This is how he acted on his first important deal." Trump later even reported the incident in his book.

"Give them the old Trump bullshit," he told the architect Der Scutt before a presentation of the Trump Tower design at a press conference in 1980. "Tell them it is going to be a million square feet, sixty-eight stories." "I don't lie, Donald," the architect replied.

Eventually Trump bought out the Equitable Life Assurance Company's share of the commercial space in Trump Tower. "He paid Equitable $60 million after an arm's-length negotiation," a top real-estate developer told me. "The equity for the entire commercial space was $120 million. Suddenly, Donald was saying that it was worth $500 million!"

When *The Art of the Deal* was published, he told the *Wall Street Journal* that the first printing would be two hundred thousand. It was fifty thousand fewer than that.

When Charles Feldman of CNN questioned Trump in March about the collapse of his business empire, Trump stormed off the set. Later, he told Feldman's boss, Ted Turner, "Your reporter threatened my secretary and made her cry."

When the stock market collapsed, he announced that he had gotten out in time and had lost nothing. In fact, he had taken a beating on his Alexander's and American Airlines stock. "What I said was, *other than* my Alexander's and American Airlines stock, I was out of the market," Trump told me swiftly.

What forces in Donald Trump's background could have set off in him such a need for self-promotion?

Ten years ago, I went to visit Trump's father in his offices on Avenue Z on the border of Coney Island in Brooklyn. Fred Trump's own real-estate fortune had been made with the help of the Brooklyn political machine and especially Abe Beame. In the 1940s, Trump and Beame shared a close friend and lawyer, a captain in a Brooklyn political club named Bunny Lindenbaum. At that time, Beame worked in the city budget office; thirty years later he would become mayor of the city. Trump, Lindenbaum, and Beame often saw one another at dinner dances and fund-raisers of the Brooklyn political clubs. It is impossible to overestimate the power of these clubs in the New York of the 1950s; they created Fred Trump and gave him access to his largest acquisition, the seventy-five-acre parcel of city land that would become the thirty-eight-hundred-unit Trump Village.

In 1960, an immense tract of land off Ocean Parkway in Brooklyn became available for development. The City Planning Commission had approved a generous tax abatement for a nonprofit foundation to build a housing cooperative. Fred Trump attacked this abatement as "a giveaway." Soon after, Trump himself decided to go after the tax abatement. Although the City Planning Commission had already approved the nonprofit plan, Lindenbaum went to see Mayor Robert Wagner, and Beame, who was in Wagner's camp, supported Trump.

Fred Trump wound up with two-thirds of the property, and within a year he had broken ground on Trump Village. Lindenbaum was given the City Planning Commission seat formerly held by Robert Moses, the power broker who built many of New York's highways, airports, and parks. The following year, Lindenbaum organized a fund-raising lunch for Wagner, who was running for reelection. Forty-three builders and landlords pledged thousands of dollars; Trump, according to reporter Wayne Barrett, pledged $2,500, one of the largest contributions. The lunch party made the front page of the newspapers, and Lindenbaum, disgraced, was forced off the commission. But Robert Wagner won the election, and Beame became his comptroller.

In 1966, as Donald was entering his junior year at the Wharton business school, Fred Trump and Lindenbaum were investigated for their role in a $60 million Mitchell-Lama mortgage. "Is there any way of preventing a man who does business in that way from getting another contract with the state?" the investigations-commission chairman asked about Trump and Lindenbaum. Ultimately, Trump was forced to return $1.2 million that he had overestimated on the land—part of which money he had used to buy a site nearby on which to build a shopping center.

Fred Trump's office was pleasantly modest; the rooms were divided by glass partitions. The Trump Organization, as Donald had already grandly taken to calling his father's company, was a small cottage on the grounds of Trump Village. At the time, Donald told reporters that "the Trump Organization" had twenty-two thousand units, although it had about half that number. Fred Trump was seventy-five then, polite, but nobody's fool. He criticized many of his son's early deals, warning him at one point that expanding into Manhattan was "a ticket on the *Titanic*." Donald ignored him. "A peacock today, a feather duster tomorrow," the developer Sam Lefrak is said to have remarked of Donald Trump. But ten years ago it was clear that Donald was the embodiment of his father's dreams. "I always tell Donald, 'The elevator to success is out of order. Go one step at a time,'" Fred Trump told me. "But what do you think of what my Donald has put together? It boggles the mind!"

Donald Trump has always viewed his father as a role model. In *The Art of the Deal*, he wrote, "Fred Trump was born in New Jersey in 1905. His father, who came here from Sweden ... owned a moderately successful restaurant." In fact, the Trump family was German and desperately poor. "At one point my mother took in stitching to keep us going," Trump's father told me. "For a time, my father owned a restaurant in the Klondike, but he died when I was young." Donald's cousin John Walter once wrote out an elaborate family tree. "We shared the same grandfather," Walter told me, "and he was German. So what?"

Although Fred Trump was born in New Jersey, family members say he felt compelled to hide his German background because most of his tenants were Jewish. "After the war, he thought that Jews would never rent from him if they knew his lineage," Ivana reportedly said. Certainly, Fred Trump's camouflage could easily convey to a child the impression that in business anything goes. When I asked Donald Trump about this, he was evasive: "Actually, it was very difficult. My father was not German; my father's *parents* were German . . . Swedish, and really sort of all over Europe . . . and I was even thinking in the second edition of putting more emphasis on other places because I was getting so many letters from Sweden: Would I come over and speak to Parliament? Would I come meet with the president?"

Donald Trump appears to take aspects of his German background seriously. John Walter works for the Trump Organization, and when he visits Donald in his office, Ivana told a friend, he clicks his heels and says, "*Heil* Hitler," possibly as a family joke.

Last April, perhaps in a surge of Czech nationalism, Ivana Trump told her lawyer Michael Kennedy that from time to time her husband reads a book of Hitler's collected speeches, *My New Order*, which he keeps in a cabinet by his bed. Kennedy now guards a copy of *My New Order* in a closet at his office, as if it were a grenade. Hitler's speeches, from his earliest days up through the Phony War of 1939, reveal his extraordinary ability as a master propagandist.

"Did your cousin John give you the Hitler speeches?" I asked Trump.

Trump hesitated. "Who told you that?"

"I don't remember," I said.

"Actually, it was my friend Marty Davis from Paramount who gave me a copy of *Mein Kampf*, and he's a Jew." ("I did give him a book about Hitler," Marty Davis said. "But it was *My New Order*, Hitler's speeches, not *Mein Kampf*. I thought he would find it interesting. I am his friend, but I'm not Jewish.")

Later, Trump returned to this subject. "*If* I had these speeches, and I am not saying that I do, I would never read them."

Is Ivana trying to convince her friends and lawyer that Trump is a crypto-Nazi? Trump is no reader or history buff. Perhaps his possession of Hitler's speeches merely indicates an interest in Hitler's genius at propaganda. The Führer often described his defeats at Stalingrad and in North Africa as great victories. Trump continues to endow his diminishing world with significance as well. "There's nobody that has the cash flow that I have," he told the *Wall Street Journal* long after he knew better. "I want to be king of cash."

Fred Trump, like his son, has never resisted exaggeration. When Donald was a child, his father bought a house that "had nine bathrooms and columns like Tara," Fred Trump said. The house, however, was in Queens. Donald would someday envision a larger world. It was Donald's mother, Mary, who revered luxury. "My mother had a sense of the grand," Trump told me. "I can remember her watching the coronation of Queen Elizabeth and being so fascinated by it. My father had no interest in that kind of thing at all."

Donald Trump often went with his father to construction sites, for they were extraordinarily close, almost kindred spirits. In family photographs, Fred and Donald stand together, often arm in arm, while Donald's sisters and younger brother, Robert, seem off in the ether. Ivana has told friends that Donald even persuaded his father to put him in charge of his three siblings' trust funds.

Donald was one of five children, the second son. As a child, he was so boisterous that his parents sent him away to military school. "That was the way it worked in the Trump family," a longtime friend told me. "It was not a loving atmosphere." Donald was chubby then, but military school slimmed him down. He became forceful, and grew even closer to his father. "I had to fight back all the time," Trump once told me. "These guys like my father are tough. You have to be hitting back! Otherwise they don't respect you!"

Family members say that the firstborn son, Fred junior, often felt shut out by the relationship between Donald and his father. As a young man, he announced his intention to be an airplane pilot. Later, according to a friend of Ivana's, Donald and his father often belittled Fred junior for this career choice. "Donald would say, 'What is the difference between what you do and driving a bus? Why aren't you in the family real-estate business?'" Fred junior became an alcoholic and died at age forty-three. Ivana has always told her close friends that she believed the pressure put on him by his father and his brother hastened his early death. "Perhaps unknowingly [we did put pressure on him]," Trump told me. "We assumed that [real estate] came rather easy to us and it should have come easily to him. I had success, and that put pressure on Fred, too. What is this, a psychoanalysis of Donald?"

Donald's relationship with Robert has also had troubled moments. Robert, who did go into the family business, has always been "the nice guy," in his brother's shadow. There has been additional friction between Robert's wife, Blaine, and Ivana. Blaine is considered a workhorse for New York charities, and Robert and Blaine are extremely popular—"the good Trumps," they are called. "Robert and I feel that if we say anything about the family, then we become public people," Blaine told me. The brothers' suppressed hostility erupted after the opening of the Taj Mahal. "Robert told Donald that if he didn't give him autonomy he would leave," Ivana told a friend. "So Donald did leave him alone, and there was a mess with the slot machines which cost Donald $3 million to $10 million in the first three days. When Donald exploded, Robert packed his boxes and left. He and Blaine went to her family for Easter."

As his father had had Bunny Lindenbaum for his fixer, Donald Trump had Roy Cohn, the Picasso of the inside fix. "Cohn taught Donald which fork to use," a friend told me. "I'll bring my lawyer Roy Cohn with me," Trump often told city officials a decade ago, before he learned better. "Donald calls me fifteen to twenty times a day," Cohn once told me. "He has a maddening attention to detail. He is always asking, 'What is the status of this? What is the status of that?'"

In a Trump tax-abatement case, according to Cohn's biographer Nicholas von Hoffman, the judge was handed a piece of paper that looked like an affidavit. It had just one sentence on it: "No further delays or adjournments. Stanley M. Friedman." By then Friedman had become the county leader of the Bronx. It wasn't necessary to exchange money for such favors. This was a classic "marker"; the power of suggestion of future favors was enough.

Friedman had also been crucial to Trump's plans for the Commodore Hotel. "In the final days of the Beame administration," according to Wayne Barrett, "Friedman rushed a $160 million, forty-year tax abatement . . . and actually executed the documents for the lame duck Beame." Friedman had already agreed to join Cohn's law firm, which was representing Trump. "Trump lost his moral compass when he made an alliance with Roy Cohn," Liz Smith once remarked.

In New York, Trump soon became known for his confrontational style. He also became the largest contributor to Governor Hugh Carey of New York, except for Carey's brother. Trump and his father gave $135,000. He was moving quickly now; he had set himself up in a Fifth Avenue office and a Fifth Avenue apartment and had hired Louise Sunshine, Carey's chief of fund-raising, as his "director of special projects." "I knew Donald better than anyone," she told me. "We're a team, Sunshine and Trump, and when people shove us, we shove harder." Sunshine had raised millions of dollars for Carey, and she had one of the greatest address books in the city. She took Donald to meet every city and state power broker and worked on the sale of the Trump Tower apartments.

Real-estate tax is immensely complicated. Often profit-and-loss accounting does not run parallel with cash flow. Sometimes a developer can have tremendous cash flow and yet not report taxable earnings; tax laws also permit developers to have less cash flow and greater taxable earnings. It is up to the developer. When Donald Trump broke ground on a new apartment building at Sixty-first Street and Third Avenue, Louise Sunshine was given a 5 percent share of the new Trump Plaza, as it was called.

There was some friction in Sunshine's relationship with her boss. As a result of Trump's accounting on Trump Plaza, Louise Sunshine, according to a close friend, would have had to pay taxes of $1 million. "Why are you structuring Trump Plaza this way?" she reportedly asked Donald. "Where am I going to get $1 million?" "Sell me back your 5 percent share of Trump Plaza and you can have it," Trump said.

Sunshine was so stunned by this that she went to her friend billionaire Leonard Stern for help. "I wrote out a check for $1 million on the spot so that my close friend would not find herself squeezed out by Donald," Stern told me. "I said to Louise, 'You tell Trump that unless he treats you fairly you will litigate! And as a result, the details of his duplicitous treatment would not only come to the attention of the public but also to the Casino Control Commission.'" Louise Sunshine hired Arthur Liman, who would later represent the financier Michael Milken, to handle her case. Liman worked out a settlement: Trump paid Louise Sunshine $2.7 million for her share of Trump Plaza. Sunshine repaid Leonard Stern. For several years, Trump and Sunshine had a cool relationship. But in fine New York style, they are now friends again. "Donald never should have used his money as a power tool over me," Sunshine told me, adding, "I have absolved him."

Like Michael Milken, Trump began to believe that his inordinate skills could be translated into any business. He started to expand out of the familiar world of real estate into casinos, airlines, and hotels. With Citicorp as his enabler, he bought the Plaza and the Eastern shuttle. He managed them both surprisingly well, but he had paid too much for them. He always had the ready cooperation of the starstruck banks, which would later panic. A member of the board of the Chase Manhattan Bank recently demanded at a meeting, "What in God's name were you thinking of to make these loans?" No satisfactory answer was forthcoming; the Rockefeller bank had once kept Brazil afloat, too. The bankers, like the Brooklyn-machine hacks from Trump's childhood, were blame shufflers, frantic to keep the game going.

"You cannot believe the money the banks were throwing at us," a former top legal associate of Trump's told me. "For every deal we did, we would have six or eight banks who were willing to give us hundreds of millions of dollars. We used to have to pick through the financings; the banks could not sign on fast enough to anything Donald conceived."

"He bought more and more properties and expanded so much that he guaranteed his own self-destruction. His fix was spending money. Well, his quick fix became his Achilles' heel," a prominent developer told me.

Trump's negotiations, according to one lawyer who worked on the acquisition of the Atlantic City casino of Resorts International, were always unusually unpleasant. After the success of *The Art of the Deal*, Trump's lawyers began to talk about "Donald's ego" as if it were a separate entity. "Donald's ego will never permit us to accept that point," one lawyer said over and over again during the negotiations. "The key to Donald, like with any bully, is to tell him to go fuck himself," the lawyer told me. When Mortimer Zuckerman, the chairman and CEO of Boston Properties, submitted a design that was chosen for the site of the Fifty-ninth Street coliseum, Trump became apoplectic. "He called everyone, trying to get his deal killed. Of course, Mort's partner was Salomon Brothers, so Trump got nowhere," a person close to Zuckerman remembered.

One image of Ivana and Donald Trump sticks in my memory. Wintertime, three years ago. They were at the Wollman Rink. Donald had just fixed it up for the city. He had been crowing in the newspapers about what dummies Mayor Koch and the city had been, wasting years and money and coming up with nothing on the skating rink. Trump had taken over the job and done it well. If he grabbed more of the credit than he deserved, no one really held it against him; the rink was open at last and filled with happy skaters.

Ivana was wearing a striking lynx coat that showed her blonde hair to advantage. Their arms were around each other. They looked so very young and rich, living in the moment of their success. A polite crowd had gathered to congratulate them on the triumph of the rink. The people near Donald appeared to feel enlivened by his presence, as if he were a hero. His happiness seemed a reflection of the crowd's adulation.

Next to me a man called out, "Why don't you negotiate the SALT talks for Reagan, Donald?" Ivana beamed. The snow began falling very lightly; from the rink below you could hear "The Skaters' Waltz."

Some months before the Trumps' separation, Donald and Ivana were due at a dinner party being given in their honor. The Trumps were late, and this was not a dinner to be taken lightly. The hosts had a family name that evoked the very history of New York, yet as if they had recognized another force coming up in the city, they were honoring Donald and Ivana Trump.

Trump entered the room first. "I had to tape the Larry King show," he said. "I'm on Larry King tonight." He seemed very restless. Trump paid little attention to his blonde companion, and no one in the room recognized Ivana until she began to speak. "My God! What has she done to herself?" one guest asked. Ivana's Slavic cheeks were gone; her lips had been fluffed up into a pout. Her limbs had been resculpted, and her cleavage astonishingly enhanced. The guests were so confused by her looks that her presence created an odd mood.

All through dinner Donald fidgeted. He looked at his watch. He mentioned repeatedly that he was at that moment on the Larry King show, as if he expected the guests to get up from their places. He had been belligerent to King that night, and he wanted the guests to see him, perhaps to confirm his powers. "Do you mind if I sit back a little? Because your breath is very bad—it really is," he had told Larry King on national TV.

"Come on, Arnold! Pose with me! Come on!" Ivana Trump called out to the designer Arnold Scaasi on a warm night this past June. They were at the Waldorf-Astoria, at an awards ceremony sponsored by the Fragrance Foundation, and Ivana was a presenter. The carpet was shabby in the Jade Room; the paparazzi were waiting to pounce. PR materials covered the tables of this "must do" event, of the kind that often passes for New York social life. The most expensive couture dress looked, under the blue-green tint of the lights, cheap.

I was surprised that she appeared. The day before, her husband's crisis with the banks had provided the headlines on all three of the local tabloids. TRUMP IN A SLUMP! cried the *Daily News*. One columnist even said Trump's problems were the occasion for city joy, and proposed a unity day. "Ivana! Ivana! Ivana!" the photographers called out to her. Ivana smiled, as if she were a presidential candidate. She wore a full-skirted mint-green satin beaded gown; her hair was swept off her face in a chignon. However humiliated for her children's sake she may have felt by the bad publicity, she had elected to leave them at home that night. Ivana was at the Waldorf by 6:15 p.m., greeting reporters and paparazzi by name. She could not afford now to alienate the perfume establishment by canceling, for soon she would be merchandising a fragrance, and she would need their goodwill.

Ivana seemed determined to keep her new stature in the city

of alliances, for her financial future depended on her being able to salvage the brand name. As a woman alone, with a reduced fortune, Ivana was entering a tough world. She had no Rothkos to hock and no important jewels. But she did have the name Ivana, and she was making plans to market scarves, perfumes, handbags, and shoes, as once her husband had been able to market the name Trump.

Several feet away from us, the local CBS reporter was doing a stand-up for the evening news. The reporter was commenting on the unraveling of the Trump empire while Ivana was chatting with Scaasi and Estée Lauder. Lauder, a tough businesswoman herself, had reportedly told Ivana several months earlier, "Go back with Donald. It is a cold world out here." I was reminded of a crowd scene in Nathanael West's *Day of the Locust.* Ivana even allowed the CBS reporter to shove a microphone into her face. "Donald and I are partners in marriage and in business. I will stand beside him through thick or thin, for better or worse," she told the reporters with bizarre aplomb. Ivana had become, like Donald, a double agent, able to project innocence and utter confidence. She had, in fact, almost turned into Donald Trump.

"To tell you the truth, I've made Ivana a very popular woman. I've made a lot of satellites. Hey, whether it's Marla or Ivana. Marla can do any movie she wants to now. Ivana can do whatever she wants," Donald Trump told me on the phone.

"New York City is a very tough place," Ivana Trump told me years ago. "I'm tough, too. When people give me a punch in the nose, I react by getting even tougher." We were walking through the rubble of the Commodore Hotel, which would soon reopen as the Grand Hyatt. Ivana had been given the responsibility of supervising all the decoration; she was hard at it, despite the fact that she was wearing a white wool Thierry Mugler jumpsuit and pale Dior shoes as she picked her way through the sawdust. "I told you never to leave a broom like this in a room!" she screamed at one worker. Screaming at her employees had become part of her hallmark, perhaps her way of feeling power. Later, in Atlantic City, she would become known for her obsession with cleanliness.

The phrase "Stockholm syndrome" is now used by Ivana's lawyer Michael Kennedy to describe her relationship with Donald. "She had the mentality of a captive," Kennedy told me. "After a while she couldn't fight her captor anymore, and she began to identify with him. Ivana is deaf, dumb, and blind when it comes to Donald." If Donald worked eighteen-hour days, so would Ivana. The Trumps hired two nannies and a bodyguard for their children. She went to work running Trump Castle casino in Atlantic City, often spending two or three days a week there supervising the staff.

Determined to bring glamour to Trump Castle, she became famous for her attention to appearances, once moving a pregnant waitress, desperate for big tips, off the casino floor. The woman was placed in a distant lounge and given a clown's suit to disguise her condition.

In New York, Ivana did not resist her husband's grandiosity. Soon after Trump Tower was completed, the Trumps took possession of their triplex. Ivana's lawyers often talk about her love of the domestic arts and describe her homemade jams and jellies. Yet the kitchen of her city apartment, which she designed, is tiny, no more than a kitchenette, tiled with gold linoleum. "The children's wing has a kitchen, and that is where the nanny cooks," a friend said. The Trump living room has a beige onyx floor with holes carved out to fit the carpets. There is a waterfall cascading down a marble wall, an Italianate fountain, and the famous murals. Their bedroom had a glass wall filled with arrangements of silk flowers. After a time, Ivana tired of the décor. She called in a renowned decorator. "What can I do with this interior?" she reportedly asked him. "Absolutely nothing," he said.

Christmas Eve, three years ago. Ivana had received another stack of legal documents the size of a telephone book. "What is this?" she is said to have asked Donald. "It is our new nuptial agreement. You get $10 million. Sign it!" "But I can't look at this now, it's Christmas," Ivana said. Donald pressed her, according to Kennedy. Trump seemed extraordinarily concerned that she sign the papers, perhaps because an Atlantic City photographer was threatening to blackmail him with photos he had taken of him and Marla Maples. However efficiently Ivana ran Trump Castle, she seemed terrified of her husband. She signed the papers giving her $10 million and the mansion in Greenwich, Connecticut. Later, Trump would tell reporters, "Ivana has $25 million."

The tactics he used in business he now brought home. "Donald began calling Ivana and screaming all the time: 'You don't know what you are doing!'" one of Ivana's top assistants told me. "When Ivana would hang up the phone, I would say, 'How can you put up with this?' and Ivana would say, 'Because Donald is right.'" He began belittling her: "That dress is terrible." "You're showing too much cleavage." "You never spend enough time with the children." "Who would touch those plastic breasts?" Ivana told her friends that Donald had stopped sleeping with her. She blamed herself. "I think it was Donald's master plan to get rid of Ivana in Atlantic

City," one of her assistants told me. "By then, Marla Maples was in a suite at the Trump Regency. Atlantic City was to be their playground."

Ivana had once warned her husband against Atlantic City. "Why expand somewhere where there is no airport?" Trump, however, was determined to invest there, even though Las Vegas associates had told him that Nevada gaming had profit factors that could total $200 million a year. But by now Marla Maples was in Atlantic City, and it was close to New York. Trump had become, according to one friend, "so focused on Marla he wasn't paying attention to his business."

Though Ivana had established herself in Atlantic City to please Donald, her presence there now, with Marla on the scene, was an inconvenience to him. With the acquisition of the Plaza Hotel, he could deliver an ultimatum: "Either you act like my wife and come back to New York and take care of your children or you run the casino in Atlantic City and we get divorced."

"What am I going to do?" she asked one of her assistants. "If I don't do what he says, I am going to lose him."

Trump even called a press conference to announce Ivana's new position as the president of the Plaza Hotel: "My wife, Ivana, is a brilliant manager. I will pay her one dollar a year and all the dresses she can buy!" Ivana called her friends in tears. "How can Donald humiliate me this way?"

"I think Marla is very different from her image," Donald Trump told me in July. "Her image is that of a very good-looking buxom blonde." A Donna Rice? "She's much different than that. She's smart, she's very nice, and not ambitious. She could have made a fortune in the last six months if she had wanted to!"

"How could you have allowed Marla to be the No Excuses jeans girl?" I asked Trump. "Because I figured she could make $600,000 for doing one day's work. For the negative publicity, I thought, that $600,000 she can live on the rest of her life," Trump told me.

This past February, Trump took off for Japan, telling reporters he would be attending the Mike Tyson fight. His real motive was reportedly to meet with bankers to try to sell the Plaza, for Arthur Andersen's November audit had been dire. As he was flying back, he was radioed on the plane. Liz Smith had broken the story of the Trumps' separation. The entire sordid history of Marla Maples and Ivana fighting on the Aspen ski slopes was all over the papers. Ivana had done to Donald what years ago he had done to Jay Pritzker in Nepal. From the airplane, Trump called Liz Smith. "Congratulations on your story," he told her sarcastically. "I have had it with Ivana. She's gotten to be like Leona Helmsley." "Shame on you, Donald!" Smith replied. "How dare you say that about the mother of your children?" "Just write that someone from Howard Rubenstein's office said it," Trump told Smith, referring to his well-connected press agent. ("I never said that," Trump told me. "Yes, he did," said Smith.) The Japanese bankers with whom Trump had negotiated a tentative sale suddenly backed off. "The Japanese despise scandal," one of their associates told me.

Several weeks later, Donald called Ivana. "Why don't we walk down Fifth Avenue together for the photographers and pretend that this entire scandal has been a publicity stunt? We could say that we wanted to see who would side with you and who would side with me." As the press became more sympathetic to Ivana, Donald would scream at his lawyers, "This is bullshit!"

Ivana began to repair old feuds all over town. "We can be friends now, Leonard, can't we?" she said at a recent party, according to a friend of Leonard Stern's. "Your problem was with Donald, never me. I always liked you."

Trump's lawyers tried mightily to catch up with Ivana. "Donald saw a bill this week that Ivana charged $7,000 worth of Pratesi sheets for their daughter, Ivanka," one lawyer said. "He called in a rage. 'Why does a seven-year-old need $7,000 worth of sheets?' She charged a $350 shirt at Montenapoleone. Who was that for, her new best friend, Jerry Zipkin?" The lawyer described Ivana's bills from Carolina Herrera: "We will get a bill for $25,000, and Ivana will have photocopied over the invoice, so instead of one dress at $25,000, in her own handwriting she will write, 'Six items for $25,000.'" (A spokesman for Ivana says that this is completely untrue.)

The scandal was seriously affecting the Trump children. Donny junior was being ridiculed at the Buckley School. Ivanka had been in tears at Chapin. When Donald and Marla Maples attended the same Elton John concert, Donny junior cried, for his father had told the children he would give Marla Maples up. "The children are all wrecks," Ivana told Liz Smith. "I don't know how Donald can say they are great and fine. Ivanka now comes home from school crying, 'Mommy, does it mean I'm not going to be Ivanka Trump anymore?' Little Eric asks me, 'Is it true you are going away and not coming back?'" However cavalier Ivana's public behavior was, in private she often cried. Once her husband's coconspirator, she told friends that she now felt she was his victim.

On the Saturday of Donald Trump's forty-fourth-birthday celebration, I tried to take a walk on the West Side yards above Lincoln Center in Manhattan. The railroad tracks were rusty, the land was overgrown. The property stretched on, block after block. It was cool by the Hudson River that morning, with a pleasant breeze whipping over the water. The only sign of Trump was a high storm fence topped with elaborate curls of barbed wire to keep out the homeless people who live nearby. It was on this land, at the height of his megalomania, that Trump said he would erect "the tallest building in the world," a plan that was successfully thwarted by neighborhood activists who were resistant to having parts of the West Side obscured in shadow. "They have no power," Trump said at the time, baffled that anyone would resist his grandiose schemes.

Ivana had left for London to take part in one more public-relations event promoting the Plaza, only this time her friends the Baron and Baroness Ricky di Portanova were rumored to be paying the bill. Ivana had had her New York media campaign orchestrated by John Scanlon, who had handled public relations for CBS during the Westmoreland libel case. In London, she was cosseted by Eleanor Lambert, the doyenne of fashion publicists. A story went around London that she couldn't afford her hotel and had moved in with a friend on Eaton Square. She was treading the same ground as Undine Spragg, who so carefully calculated her rise in Edith Wharton's *The Custom of the Country*. Sir Humphry Wakefield assembled a list of titled guests for a dinner, but there was friction between him and Ivana. When the guests, including the Duchess of Northumberland, arrived, many of them were displeased that they had been lured to a dinner that, to their surprise, was in honor of Ivana Trump. "Humphry will pay for this," one guest reportedly said.

That Saturday, New York seemed oddly vacant without the Trumps. Donald had left for his birthday party in Atlantic City. Hundreds of casino employees had been told to be on the Boardwalk to greet him, since Manhattan boosters were in short supply. The day before, he had defaulted on $73 million owed to bondholders and bankers. Clowns and jesters borrowed from Trump's Xanadu attempted to entertain the waiting employees and reporters underneath Trump's minarets and elephants, which soon might be repossessed.

Trump arrived very late, flanked by his bodyguards. His face was hard, his mouth set into a line. With an elaborate flourish, Trump's executives pulled a curtain to reveal his birthday tribute, a huge portrait of Donald Trump, the same image the Japanese stared at in his Manhattan tower. The size of the portrait was unsettling on the Atlantic City Boardwalk: ten feet of the Donald, leaning forward on his elbow, his face frozen in the familiar defiant smirk.

Within days, the bankers agreed to give Trump $65 million to pay his bills. Much of his empire would probably have to be dismantled, but he would retain control. His personal allowance would now be $450,000 a month. "I can live with that," Trump said. "However absurd this sounds, it was smarter to do it this way than to let a judge preside over a fire sale in a bankruptcy court," one banker told me. Trump crowed about the bailout. "This is a great victory. It's a great agreement for everybody," he said.

Not exactly. Trump's bankers were said to be so upset at Trump's balance sheet—he was reportedly over half a billion dollars in the hole—that they demanded he sign over his future trust inheritance to secure the new loans. Trump's father, who had created him by helping him achieve his first deals, now seemed to be rescuing him again. "Total bullshit," Trump told me. "I have been given five years by the banks. The banks would never have asked me for my future inheritance, and I would never have given it."

Soon after, Trump announced that the French department store Galeries Lafayette would take over the vast space Bonwit Teller had vacated in Trump Tower. "This is in no way a comeback," Trump told me. "Because I never went anywhere."

I was still searching for Donald Trump. On a rainy Thursday in July, I went down to federal court, where he was set to testify in a civil case in which he was a defendant. Along with his contractor, Trump had been accused of hiring scores of illegal Polish aliens to do the demolition work on the Trump Tower site. "The Polish brigade," as they came to be called, had been astonishingly exploited on the job, earning four dollars an hour for work that usually paid five times that.

The last time I had been in this neighborhood was to hear the verdict in the John Gotti trial. I had come to know the area well. The guard inside greeted me by name. I was often here dipping in and out of the courtrooms to observe the notorious figures of the last decade. I thought of Bess Myerson, Michael Milken, Ivan Boesky, Leona Helmsley, Imelda Marcos, and Adnan Khashoggi, shattered and brought down in the crazy kaleidoscope of the 1980s.

Each one had, at one time in his or her life, been thought to be like Donald Trump, a figure of greatness, anointed with special powers. In front of the courthouse, the police barricades were up. So many celebrities passed through these revolving doors that the yellow sawhorses were left routinely on the massive courthouse steps.

I thought about the ten years since I had first met Donald Trump. It is fashionable now to say that he was a symbol of the crassness of the 1980s, but Trump became more than a vulgarian. Like Michael Milken, Trump appeared to believe that his money gave him a freedom to set the rules. No one stopped him. His exaggerations and baloney were reported, and people laughed. His bankers showered him with money. City officials almost allowed him to set public policy by erecting his wall of concrete on the Hudson River. New York City, like the bankers from the Chase and Manny Hanny, allowed Trump to exist in a universe where all reality had vanished. "I met with a couple of reporters," Trump told me on the telephone, "and they totally saw what I was saying. They completely believed me. And then they went out and wrote vicious things about me, as I am sure you will, too." Long ago, Trump had counted me among his enemies in his world of "positives" and "negatives." I felt that the next dozen people he spoke to would probably be subjected to a catalogue of my transgressions as imagined by Donald Trump.

When I got to the courtroom, Trump had gone. His lawyer, the venerable and well-connected Milton Gould, was smiling broadly, for he appeared to believe that he was wiping the floor with this case. Trump had said that he knew nothing about the demolitions, that his contractor had been "a disaster." Yet one FBI informant testified that he had warned Trump of the presence of the Polish brigade and had told him that if he didn't get rid of them his casino license might not be granted.

I wandered down to the press room on the fifth floor to hear about Trump's testimony. The reporters sounded weary; they had heard it all before. "Goddamn it," one shouted at me, "we created him! We bought his bullshit! He was always a phony, and we filled our papers with him!"

I thought about the last questions Donald Trump had asked me the day before on the telephone. "How long is your article?" "Long," I said. Trump seemed pleased. "Is it a cover?" he asked.

FRANCE'S SCARLET LETTER

JUNE 2003

"I tried to bring the techniques of simple police interrogation. Ask the name, the address, the phone number, the place of the attack."

It would take many months for David de Rothschild to realize that what was happening to Jews in France was a powerful predictor of a war that was coming down history's long stream. In May 2001, when he and a group of French business leaders arrived in Jerusalem for meetings with Prime Minister Ariel Sharon and members of his Cabinet, he reluctantly agreed to speak to a reporter from the *Jerusalem Post*. Then fifty-eight and the head of the French branch of his family's banking dynasty, he was just beginning to be aware of a wave of attacks on French Jews by French Muslims that would escalate into an unimaginable nightmare and affect France, the United States, and the Muslim and Jewish populations of both countries.

Rothschild was actively involved in Jewish organizations in France, but, as he told friends, he was not particularly *croyant,* or religious, by nature. In restaurants, however, if he overheard a conversation that struck him as anti-Semitic, he was known to walk over to the table and silently present his card. That day in Jerusalem, he did not yet comprehend how dangerous the situation in France had become. The facts were these: Between January and May 2001 there had been more than three hundred attacks against Jews. From Marseille to Paris, synagogues had been destroyed, school buses stoned, children assaulted. Yet very few of the incidents had been reported in the French media, which have a distinctly pro-Palestinian tilt. So Rothschild was largely uninformed concerning the accurate numbers. He and his friends were still operating in a near vacuum, because of what is called in France *la barrière du silence,* which minimizes and mystifies reporting on French Jewish matters and the Middle East.

Rothschild would later be disturbed that he had not been made more aware faster of the degree of violence, which would be perceived outside France as the return of classic anti-Semitism and anti-Americanism and would infect France and much of Europe over the next two years. By the spring of this year, the number of hate crimes had risen above one thousand, and the relationship of the United States, poised to declare a war on Iraq, and France, implacably opposed to such a war, was glacial.

About six million Muslims live in France, nearly 10 percent of the population, a potential voting bloc. In contrast, there are only about 650,000 Jews, but it is the third-largest Jewish population in the world, after Israel and the United States. The victims of the attacks appeared to live mostly in working-class areas in the *banlieues,* or suburbs, on the outskirts of Paris, a laboratory of assimilation where much of the unemployed Muslim population also lives. The situation, Rothschild later told me, was fraught with complexity. In addition to a large number of distinguished Arab intellectuals, France was also home to cells of terrorists, fundamentalist imams, and firms with strong business ties to Baghdad. When Rothschild arrived in Israel in May 2001, he had also left behind him another, subtler struggle, going on behind closed doors, between the establishment Ashkenazi Jews of central Paris and the *pieds-noirs,* French citizens formerly of North Africa, many of them lower-middle-class Sephardic Jews who live in the suburbs. The Sephardic communities in the Paris outskirts were the principal targets of anti-Western paranoia spewing up out of the Middle East. A widely shared position of the upper-class Jewish establishment in France was to let such things alone and not *jeter de l'huile sur le feu* (throw oil on the fire).

Rothschild and the Jewish intellectual establishment would be caught in the vise of a vicious debate at a time of intense political correctness in France. Their country was marginalized as a world power and was owed billions of dollars by Iraq for the brisk trade between the two countries. In addition, before the 1991 Gulf War, France had been a major supplier of weapons to Iraq. Yet France trumpeted its moral superiority. By the time Rothschild saw the reporter from the *Jerusalem Post,* France was too busy "feeding the crocodile," as one historian remarked, to notice the danger that lurked within. In May 2001, Rothschild was worried principally about the growing popularity of Jean-Marie Le Pen, the far-right-wing candidate for president. Notoriously anti-Semitic— Hitler's gas chambers were a "minor detail" in World War II, he has said—Le Pen had won 15 percent of the vote in 1995 on an antifor-eigner hate platform, and was strong in the polls for the 2002 elections. Rothschild believed, he told the reporter in Jerusalem, that the wave of attacks was likely coming from "neo-Nazis, a hostile, aggressive, anti-Semitic, right-wing population, among which you may have some Muslims. But it's not being led by the Muslims."

Rothschild was careful with his language. "The Muslims who have chosen France live there normally, not with the aim of doing any terrorist activity," he said. "I promise you that in the last ten, fif-teen years I haven't received any kind of anti-Semitic letter, any swas-tika, nothing like that. . . . Possibly because I am privileged, possibly because I live in a protected environment. . . . I personally do not feel anti-Semitism." Within hours of its publication, his comment would rocket through emails in the working-class areas of Paris and be talked about in catastrophic terms, inflaming an oddball activist cop who had taken the plight of France's Jews as his mission. It was but one small piece of a dilemma that would grow imperceptibly into a cataclysm as America and France came to a stunning break in their relationship on the eve of the U.S.-led war with Iraq. Roth-schild was still trying to analyze the mystery that had led to an inter-national crisis when he spoke on the phone with me this past March. His voice rose as he said, "Who was inhibited to talk? Why did it take so long? Whose fault was it? What was the reason?" He concluded sadly, "These are questions that are hard to answer."

I have a story to tell. It begins on the northern outskirts of Paris in the town of Le Blanc-Mesnil in October 2000. Le Blanc-Mesnil is half a dozen stops on the Métro line from Charles de Gaulle

Airport, a community of matchbox row houses with red tile roofs and cafés where the menu of falafel specialties is written in French and Arabic. It is inhabited by factory hands, accountants, teachers, and garment-industry workers. Along with Drancy, St.-Denis, and a cluster of other towns, Le Blanc-Mesnil is part of District 93, the "Red belt" historically governed by Communist mayors, where for years the underboil of ethnic hatred has been rumbling. Since the 1980s, thousands of Muslim immigrants have moved into the Red belt, a former outpost of French colonials and Sephardic Jews who had emigrated from Algeria, Tunisia, and Morocco decades earlier.

In October 2000, seven months before Rothschild visited Jerusalem, Sammy Ghozlan was home on Avenue Henri Barbusse in Le Blanc-Mesnil, planning the coming appearances of his dance bands. Ghozlan had just retired from the French police force after a long career as commissioner of the department of Seine–Saint-Denis. He was at the top of his game, known all over the Jewish community of Paris as *le poulet casher,* the kosher chicken, "*poulet,*" like "*flic,*" being slang for "cop." Ghozlan was a *pied-noir* reared in Algeria. His father had been a police officer in Constantine, a man of influence until suddenly one day he was not, and fled, like thousands of others, during the Algerian war. Sammy Ghozlan was obsessed with his Frenchness. He loved Voltaire and drank the best wines. Ghozlan's greatest passion was music; he had played piano and violin all his life, and had developed a Vegas-style Hasidic act into a thriving business, with two Sammy Ghozlan bands working the French Bar Mitzvah and wedding circuit. Ghozlan, as conductor, always wore a fresh tuxedo, a white satin scarf, and a perfectly pleated cummerbund. What little English he knew came from lip-synching to Wayne Newton and John Travolta. "I Will Survive" was his signature closer. He was deeply religious and would not pick up the telephone from sundown Friday until sundown Saturday.

Early in his police career, Ghozlan had become a minor celebrity when he stopped the violence in the projects at Aulnay-sous-Bois, the next town over. He was like a detective in a film noir; his method was to negotiate, to suggest to his adversary that they were allies. He was convinced that success had come to him because he understood the nuances of the term *compte à régler* (a score to settle). For the exile, life in the *banlieues* was all about settling scores. Ghozlan had learned Arabic in Algeria and spoke it frequently in the streets so that he could put himself in the skin of the Arabs he had grown up with. "When the Arabs arrived in France, they were humiliated by the French," he said. "They were not appreciated. They suffered a lot because of that. This is the reason for their rage. They want to take their revenge for the Algerian war." It was, he said, a way to show their identity.

On the night of October 3, 2000, Ghozlan was already missing police work, but his wife, Monique, had lectured him about not second-guessing or dropping in on the new commissioner of Seine–Saint-Denis. It was time to move on, she told him; he had no reason not to. He was making 5,000 euros per Bar Mitzvah and had months of bookings in France and Switzerland. Besides, mandatory retirement was not negotiable in France. At fifty-eight he was ready to hit the Sephardic European party circuit in his new life as not only *le poulet casher* but also the schmoozer and magnet for neighborhood crime gossip. He felt he had earned a festive third act, and he had all the celebrity he needed with a weekly show on 94.8 Judaiques FM radio. There, in his four-room office and studio up a narrow stairwell in the Fifth Arrondissement, close to the Pantheon and the Sorbonne, he could let fly, showcasing Jewish pop stars such as Enrico Macias, promoting the Ghozlan bands, and dispensing crime-protection advice to callers.

That same night at a two-room synagogue in Villepinte, a few towns away from Le Blanc-Mesnil, smoke billowed up from the kitchen and out the classroom windows of the religious school. Jacques Grosslerner, a leader of the Jewish community, immediately reached out to the most experienced person he could think of—Ghozlan. "There is a fire at Villepinte," Grosslerner told him. "Are you au courant?" It was ten o'clock. Ghozlan dialed the prefect of the district and repeated the question: "Are you au courant?" Then he got in his car and drove to Villepinte. The prefect reached Ghozlan on his cell phone. "It is nothing more than a trash fire," he told him. At the synagogue an hour later, however, Ghozlan ran into a detective he knew who told him, "It is no trash fire. We found six Molotov cocktails."

Ghozlan went right to work. He dug a plastic bag out of his car and swept up bits of charred wood, blackened brick, and ash. Within months he would be on a collision course with the French police and several members of the establishment in Paris who ran major Jewish organizations. In Le Blanc-Mesnil, with no resources to draw on except his black plastic address book, Ghozlan was quickly enmeshed in the rising tide of what French Jewish intellectuals would tag "soft-wave anti-Semitism," a new form disguised as anti-Americanism and pro-Palestinianism. It would soon grow into a constant fear on the part of French Jews, a concern bordering on panic in synagogues across suburban America, and forums and articles in the American media. In Europe, however, terms recalling the Nazi era, such as Kristallnacht, were raised only occasionally, and then in a context that portrayed the Israelis as the new storm troopers. The title of an editorial in the *New York Daily News* was succinct: "The Poison's Back: Europeans Call It Anti-Zionism, but It's Really the Old Anti-Semitism."

Ghozlan could not foresee any of this as he quietly gathered soot and brick from Villepinte in the moonlight. But for the first time since he had escaped Algeria as a teenager—"You have three days to leave," an Algerian policeman had told his family—he was feeling an unease that bordered on dread. Over the next ten days, four more synagogues were burned in greater Paris, and nineteen arson attempts were reported against synagogues and Jewish homes and businesses. It occurred to Ghozlan that soon he might be back in police work. Within months he had set up a hotline and a one-man investigative unit called SOS Truth and Security to monitor the trouble. He financed the operation with the money he made from the Ghozlan Hasidic bands.

On the afternoon of October 7, 2000, Clément Weill-Raynal, a reporter and legal correspondent for the France 3 television network, was walking through the Place de la République when he saw hundreds of people massed for a demonstration. Paris is the city of demonstrations—there are so many that a caption in the

Economist once satirized the French love of public display as "Another Day, Another Demo." At first Weill-Raynal tried to ignore the noise, the agitation, and the flags of Hezbollah, Hamas, and certain far-left organizations. "They were shouting, 'Death to the Jews! Kill the Jews! Sharon is a killer!' It was the moment when we had arrived at the point that I was afraid of for many years. The junction of leftists, pro-Palestinians, and Arabs had created a new form of anti-Semitism," Weill-Raynal said.

Anti-Semitism in France had been considered a right-wing phenomenon that historically had its roots in the Vatican and the libel of the greedy Jew as Christ-killer. It had fueled the crowds howling "Death to the Jews!" in the streets near L'École Militaire during the Dreyfus Affair in 1895, and seethed through Vichy with the deportation of seventy-six thousand French Jews to the death camps. The new form of anti-Semitism, Weill-Raynal understood, was different: It was coming from the left, part of the movement known in France as *le néo-gauchisme*, and it was connected to the country's socialist politics and the difficulties of assimilating the large French Muslim population. It was camouflaged as anti-Israel politics, but the issue was immense and complex. Only in recent years has France recognized ethnic subcultures. It is illegal to count race or ethnicity in its census figures, and impossible to record accurate figures for its minorities. There is a spirit of universality in the school system, and a national curriculum. The Jewish issue was a dim, secondary preoccupation if it registered at all in French minds.

Although there were Jews on every level of political influence and intellectual stature in the country, the policy of modern France toward its Jews had been set during the time of Napoleon. "The

Jews should be denied everything as a nation," remarked Count Stanislas de Clermont-Tonnerre in 1789, "but granted everything as individuals." Frenchness was what mattered. As one writer said to me, "I am French first, Jewish second." The most powerful Jews in France rarely identified themselves as Jews. To do so was being "Judeocentric," a term used with contempt. Additional complicating factors were a long-standing French-intellectual romantic attraction to Third World guerrillas, guilt over the slaughter in the Algerian war, and France's need for Iraq's oil and trading alliances from Saudi Arabia to Morocco. All of this was filtered through the thrum of dormant traditional anti-Semitism, which could be revived without much provocation. "Old wine in new bottles," one historian called it.

After fifteen years at France 3, Weill-Raynal was well aware of the slanted coverage concerning the Palestinian-Israeli struggle. "We are not Israel," he told me. "The motto 'Jews is news' is a joke around here." Members of his family had been deported to the Nazi death camps from Drancy, but he was closer in spirit to the "assimilated" Jews of central Paris.

Weill-Raynal had been initiated early into an understanding of the barrier of silence in the media. The standard was set at *Le Monde,* which characterizes the Israeli settlers as "*colons*" (colonizers). In 1987, in the days after the first intifada—the fight waged in the West Bank and Gaza settlements—Weill-Raynal was told by his editors not to file reports on the Middle East.

"You are too biased," one told him.

"I asked them, 'How am I biased?' The answer was simple. I was Jewish."

The editor explained, "You cannot be fair."

"It is a story I know very well. I know the country. I know the people. I know the roots of the problem," Weill-Raynal said.

"No," the editor insisted. "You are too biased."

Frustrated, Weill-Raynal began to keep meticulous notes on Agence France-Presse, the wire service, a major source of information in the country. He immediately noticed an item the service used over and over to explain the violence in the Middle East, a controversial visit Ariel Sharon had made to the Temple Mount, the shrine known to Muslims as the Noble Sanctuary, in September 2000. "This ran again and again without any counterexplanation of the terrorist attacks or the provocation," Weill-Raynal said. "There was no subsequent reporting to place the visit in context. On the anniversary of the second intifada, they put out a revised report, and it was almost as biased. Now the news agency explained that, yes, in fact there were two versions of this incident—the Palestinian and the Israeli. It was as if it was inconceivable that the French might understand that there was a conflicting point of view."

Just days after the demonstration, Weill-Raynal received a barrage of phone calls from Sammy Ghozlan about the burning of a synagogue in Trappes. "This is very serious," Ghozlan said before he rang off to call *Le Parisien*, a tabloid that covers Paris and suburban news. Weill-Raynal knew Ghozlan as an activist and a minor local celebrity—the Sephardic Columbo with his Hasidic bands.

"What is this so-called synagogue burning at Trappes?" an editor had asked him.

"It is not 'so-called,'" Weill-Raynal had said. "It is an anti-Semitic attack."

"It was a true French moment," Weill-Raynal told me. "The editor immediately changed the subject and turned to the reporter next to me. He said, 'Georges, what are you working on?' The next day *Libération,* a left-wing paper, ran it on the front page. The editor came to me and said, 'You were right.'" But no assignment to report the attack was forthcoming.

As Weill-Raynal walked through the Place de la République that day, he was sickened by the screams of "Kill the Jews!" Hundreds of protesters crowded the streets in front of the Holiday Inn on the Right Bank. TV cameras focused on signs that read SHARON KILLER. For years, he says, he had accumulated reams of skewed reporting from Agence France-Presse. Returning to his apartment near the Place de la Bastille, he turned on the TV. "It was catastrophic," he said. "No one had reported what I saw, what I heard. No one had felt it was newsworthy to report 'Kill the Jews.'" Weill-Raynal realized that in all of Paris there was only one potential outlet for his dispatch, Judaiques FM. Jewish radio had arrived in Paris when the socialist government of the 1980s changed the licensing restrictions. The station, with a sizable audience in France, has become a powerful independent outlet of information for intellectuals and journalists. When I visited the studio, it seemed to be out of a different era. Just a few blocks from the Sorbonne, it could have been at a radio station in wartime London or Nepal.

"How should we identify you?" the news announcer asked Weill-Raynal when he rushed in to make his report. "Suddenly I heard myself say, 'Clément Weill-Raynal, president of the Association of Jewish Journalists of the French Press.' It was the moment when I knew I had to declare myself as a Jew. I said, 'I want to get on and denounce a situation in Paris yesterday. The police were there. The Movement Against Racism and for Friendship Between People was there. They shouted "Kill the Jews!" in front of the statue of the République. This is a scandal. Nobody stopped it. No one has denounced it.' And you know, once in your life, you are the right man at the right time."

Just then Henri Hajdenberg, the president of Le Conseil Représentatif des Institutions Juives de France (CRIF), France's main Jewish organization, was in his car. His brother had been a backer of another Jewish station, and Hajdenberg often tuned in to Judaiques FM for the news. "He heard me on the radio," Weill-Raynal said. The next day, when Hajdenberg met with French president Jacques Chirac, he said, "Mr. President, I heard that demonstrators were shouting 'Kill the Jews!' at the Place de la République." As he left the Élysée Palace, Hajdenberg stopped to tell several reporters about the incident. "The president was shocked when I told him what had happened," Hajdenberg told them. Later a member of the French parliament asked Lionel Jospin, the prime minister, for an explanation, but Jospin refused to investigate the incident. Weill-Raynal said, "I asked the question 'Why has this taken days?' and the answer was 'It's not so simple.'"

I met Sammy Ghozlan last September, a few days before the Jewish holidays. The Paris hotels were packed; the art dealers were in town for the antiques fair. As I left New York, Ed Koch, the former mayor of the city, had summoned his rhetoric against the French on his weekly radio show, angrily supporting boycotts. There were rumors of Jews wearing yarmulkes being beaten to death on the Champs-Élysées, and of killer apes unleashed to attack yeshiva boys. It was difficult to imagine that the Paris of *Amélie* had turned into Badenheim, 1939. Surely, I thought, this was shock-jock exaggeration.

Ghozlan was late for our meeting. I waited in a kosher pizzeria in the Nineteenth Arrondissement, an area of shuls and Orthodox schools with a large Muslim population. Middle Eastern pastries glistened in the windows of the bakeries. The weather was warm, and the door of the pizzeria was open, so I could hear Ghozlan's voice before he actually walked in. "*Désolé, désolé,*" he mumbled like a chant as the door banged behind him. His white suit was rumpled; his gray Hush Puppies were scuffed. His reputation stuck out all over him. I knew he was thought to be—depending on who was offering an opinion—at the intersection of paranoia and truth, a one-man crime agency, and a folk hero of the *banlieues*. He resembled a tough, beat-up Yves Montand—hidden and canny, the receptacle of hundreds of lyrics memorized in the middle of the night, rehearsals, microphones, sound checks. Ghozlan had a clipped mustache, a low forehead, and thick dark hair; he was husky, but he moved with the agility of a dancer. He projected urgency, perpetual agitation. I imagined him leading his orchestra, a singing detective racing through lyrics at frenetic speed. The more time we spent together, the more I realized that what preoccupied him was his scrim of the past, the fear that the Algerian war would be refought in Paris.

I followed him out of the restaurant to a pastry shop at the next corner. The owner of the pizzeria recognized him from TV and followed us out. "*Nous avons peur, Monsieur Ghozlan,*" he said. "We are being attacked every day." He stood very close to the retired policeman, as if proximity would provide safety. It was clear that he had no confidence in the local authorities. Ghozlan handed him the card for the hotline. "Call us," he said.

The pastry shop was deserted. Ghozlan placed police dossiers, files, and stacks of paper on a tray table of hammered Moroccan brass between us. He handed me a thick white plastic binder, the kind a high-school student might carry. In it were hundreds of reports, carefully written out by hand. At the top of each page were the words "SOS Vérité-Sécurité" and, underneath, a box: "*Formulaire de Déclaration*." A 2002 report from the Tenth Arrondissement read:

> I was in a taxi with my husband and I arrived in front of my building. I gave the money to the taxi driver and asked for a receipt and my husband went out of the car and I was waiting. She refused to give me the receipt and said, "You are a dirty Jew." And then she spit at me, *proférant des menaces en arabe* [threatening me in Arabic]. She took off in the car and beat me with clothes she had in the front seat. Then she told me that her sons would kill me. I tried to call for help, but the taxi was moving too fast. At a red light, a young man saw me and came and helped me. He offered to be a witness. . . . The incident was shocking. Part of my family was deported to Auschwitz and did not come back. . . . And this is the first time something like this has happened to me. . . . Please do not mention my name. I am afraid that her sons will come to kill me.

A report from the town of Fontainebleau said, "Two 13-year-olds on their way to synagogue were hit with paddles. We will kill you." An insult hurled at a teacher: "When the Messiah comes, each

Jew will have 10,000 goyim as slaves!" Another provocation at a different school: "Have you read *The Protocols of the Elders of Zion*?... Jews feast on the blood of non-Jewish children. They bake it in their matzohs. There is truth that they are all conspiring."

Ghozlan drew a diagram to explain an episode that had happened in Sarcelles, a fifteen-minute drive from Le Blanc-Mesnil. "There was a school bus... maybe you heard about it? They came, they attacked it. The schoolchildren were shocked and scared. I heard that the police said, 'It is expected because of what Israel does to the Palestinians. *C'est normal.*'"

His voice rose. "The president of France has said, 'There is no anti-Semitism in France.' What is the burning of the synagogue at Trappes? What are the Molotov cocktails thrown at the Jewish school in Créteil? And what are all of these?" He picked up the white plastic binder, flipped the pages, adjusted a pair of half-glasses on his nose, and began to read: "'*Sale Juif*' [dirty Jew] written on walls in Drancy... Students wearing kippa attacked outside the schools..."

Out there. The phrase leaped at me from my first days in Paris. "We don't go out there," I was told at a dinner in a grand apartment in the Sixteenth Arrondissement, and there was a whiff of contempt in the tone. "The attacks are all happening out there," said a doctor's wife, an active member of the Temple Beau Grenelle, which journalists and ministers attend.

I had come to investigate two questions: Had France become an anti-Semitic country? How would the policies of France affect the United States? I quickly sensed an odd, split-screen reality, a double narrative, two worlds of Paris, rarely colliding, trying to come to terms with a potential disaster. Anti-American best-sellers filled the windows of the bookshops on the Boulevard Saint-Michel. France was facing its fears of a République d'Islam on French soil. A work with a similar title was selling briskly in the stores, as was *Dreaming of Palestine,* a young-adult best-seller published by Flammarion glamorizing suicide bombers. Teachers in the suburbs have been shocked to discover girls in the bathroom praying to Mecca as if they were performing an illicit act rather than simply practicing their religion. Some of the classes were 70 percent Muslim. Seminars on how to teach history, particularly World War II, were held for teachers who had experienced violence in their classes when they brought up the subject of Hitler and the Jews. Gang rapes—another frequent problem in the working-class suburbs— occupied the school authorities. All over the *banlieues,* I heard the code of modern France—Judeophobia, Judeocentric, *anti-feuj,* a term from a pidgin French called Verlan, the protest language of the *banlieues.* "*Feuj*" is a backward spelling of "*Juif.*"

Raising the subject of the hundreds of attacks on Jews was tricky in central Paris. It was impossible not to think I had somehow gone back in time to a world captured very well by Laura Hobson in her 1946 best-seller, *Gentleman's Agreement,* where the word "Jewish" was said in whispers. Every now and then some unpleasant remark would remind you that you were in the country that created the Dreyfus Affair, but mainstream French Jews do not make waves. Occasionally I heard someone say, "This is not Vichy." It was a way to mute the drama of the alarming numbers, a method of self-reassurance that made the speaker seem above the fray of the statistics: nothing to be alarmed about. The attacks were happening out there, as if that were Iceland, far away from the three-star restaurants and the Matisse-Picasso show at the Grand Palais.

"Out there" is, in fact, ten Métro stops from the Place de la Concorde. It is a territory of class identification, behind a Maginot Line of French snobbism and disconnection, a Gallic sense of the insider and the other. It contains towns that are full of memories of France's Vichy years—Drancy, where Simone de Beauvoir pushed food parcels through a barbed-wire fence to friends being deported to Auschwitz; Les Lilas, with its wedding-cake Hôtel de Ville, where Free French forces celebrated the Liberation.

News travels fast in the *banlieues*. All that autumn and into the winter of 2001 and the following year, the attacks intensified, linked in severity to the politics of the Middle East. In Le Blanc-Mesnil, Ghozlan was getting nowhere with the French police. He distributed his SOS forms in schools, community centers, and synagogues, and installed another telephone line at home. On the weekends, volunteers from his synagogue and his daughters—one of them a lawyer who handles Arab divorce cases—helped him. He became increasingly harried. He had calls to make to the authorities, e-mails to send. The pages in his white notebook grew—stones thrown through windows, fires set in schools, boys wearing yarmulkes attacked at Métro stops. Several times a week he would leave his house in his gray Renault and drive the roads he had been traveling for years to the police headquarters of Seine–Saint-Denis. The small houses along the way were neatly appointed, with assists from the Republic, their decent façades disguising the lack of jobs within. He went to see the chief of police and began to hear such new euphemisms as *les desperados de cage d'escalier* (desperadoes of the stairwell) along with the traditional term *les voyous* (vandals).

"*Sauvageons,*" in Jean-Jacques Rousseau's sense of noble savages, had become a politically correct term for Arabs, along with "*les jeunes*" (the young).

"Look, Sammy," the chief told him, "they are doing the same things to the cops that they do to the Jews. They throw washing machines down from their apartments at police cars. They run into us." "I understood it," Ghozlan later told me. "They worried about appearing heavy-handed. There was a fear that they would be called thugs and Nazis. Several of my friends mentioned to me that they were afraid of creating a situation like in Los Angeles—another Watts."

That February, in Sarcelles, flaming objects were thrown into the Tiferet Israel School, destroying the building. In April, at Garges-les-Gonesse, firebombs were hurled at the synagogue. From Nice to Marseille, anti-Semitic mail was delivered. In the offices of CRIF, located in the Fifth Arrondissement several blocks from the popular food market on the Rue Mouffetard, an envelope arrived filled with white powder and a message: "The biological war against the Jewish lobby has begun."

In London in December 2001, in a now famous conversation at the publisher Conrad Black's, the French ambassador, Daniel Bernard, called Israel "that shitty little country" and refused later to apologize. Then, in Paris, a Hanukkah screening of a Harry Potter movie reserved by the Jewish National Fund was canceled by the theater because of fears of Muslim violence. Very few of these episodes were reported in the mainstream press, but emails bombarded the office of Abraham Foxman, the national director of the Anti-Defamation League, in New York. Foxman had long understood the delicacy of navigating within the French establishment.

With a budget of $50 million, the ADL, headquartered in an eleven-story building across from the United Nations, has resources and a network of intelligence operatives that are inconceivable to most French Jewish officials. A little-known fact about French Jews is how underfunded their organizations are. Each year the Rothschild family contributes a significant amount of money to fund myriad budget requests—security guards, employees, operating expenses—to protect the Jews of France.

"What we are talking about here is the need to understand that Jewish France has been traditionally controlled by the *Hofjuden,* the Jews of the court," Shimon Samuels said to me the day we met. Samuels is an expert on the subject. He arrived in Paris from Jerusalem in 1980 and in 1988 set up an office of the Simon Wiesenthal Center, the organization responsible for tracking down many former Nazis. Trained in London and Jerusalem as a political scientist, Samuels was convinced that the new rise of Muslim fundamentalism had become a graver concern to the world than the capture and prosecution of octogenarians. He had the overview of a professor and used German words to describe the oddity of the French Jewish social structure. As the head of the Paris office of the Wiesenthal center, he monitored potential terrorist and anti-Semitic activity throughout the world.

Getting in communication with Samuels is a daunting task. His email cannot be accessed in many of the strange places he travels, and his cell phone message system is often overloaded or impenetrable. Emails I sent him bounced back to me, and I got used to phones that didn't ring and recordings that explained that Mr. Samuels was unable to receive messages. Much of his year is spent in zones of possible terrorist activity; he can "get by" in twelve languages. Rarely in Paris, he is a man in airplanes or at conferences in Third World countries. In Durban, where he participated in the UN World Conference Against Racism in 2001, he was expelled from the room. Later he witnessed demonstrators marching to a synagogue screaming, "Hitler should have finished the job!" It is his occupation to monitor the hate surging up in Islamic fundamentalist quarters. A tireless lobbyist, he has an ability to forge political compromises. With me, the phrase he used to describe French indifference concerning what was happening in their country was "the black box of denial," and he spoke of "the many-headed hydra" behind the attacks. He often sounded harried and snappish, the stern and rumpled professor who had no time for lengthy explanations. He understood that, for the establishment Jews of France, religion was secondary to their Frenchness. They maintained their status by being *Hofjuden,* skilled at *shah shtil,* the ability to whisper into the ear of the king.

Samuels is British and spent his early years in Warwickshire, in the English countryside, with a family that sent him to Sunday school. Coming home one afternoon, he and his cousin were attacked by local boys, who stoned them and tied them to a cross in a field. "Incredibly, I wiped the event from my mind, as if it didn't happen," he told me. Immediately after that, he rejoined his parents in London. Years later he visited his grandparents' grave, only to find that it had been desecrated. When he called the burial society to complain, he was told, "A storm destroyed it." "The storm stopped on the Jewish side of the cemetery?" he demanded. "Suddenly what happened to me as a child came back in excruciating detail," he said, "and I understood for the first time in my life why I do what I do."

Samuels did not look forward to attending the CRIF annual dinner. CRIF always invited the prime minister and his Cabinet, and several hundred people attended the formal evening. For Samuels, the dinner was everything he disliked about working in France. A few months after his arrival in 1980, a bomb had been exploded outside the Rue Copernic synagogue in Paris. Four people walking in the neighborhood were killed. "Two innocent French persons were killed," the then prime minister, Raymond Barre, had remarked. He was widely criticized for the implication that Jewish victims were an altogether different species from the French. Before setting up the Wiesenthal office in Paris, Samuels had worked as the deputy director of a strategic political-science institute in Israel. By the end of the 1970s, he had begun to have a strong sense of the rise of terrorism in Islamic fundamentalist sects.

In the winter of 2001, Samuels was having to navigate his own complex relationships within the French Jewish establishment, which was not ready to share fully his alarm at the attacks on Jews in the *banlieues*. Their focus was still on the traditional, Vichy model of historical right-wing anti-Semitism, and their concern centered on Jean-Marie Le Pen, who appeared to them to be a resurrection of the old hatreds. In 2002 he would pull roughly 20 percent of the national vote in the first round of the presidential election.

For Samuels, the differences between the old and new forms of anti-Semitism manifested themselves when he pressed the case for reparations for French victims of the Holocaust. "Jews should not be about money," a leader of a prominent Jewish organization told him. "It reinforces a negative stereotype." Samuels was told he was *un traître*, a traitor, and berated for his American pushiness in trying to collect restitution for victims. In the late nineties, Samuels assisted a team of New York lawyers pursuing a class-action lawsuit against French banks for hundreds of victims. The case had further established Samuels as a scrappy outsider, *trop américain*, in certain powerful circles. On the subject of the CRIF dinner, he was not hesitant about voicing his opinion. "The Jewish community should set itself as an objective that they do not need a dinner with the prime minister," he told me. "It sets in motion a set of political mortgages, where the prime minister has to give an accounting. And the Jews, like in medieval times, come to the court with their pleas. It is humiliating . . . an event in which the community is put into the position of having to be a supplicant."

All these reasons and more drew Shimon Samuels to Sammy Ghozlan. Samuels knew Ghozlan by reputation; he had been recruited during François Mitterrand's administration to help investigate the 1982 bombing at Jo Goldenberg's, a famous Jewish restaurant in the Marais district of Paris, and he had been the subject of a lengthy article in *Le Matin* magazine. The film director Alexandre Arcady had used the character of a Sephardic cop named Sammy in a Nazi-art-caper movie called *K*, based on a detective novel, but Samuels had never seen it or heard of the book. He knew of Ghozlan mainly through the flyers for his "*grand orchestre de variétés*" and the cards distributed at Bar Mitzvahs that showed Sammy posed behind drums in a tuxedo with his band, with "*Groove, Funck,*

Hassidiques, Israélien . . . Oriental" written in bold yellow letters at the top. When the two men met at the CRIF dinner, Samuels mentioned his midlife attempt to learn to play the clarinet. "Ghozlan reminded me of a Pancho Villa type, very uncharacteristic of French Jews," Samuels later said. "He had no pretense of being an intellectual." Ghozlan told Samuels he had been incensed that the Jewish leadership had fought him when he took on the claimants' case against French banks. Samuels understood immediately that Ghozlan could be a useful ally. "He had come with the police background and was trying to do—with no real help!—exactly what we were doing, analyze documents, work his sources. . . . I thought the Jewish organizations had missed out on an effective intelligence operation in the *banlieues*." It would take months, however, for Samuels, forever circling the globe, to be able to forge an official relationship with the cop from the suburbs.

By the winter of 2001, the situation had become untenable. The attack on the World Trade Center appeared to set off a fresh wave of violence. More and more, in the late afternoon, Monique Ghozlan would find her husband at the *consistoire*, which regulated synagogues and all aspects of Jewish life, giving interns and volunteers recommendations on how to take calls from attack victims.

Monique and Sammy live in a stone house behind a hedge, within walking distance of their small synagogue. The house is decorated with a collection of North African silver they brought from Algeria and family portraits, including one of Sammy's grandfather, who was once the chief rabbi of Algeria. At the turn of the twentieth century, the Ghozlans were orchardists who had large properties in the country. Monique, whom Sammy met when he was in the Boy Scouts, has pineapple-blond hair and a perpetual tan. The daughter of a bar owner and the mother of three grown daughters and one son, she resembles the actress Dyan Cannon, with hair that cascades to her shoulders. As Sammy worked the phones in the late afternoon, Monique, home from her job teaching first grade, would cook couscous, fava beans, and fish—traditional Sephardic foods.

The Sephardim have a hermetic culture with entirely different rituals from those of Ashkenazi Jews. Considered by many to be more religious than their Eastern European counterparts, France's Sephardim never experienced massive pogroms or, for that matter, Europe's secular enlightenment; Spinoza was Sephardic, but there was no Sephardic Freud or Marx. Revered as "the muscle Jews" by the early Zionist leader Theodor Herzl, the Sephardim were thought to be free of the victim complexes of Eastern Europeans. "We are not always as educated, and we like to drink and have big parties, but we are not depressives," Sammy told me. In the small shuls on the outskirts, there is chaos during the service, with children running from family to family and men gossiping through the chanting of the Torah as if they were conducting business in a bazaar. Sephardic families are often large, and first cousins are permitted to marry. Since the Algerian war drove them to France in the 1960s, Sephardim can now be found at every level of education and accomplishment in French society—Nobel laureates, government ministers, distinguished intellectuals—and many of them have intermarried with Ashkenazi Jews. According to a recent survey, 70 percent of the Jews in France are Sephardic.

———

Still, it did not take much to make Ghozlan see himself as an out-sider, misunderstood by the French elite. He had a title, security adviser, which sounded impressive, but he had no office and no private phone. A special green telephone had been installed at the *consistoire*, and all calls received by volunteers were reported to Ghozlan. "I tried to bring the techniques of simple police interrogation," he said. "Ask the name, the address, the phone number, the place of the attack." He was often understandably frustrated. The idea that by the winter of 2001 this jerry-built detective agency was monitoring more than two hundred incidents throughout France was shocking to Ghozlan. A rabbi had been beaten up, urine had been thrown at Jewish students on a playground, and fires had been set, yet few of the incidents were reported immediately to the police. It was detective work at its most primitive, on scraps of paper. Failure was unthinkable to Ghozlan, however, and he knew how to deal with the French bureaucracy. But lobbying through ethnic organizations was frowned upon in France and was considered an act with vulgar American overtones. The officials of many Jewish organizations were averse to such aggressive tactics.

At home Ghozlan had a large-screen television for his ninety-two-year-old mother, who lived with him. Ghozlan and his mother never missed an episode of *NYPD Blue*, dubbed into French, and it galled him that he was forced to operate without support or equipment of any kind. He looked for a storefront to use as a base for his operation, but he knew that that, too, would be primitive—two rooms tucked in the back of a Jewish center in an out-of-the-way arrondissement. On Fridays after his broadcast, he would drive to Rue Broca to check on his volunteers, only to find the interns had missed a call or were on an extended lunch break, indicating that they were oblivious to the seriousness of what seemed to them minor incidents. He began to seethe at the injustice and remembered every remark that seemed to diminish his work. One official told him, "There is no anti-Semitism unless someone dies."

Shortly after David de Rothschild made his remarks to the *Jerusalem Post,* Ghozlan's cell phone rang. When he learned that Rothschild had said there was no significant anti-Semitism in France and that neo-Nazis were most likely responsible for the attacks, Ghozlan erupted. "It was clear to me that Rothschild and the Ashkenazi Jews would never understand our situation. I wanted to start a Jewish security force," he told me.

As Jean-Marie Le Pen mounted his campaign in 2002, the tally of anti-Semitic attacks had risen to more than 350. The official line of the government continued to be "There is no anti-Semitism." "How can they say this with a straight face?" the reporter Christopher Caldwell would later demand in the *Weekly Standard.*

You get to the house of Samuel Pisar, who is a survivor of Auschwitz, through an elaborate private entrance on the Square Foch. A grander address does not exist in Paris. Pisar made his fortune as an international lawyer; he was one of the last people to speak to the troubled media mogul Robert Maxwell before he went over the side of his yacht. He lives surrounded by Rothkos in a house of flawless modernity. Presidents Chirac and Mitterrand have often invited him to speak publicly on Jewish matters. As the attacks on Jews mounted, Pisar began to send frequent emails to Abraham Foxman in New York, reporting the endless debates raging privately in elite circles. Foxman had one word of advice: Mobilize. It was therefore up to Pisar to help galvanize a paralyzed French establishment that could equivocate with dexterity, extending arguments for months. In the period following the attack on the World Trade Center, Frenchmen began to speak of "*la benladenisation des banlieues.*" They also noted that terrorist Zacarias Moussaoui, awaiting trial for his part in the 9/11 attacks, was a product of the *banlieues,* as were various terrorists arrested for attacks that had taken place from Strasbourg to Béziers, on the Belgian border.

Roger Cukierman often made his way to Square Foch to engage in lengthy discussions. Of all the Jewish officials in Paris, Cukierman, the head of CRIF, had the sharpest insights into the anti-Semitic problem, but he was cautious by nature. A former chairman of the Rothschild bank in Paris, he is often in Israel, where his son runs an investment house. Cukierman put the highest premium on respectability and did not want to be considered pro-Zionist. All that winter of 2002, behind closed doors within the elite Jewish community, a fierce struggle was going on.

"I urged Cukierman to go to the United States and see the great Jewish organizations," Pisar told me. "I wanted him to meet Abe Foxman, and the Bronfmans [founders of Seagram and patrons of many Jewish organizations], and I wanted him to learn how the American Jewish organizations handle these things." Pisar knew that Cukierman, despite his prestige in France, had never been totally free of worry as to how he was perceived. "After the Holocaust, European Jews carried with them the syndromes of the ghettos," Pisar said. "There were many Jews here who said, 'We have to do something,' but others said, 'Don't rock the boat.' In America they don't speak that way. No one says, 'Don't rock the boat.'"

"I was very impressed by what I saw at the ADL," Cukierman told me. He had been in New York on many occasions, but the size and scope of the operation startled him. For starters, there was the outward symbol of the ADL's gray brick office building in the United Nations Plaza. Foxman's worldwide staff of intelligence agents shared information with the government, turned out press releases, put pressure on Congress, and had access to the leading editorial pages across the country. Cukierman and the group with him from Paris suddenly realized that Americans who happened to be Jewish felt wholly comfortable in their country and their communities. "When I got back," Cukierman said, "the first thing I did was to almost triple the budget of CRIF."

In February 2002, Cukierman submitted a searing and prophetic editorial to *Le Monde,* in the form of an open letter to President Jacques Chirac:

> The leaders of the country like to play down anti-Jewish acts. They prefer to see these as ordinary violence. We are deluged with statistics designed to show that an attack against a synagogue is an act of violence and not anti-Semitism. Some Jews who have lost touch with reality like to buttress their personal status by turning a deaf ear and a blind eye to danger, in order to curry favor with the public consensus. . . . Judicial authorities don't like to mete out strong punishment for acts of anti-Jewish violence, even when the perpetrators are caught red-handed: a three-month suspended sentence or nothing for

an attack on a Jewish place of worship, compared to a year for burning a straw cottage in Corsica.

Why this laxness? Because this violence, perpetrated by only one side, is linked to the conflict in the Middle East. Because too often Jew and Israeli mean the same thing.... Because the Muslim population is all-important.... Once again, we are the scapegoat. It's a part we no longer are prepared to play.

All over Paris, there was suddenly a flurry of activity—Shimon Samuels called it a derby race—as groups began to mobilize. As the election in which Le Pen was running neared its end, two hundred thousand protesters marched in the streets of Paris. The American Jewish Congress called for a boycott of the Cannes Film Festival. But the menace continued. Three men who burned a synagogue in Montpellier—identified as "Morad," "Jamel," and "Hakim"—were described by the prosecutor not as anti-Semites but as being "like a lot of petty delinquents, animated by a spirit of revenge, who try to ennoble their excesses by using a political discourse." Around the time Cukierman's editorial was published, individuals who broke into a synagogue in Créteil were given a three-month suspended sentence.

There are 130,000 police officers in France, according to Christopher Caldwell, but the police union is so strong that less than half of the force is assigned the beat, and only 10,000 are available for duty at any given time. Law-enforcement officials refer to the worst areas of the *banlieues* as "*zones de non-droit*" (lawless areas) and often refuse to go there. Even when police make arrests, according to Caldwell, liberal judges frequently let the criminals go, and 37 percent of the sentences are not carried out.

Victims are reluctant to be interviewed. You hear stories of people who named their attackers to the police and were later beaten up. It took me days to arrange to see a father whose two daughters were attacked in their school in central Paris. A well-known gerontologist, he insisted that I not use his name. I met him at his medical center, not far from the Marais. "My daughters were thirteen and fifteen and were surrounded by a group of students at school. A group of boys knocked them to the ground, covered them with food, and shouted, 'Dirty Jews.' What happened next was this: The attackers and other students threatened to kill the girls if they said anything, and for days my daughters received death threats." Two of the attackers were expelled, only to be reassigned to a school a short distance away, but the family kept receiving threats. At the end of the school year they moved to another arrondissement. "I could not put my daughters in any more danger," he said. "They completely changed. They had been close to so many diverse people in their school, and now they have pulled within themselves and just want to be with other Jewish students."

A history teacher named Barbara Lefebvre called Ghozlan's hotline when a student at her school insulted her. "I did not know where to turn," she told me. "I knew that no one in the school would address my concerns." One of the students had called her "a dirty Jew." "I went to one of the heads of the school and told her I was insulted as a teacher, a woman, a Jew, and a civil servant. I asked her to report it to the authorities, as I had done. She said, 'I do not have that power.'" Like the gerontologist, Lefebvre was concerned about reprisals and asked me not to identify her school. "Most of the school officials will say to the teachers, 'Don't talk about it.' It is to protect their reputation. Every pupil has a notebook with his picture in it. Many of the kids took their pictures off and put on the face of bin Laden. . . . And nobody said anything until a teacher saw it. They are afraid. But afraid of what? For those of us who have stepped forward, I say, we are not courageous. It is a duty."

Lefebvre told her story on the Jewish radio station and was contacted by another teacher, who used the pseudonym Emmanuel Brenner. A professor of history, Brenner developed a tutorial for teachers on how to teach World War II. "The problem of violence was so intense," he told me, "that I asked several of the teachers to compile their stories." He had collected them in a book called *Les Territoires Perdus de la République* (The Lost Territories of the Republic). *L'Express* had published an extract, but, Brenner told me, it was months before the book was mentioned by French television and *Le Monde.*

Only three of the seven teachers who contributed to the book used their own names. One, Iannis Roder, arrived at my hotel after school one day. "In my class, the students will not obey a woman," he said. "One child yelled at a woman whose name was Rabin, 'Jew! Jew!' I live with these children during the day, and when I tell my family about it, they are frightened. But when I talk to some journalists, they say, 'That can't be true.'" Roder said one reporter told him, "You are only seeing anti-Semitism because you are a Jew."

Driving to Trappes, near Versailles, you pass housing projects where unemployed Muslims live. The small shul in town is down the block from one. Here, in October 2000, the synagogue was destroyed, and it is only slowly being rebuilt. There are black smoke marks all over the roof. "Arrests were made," the head of the Jewish community tells me. "Many people were questioned." But there was no prosecution. Later I visit the office of Ariel Goldmann, a criminal lawyer who has boxes of files concerning the incident. The authorities suggested that someone may have accidentally put a cigarette into a trash can, he says, shaking his head in disgust. Goldmann's father was the chief rabbi of Paris in the 1980s, and Goldmann often works on such cases pro bono. They are, he says, inevitably the same. Several blocks from Goldmann's office, I visit the lawyer William Goldnadel, whose clients include the Italian journalist Oriana Fallaci. "Who do you think was responsible for the pogroms in the Germany of the 1930s?" he asks. "Piano teachers? Professors? It is always the hooligans who are at the center of the violence."

Next I go to see Shmuel Trigano, the author of twelve books and part of a circle of influential thinkers that includes the philosopher Alain Finkielkraut, the writer Michel Gurfinkel, and the philosopher and activist Bernard-Henri Lévy. "I was outraged by what was going on here," he tells me, "and I began to keep a detailed list of all the attacks to publish in a new quarterly, which would document—in ways the French press was not doing—what was going on."

Trigano was not alone in his efforts to tabulate the attacks. Dismayed by the pro-Palestinian bias in the French press, Elisabeth Schemla, a former managing editor of *L'Express*, hired a team of journalists and set up a website, Proche-Orient.info, to ensure objective reporting on the Middle East. The site, like the Jewish radio, has become mandatory for understanding the situation in France. The day I went to see Schemla, her deputy editor, Anne-Elisabeth Moutet, used the term "*tour de passe-passe*" (three-card monte) to explain the shuffles and contradictions involved in obtaining accurate information in France. CRIF and another group, SOS Racisme, created by a moderate French Muslim group and a French Jewish student organization, were also investigating, and their efforts eventually galvanized the establishment. At the CRIF dinner in 2001, Roger Cukierman confronted the prime minister, telling him, he recalled, "'We are under attack as French citizens, and it is unacceptable.' That night I gave a list of more than 300 documented attacks to every one of the seven hundred guests." Cukierman was enraged by the French bureaucracy: According to police records, there were a mere 180 attacks.

"I want to read you something," Ghozlan said one night at his house. It was a letter from an uncle in Algeria, written in May 1962. He described being in the chic tourist area of Algiers in a crowd with many Spanish and Italian visitors:

> Massive gunfire erupted around us, the first victims fell, the ones on top of the others at our feet. Separated from my children, I was stuck between two lines of fire, one coming from the Rue d'Isly, and the other from the Rampe Bugeaud, just tens of meters apart, while the Muslim soldiers fired just meters away.... Then, with the bullets whistling by my ears, I called out for my children, who I couldn't find among the numbers of dead.... A miracle happened, [the children] had escaped and explained how a man jumped on top of them and took the bullets ... trying to protect his young son.... "You are too young to be assassinated by these bastards," he said.

Ghozlan's voice broke. "It was like this with all the families," Monique said. The uncle had later been killed in the Algerian war.

At the bottom of Ghozlan's character lurked a trip wire: He had his own score to settle. He felt condemned to repeat his history, and he recalled the phrase "*le cercueil ou la valise*" (the coffin or the suitcase), warning Jews in his homeland that they had only days to flee. The Cremieux decree had conferred French citizenship on Algeria's Jews in 1870, so at the height of the Algerian war, most Jews with government jobs left for France. The small-business owners fled to Israel.

Ghozlan's father's boss, the former Vichy official Maurice Papon, stationed in Algeria in the 1950s, would be tried in Bordeaux in 1997 and convicted of complicity in the arrests and internments of 1,690 Jews. At that time in Constantine, no one knew of Papon's past, but anyone working in the French police force operated in a shadowy zone of possible collaboration. As a child, Ghozlan knew Papon because his uncle was Papon's barber. Once, during a control operation, Ghozlan's father refused to kill a notorious leader of the Front de Libération Nationale (FLN), a revolutionary group, because it was against his moral code. As a result of that, when the FLN took over Algeria, it allowed Ghozlan and his mother and sister to leave. He took only a sweater, his high-school diploma, and a salami sandwich. "I watched the city as it became smaller. I couldn't imagine I would ever see it again."

Shortly after I arrived in Paris, Ghozlan organized a meeting in District 93 of all the Jewish leaders in that community and the chief of police. The tension in the little room was palpable. "You walk into the offices of the [assistant] mayor out here, and what is hanging there but the Palestinian flag," one Jewish leader said. The chief of police did not respond directly. "We believe we are all equal—churches, mosques, synagogues," he said. The Jewish leader countered by saying, "It is not the mosques that are being attacked." The meeting went on for hours as representatives from the Jewish community described the attacks to which they were routinely subjected. Such an event in an American city would likely have been covered in the press, but there was not a single French reporter in the room.

The day Papon, then ninety-two, was let out of prison, I spent the evening with Ghozlan at his house. He was extremely agitated, working two phones at once, dialing ministers and politicians, as he kept up a simultaneous conversation with me. "The mayor of Paris is coming to a demonstration I have organized at Drancy! And the chief of police. And the minister [of integration] Eric Raoult." He left long messages, giving the time of the demonstration and the names of the journalists he had invited. I had asked to hear him play at a Bar Mitzvah, and while he made and received calls, he projected a video of a party in a hotel ballroom. There he was in his tux, looking like Gilbert Bécaud at the Paramount, invoking old newsreels of cabaret performers during the Vichy era.

The next day I was at the CRIF office with Roger Cukierman when the telephone rang. Cukierman took the call and sounded annoyed. "I won't go myself, but I'll send a representative." When he hung up he said, "A man in the suburbs is organizing a demo."

"Do you mean Sammy Ghozlan?" I asked.

"Yes," he said. "He wants to get his picture in the newspaper all of the time."

"But isn't that good?" I asked. "Doesn't he serve a function by drawing attention to the situation in France?"

Cukierman snapped, "A totally negative function. . . . Whatever the subject, he jumps on it to get his own publicity."

By late 2002, some American antiwar intellectuals were strongly criticizing the American Jewish organizations that were trying to call attention to the situation in France. As I left for France, in the fall, Susannah Heschel warned me, "If you write about any of these attacks, you will be used for fund-raising purposes by the Jewish organizations." Heschel, the chairman of the Dartmouth Jewish Studies Program, is the daughter of the prominent Jewish scholar Rabbi Abraham Heschel. Along with Cornel West and Rabbi Michael Lerner, the editor of *Tikkun*, a liberal Jewish magazine, Heschel is a co-chair of Tikkun Campus Network, a college movement. By April of this year, however, Heschel, like Rothschild, felt that she had been misled by the lack of proper reporting. "The situation in France reminds me of the Dreyfus case. After he was found innocent, the Jews were blamed for getting him exonerated. . . . There was a clear failure of the French left to respond to Muslim anti-Semitism or to know how to criticize the victims of their own colonialism." Tony Judt, writing in a recent issue of the *New York Review of Books*, allowed that anti-Semitism is on the rise around the globe, but he cited the ADL's statistics on the number of reported American incidents, as if to imply an equivalency in the lifestyles of the middle-class American Jewish community and the Jews of the Parisian *banlieues*.

The interior minister of France, Nicolas Sarkozy, had a clear sense of the terrorist activity in his country. On the Jewish high holy days, Sarkozy visited synagogues in the vicinity of the tony suburb of Neuilly, near the Bois de Boulogne. Sarkozy's grandfather was Jewish—a figure of speech employed by Jews whose families, terrified for their lives, changed religions before or during World War II. "It is wrong that, fifty years after the Shoah, Jews have to be afraid how they think about Israel," he said. I followed him that day as he traveled with his wife, who wore a pink Chanel suit, and his deputy minister. Sarkozy was applauded in the tiny meetinghouses called *oratoires,* where, in the last century, assimilated Jews had gathered. Virtually no mention of his visits appeared in the press.

In February, Sarkozy announced that scores of potential terrorists had been arrested, and in April a Muslim *consistoire* was established. Many imams in France adhere to fundamentalism, which the demographer Michèle Tribalat and a coauthor have reported extensively on in *La République et l'Islam: Entre Crainte et Aveuglement* (The Republic and Islam: Between Fear and Blindness). The imams reported to Sarkozy's representatives that they would tell their followers the first law for Muslims is the religious law. Ghozlan had taken it on himself to try to negotiate with some of the more moderate imams, but certain Jewish organizations in France had put him on warning that he was overstepping his mandate. On the telephone, Shimon Samuels was philosophical when he told me, "Suddenly there are those who rejected Ghozlan in the beginning, but who are seeing that he is effective and what he's doing is important, and they want to take it over." If France accepted a role in the coming Middle East war, Samuels added, it would mean that the attacks that had been limited to the *banlieues* could escalate to bombs going off in supermarkets all over France.

I stayed in close communication with Ghozlan and Samuels through this past winter and into the spring. As the first bombs landed on Baghdad, Ghozlan was bracing himself for what might come next. He used the word "*ratonnade*," and I asked him to define it. "It means that as an immigrant you are being attacked for being a separate identity." He feared, he said, a sinister new way of life, where people would abandon their common Frenchness and return to medieval tribalism, marooning themselves in their separate religions and ethnic inheritances.

In January, Samuels and the Wiesenthal center announced a special UNESCO conference to address the issue of anti-Semitism—the first such conference in a decade. David de Rothschild offered his house for a reception for the world leaders who would attend. Trying to maintain a cosmopolitan overview, Rothschild told me, "If you fall into a depressed spiral and believe that there is no future and the French state is pro-Arabic, where does that lead but to wrong analysis and desperation?" In early April a new wave of anti-Semitism merged with France's anti-Israel politics and its outspoken disapproval of America's war. At demonstrations in Paris, not far from where Clément Weill-Raynal had heard the crowd cry "Death to the Jews" in October 2000, Stars of David were now intertwined with swastikas on banners. Nicolas Sarkozy's office dispatched marshals in white caps to keep the protests under control, but the new epidemic of violence grew—women clubbed in the street, rocks thrown through a synagogue window, another shul burned. One demonstrator told a reporter for the *New York Times,*

"They are the targets. They are not welcome here because of what they did to our Palestinian brothers."

Ghozlan's cell phone rang during a Bar Mitzvah he was attending. "It was a boy attacked during the demo. . . . He had approached a group carrying the Israeli and American flags intertwined with swastikas and told them they were not allowed to do that. . . . They beat him up." Ghozlan persuaded the young man to go to the police and took him to the Jewish radio station. It was clear that Ghozlan's dark prophecies had become reality. In the first week of April, *Le Monde* published a shocking poll, revealing that 30 percent of the French wanted Iraq to win the war. Mecca Cola was selling briskly all over the country, and Jacques Chirac suddenly had a new nickname on playgrounds in the *banlieues*: King of the Arabs. I had difficulty reaching Ghozlan and Samuels, and when I did, Samuels sounded as morose as Ghozlan had two years earlier. It had become impossible for the opinion-makers of France to distinguish between its NATO allies and Saddam's terrorists, he said. I mentioned the new poll to him. "You don't even know the full statistics they published," he said. "You really want to hear? Total of those disapproving of the American- and British-led intervention in Iraq: 78 percent. The city of Paris: 85 percent. The extreme left: 85 percent. The extreme right: 48 percent. Asked if they would be more supportive of the war if chemical weapons were used against American and British forces, 52 percent said no. Asked do you hope the U.S. wins, 33 percent said no."

I mentioned that I had been having trouble reaching Ghozlan. There was a reason, Samuels said; he and Ghozlan had that day decided to open an alternative headquarters in the Maison France-Israël headquarters on the Avenue Marceau, a few blocks from the

Arc de Triomphe. Ghozlan's hotline was still going strong in the *banlieues*, but it was crucial that they also have a respected presence in central Paris. "The government has endorsed Saddam Hussein as a hero," Samuels said. "The genie has been let out of the bottle." The new police station would be one block from the main police headquarters. As American tanks rolled into Baghdad, there were signs that the French situation was not completely irrevocable. The cover story of the French newsmagazine *Le Point* was headlined: HAVE THEY GONE OVERBOARD?, a reference to the anti-American posturing of Jacques Chirac and his foreign minister, Dominique de Villepin. President Chirac, riding the popularity polls for his intractable opposition to the war, stayed mute even when the citizens of Baghdad openly embraced American forces, but his prime minister, Jean-Pierre Raffarin, attempted to redress the balance: "Being against the war does not mean that we want dictatorship to triumph over democracy."

The last time I spoke on the phone with Ghozlan, he sounded as frenzied as I had ever heard him. He had just learned of a new attack and was rushing to find out the details. In the first three months of this year, he told me, he had verified reports of 326 serious incidents in Paris alone.

JUDGE MOTLEY'S
VERDICT

MAY 1994

"She often talked about the South in those days as if it were a war zone and she was fighting in a revolution. No one—be it defendant or plaintiff—was going to distract her from carrying her task to a successful conclusion."

From time to time when Constance Baker Motley is invited to recall her glory days as an NAACP lawyer in the 1950s and 1960s, she is challenged by law students who think of her as an anachronism, a holdover from a time when it was believed that undoing the pathology between the races could be accomplished largely through the courts. This was the case last October, for example, when Motley, a New York federal judge, spent a week as jurist-in-residence at the law school of the University of Indiana in Bloomington. Motley is popular on the law-school circuit; she and her former colleagues at the NAACP Legal Defense and Educational Fund ride a crest of civil-rights-era nostalgia.

On May 17, 1954, when the Supreme Court issued its unanimous ruling in *Brown* v. *Board of Education*, which overturned school segregation, Motley, then a Legal Defense Fund trial lawyer, was thirty-two years old. She was "the girl in the office" then, the drudge, but over ten years she became the only woman at the plaintiff's table in the Jim Crow South as she and other lawyers tried case after case to enforce the *Brown* decision; she helped to desegregate lunch counters, schools, and buses, and in those years she also argued ten cases in front of the Supreme Court. In Montgomery, Alabama, she recently recalled, she argued five different appeals in one day as the school boards tried to put off the evil moment of desegregation. In Jackson, Mississippi, a local paper referred to her as "the Motley woman." She was chided for her fashionable clothes. Her presence in court often brought dozens of spectators, simply to marvel at the fact that a black woman could actually be a lawyer. But the majority of the law students who gathered to hear her at Indiana last October were only vaguely aware of her importance. They weren't yet born when she traveled from courtroom to courtroom through Mississippi, Alabama, and Georgia.

A few days before Motley arrived in Indiana, Alfred Aman, the law-school dean, arranged a display of the NAACP Legal Defense Fund's achievements in the foyer of the law-school building: Among other items, news accounts of Charlayne Hunter entering the University of Georgia in 1961 and James Meredith desegregating the University of Mississippi the same year were visible in a glass case. The moot-court room at the law school was filled to capacity on the afternoon Motley delivered her lecture. That night, she spoke at a dinner given by the Black Law Students Association, or BLSA. She recalled the many school-desegregation cases that had led to and followed *Brown*, but after she spoke she was kept busy answering sharp questions about her own experiences, posed by several of the BLSA members: The narrative of Constance Motley's life seemed to contradict the reality of modem racial politics. "Shouldn't you have fought for equal schools?" one student asked her, and went on to cite the breakdown in black communities, the black-on-black crime, the miserable test scores, and the loss of pride among black men. "Your generation always used the word 'mainstream,'" another student said, and asked, "What is wrong with black culture?" Motley was brisk with the BLSA students. "I don't know what black culture is," she said, as if attempting to camouflage her irritation. When Motley returned to New York, she told me that she had been startled at being asked to defend herself. At this point in her life, she has come to expect, at the very least, a certain degree of respect for what she and the NAACP Legal Defense Fund accomplished. A mistake to fight for integration? The guiding principle of Constance Baker Motley's life has been her belief that the law is the primary instrument of social reform. "In my early days at the NAACP, I could never have imagined this situation at the colleges today," she told me.

A few weeks later, I went to visit Judge Motley at the United States Court House in downtown Manhattan. I took the elevator to the twentieth floor, but Motley was not yet in her chambers; she was in court, hearing pretrial motions on a case that involved the alleged mistreatment of a Black Muslim by prison officials.

The decor of Motley's chambers was very feminine, with floral chintz curtains and pink walls. Judge Motley's law clerk had left a stack of faded newspapers for me on the conference table. A headline on the top paper, a copy of the September 11, 1963, *New York*

Times, read "WALLACE ENDS RESISTANCE AS GUARD IS FEDERALIZED; MORE SCHOOLS INTEGRATE." The news story described the events of the previous day, when, after months of resistance by Governor George Wallace, the schools in Birmingham and two other Alabama cities were integrated. It told of a blonde high-school girl in Birmingham who had cried when she learned that black children were enrolled in her school. "I hope my momma heard, so she'll come get me," she said. The *Times* correspondent in Birmingham related that seventy-five youths had shouted, "Keep the niggers out!" "Go home!" and "Two, four, six, eight, we don't want to integrate!" I flipped through the stack of newspapers. In one, I saw a photograph, snapped in the hallway of the federal courthouse in Birmingham in 1962, that showed Motley wearing a fashionable black coat and matching hat and an elegant printed scarf. She was looking down at the floor, as if to distance herself from the mob, but she did not look particularly afraid; in fact, she appeared oddly serene.

There was also an envelope of documents referring to Constance Motley that went back as far as fifty years. They included the expected awards letters and banquet menus, and some unexpected examples of the way she handled her anger: Motley had kept a copy of every complaint she filed with the Taxi and Limousine Commission about drivers who failed to pick her up. ("Complainant, who is a Negro, charged that respondent discriminated against her . . . because of complainant's color.") Then I came to a single-spaced letter signed "Anthropologist":

Mrs. MOTLEY: When you made your plea before Judge Tuttle, how many windows did you raise to let your stinking body odor escape? How much cologne did you use to saturate your clothing with to prevent others from smelling your stinking body? . . . It is hard to see how any person with an ounce of brains would get up and argue that the nigger is equal to other races. It just is not so.

As I finished the letter, Judge Motley walked into the room. I asked her about the letter, and she told me she could hardly remember receiving it. "I used to get letters like that all the time. I wonder why I even kept it," she said.

Constance Baker Motley is seventy-two years old. When she was admitted to Columbia Law School, in 1943, her photograph ran in a rotogravure for African-Americans, and she was held up as a role model. "She's one of the few Negro women enrolled in Columbia University's famous School of Law," the caption noted. As time passed, she became the first African-American woman to be a New York state senator, a borough president (Manhattan), a federal judge. Judge Motley is tall and large-boned, but she has delicate features and dainty hands and feet. She is judicial, formal, precise. Unlike many of the civil-rights activists of her generation, she is far more comfortable discoursing on the history of the Fourteenth Amendment than delivering an impassioned speech. Given what she has been through, her dry, legalistic demeanor may be her most remarkable achievement. She has been in jail cells with Martin Luther King, Jr., where the air was so foul that she became faint; she spent long nights in Birmingham churches singing freedom songs; she stayed with Medgar Evers, and, under armed guard, in the

Birmingham home of a Legal Defense Fund attorney whose house was repeatedly bombed during the fifties and sixties; racist insults have been hurled at her by white lawyers. Yet, for all this, her memories tend to be a lawyer's memories. She focuses on the method by which school integration was actually achieved, the litigation strategies, the motions and sustaining orders, the quashing of subpoenas, the emergency appeals. It was her knowledge of the law that enabled her to transcend the emotionalism of the Jim Crow courts. In her 1992 memoir, *In My Place*, Charlayne Hunter-Gault recalls sitting with Constance Motley at the plaintiff's table in a Georgia courtroom during her attempt to enter the University of Georgia: "She barely acknowledged my presence . . . I never, for example, heard her laugh in the presence of any state or university officials, except as a barely masked form of sarcasm. It seemed as if this was the most important mission in her life. In fact, she often talked about the South in those days as if it were a war zone and she was fighting in a revolution. No one—be it defendant or plaintiff—was going to distract her from carrying her task to a successful conclusion."

Until she was a teenager, Connie Baker had never heard of Harriet Tubman or Sojourner Truth. She attended a New Haven school where she was one of the few black students. Her parents, originally from the tiny Caribbean island of Nevis, moved to New Haven at the turn of the century and became part of the clannish West Indian community there. Connie Baker had eleven brothers and sisters. Although the family was poor, the children had an air of superiority, from their parents' years at British schools. The Bakers lived on the outskirts of the Yale campus, and Connie's father was a cook at Skull & Bones; in fact, most of the Baker family was associated with Yale—her uncles also worked in the university's clubs. "They told all the little white Yalies what to do," Judge Motley's niece and namesake Connie Royster told me.

Nevertheless, Connie was once turned away from a Connecticut beach near New Haven, and some restaurants in New Haven wouldn't serve blacks. She learned about black heroes and heroines and discovered the writings of W. E. B. Du Bois at church lectures.

Last October, Judge Motley was inducted into the National Women's Hall of Fame, in Seneca Falls, New York. The list of women inducted with her included the physicist Rosalyn Yalow, who had won a Nobel Prize; the civil-rights leader and founder of the Children's Defense Fund Marian Wright Edelman; the labor organizer Dolores Huerta; and Wilma Mankiller, the chief of the Cherokee Nation. The mother of Emmett Till, a black teenager who was murdered in Mississippi in 1955, accepted an award for Rosa Parks, who had inspired the 1955–56 bus boycott in Montgomery when she refused to give up a front seat. "Rosa Parks was willing to pay the cost to save the lost," Emmett Till's mother said. Most of the women used the occasion to make political speeches, but Judge Motley spoke about a white man named Clarence Blakeslee. "There was no money for me to go to college," she said. "I went to work at the National Youth Administration, and one day I gave a speech at a black community house. Clarence Blakeslee had built the community house. He was a contractor who had done a lot of work at Yale. He had made millions of dollars, and what he did with those millions was to help educate black Americans." Blakeslee had been impressed by the teenager's speech and had asked her where she would attend college. When Connie Baker told him that her parents could not afford to send her, he offered to pay for her entire education. "Clarence Blakeslee was a white man responsible for my being here today," she said.

Connie Baker traveled to Fisk University, in Nashville, by train, riding in a Jim Crow car; she was eager to experience segregation. Her parents were frightened for her; they themselves refused to cross the Mason-Dixon Line. On her first trip home, she brought them back a "Colored Only" sign. At Fisk, she met, for the first time, black students from middle-class families in the South, who were ensconced in black communities, with their own clubs and churches. "It was my first experience in a black institution with black people who were just like white people, as we used to say," Judge Motley said of Fisk. "Their parents were college educated, they had wealth. For the first time, I met blacks who were doing something other than cooking and waiting on tables. They intended to go back into the black community." White people, however, were the standard, and Connie Baker could not understand why the Fisk students were not interested in advancing in the white world. It was, she told me, the enigma of her college days. "All of our lives, we had to be like white people. We had to dress, think, and act like white people," she recalled, yet her classmates did not want to become part of the white community.

At Columbia Law School, she began to work as a volunteer at the NAACP's Legal Defense and Educational Fund, Inc., a subsidiary that Thurgood Marshall and his mentor, Charles Houston, had created in 1939. It was usually called the Inc. Fund, for short. Marshall seemed to find little remarkable in the fact that she was a woman, and took her on as a clerk. After she graduated, in 1946, she began working full-time. Her salary was fifty dollars a week. Besides Motley, the entire staff consisted of Marshall and three other lawyers, one of whom worked part-time. At first, Motley worked on housing cases, challenging the restrictive covenants that excluded blacks from buying real estate in white neighborhoods. Marshall was then involved in several cases to integrate universities at the graduate-school level, such as the ones in which Ada Sipuel sought admission to the University of Oklahoma College of Law and Heman Sweatt to the University of Texas School of Law. It was Marshall's strategy to argue the graduate-school cases under *Plessy v. Ferguson*, the onerous 1896 Supreme Court decision that upheld existing separate-but-equal doctrine and set up the legal framework for segregation. Marshall argued that since there were no black law schools in Texas and Oklahoma, Sipuel and Sweatt should be admitted to the white institutions. Ultimately, of course, in *Brown*, the Supreme Court ruled against separate facilities, arguing that even where they were equal, segregation per se had a negative effect.

In 1949, when Connie Motley tried her first case, in Jackson, Mississippi, the people there had hardly ever seen a black lawyer before, and had never seen one who was a woman. She was married by then. Her husband, Joel Motley, was a New York real-estate broker whom she had met when they were living at the Harlem YMCA and YWCA, respectively. They had gotten married in August of 1946, and this was her first trip to the Deep South ever. Her husband worried about her. Her only experience in a courtroom had been observing the meticulous style of Charles Houston in a University of Maryland nursing-school case. Motley found it impressive that Houston wrote down every one of his exhibits and questions in advance and never deviated from his text.

Motley and her colleague Robert Carter, who is now also a federal judge, booked a Pullman to Jackson. (She had bought a new dress at Lord & Taylor for the trial.) The case was an equalization-of-salary suit originally brought by a teacher, Gladys Noel Bates. When Connie Motley walked into the courtroom in Jackson for the first time, she was appalled by a WPA mural depicting the glories of lost Dixie that covered an entire wall. She remembers staring at the white women in their crinolines and hoopskirts on one side and the darkies hoisting cotton bales on the other. She had never imagined that on her first big case, when she needed all the poise she could muster, she would have to interrogate witnesses and offer arguments while being confronted with such a spectacle. She recalls that trial as one of the few occasions when she was almost overcome with rage.

Other memories of the trial also remain vivid. "When we got to court on the first day, we saw that all the seats were taken by whites, because the black people believed that they had to sit in the balcony," she told me. "But this court did not have a balcony, so the blacks stood along the walls. After the first session, Bob Carter told the people that, unlike in state court, in a federal court you could sit anywhere you wanted. The next morning, we got there at nine o'clock, and all the seats were taken by blacks."

She went on to say, "In those days, no black lawyers ever went to court. If they had a case, they got a white lawyer to go for them. Bob and I needed a local lawyer to appear and sign the complaint. This was the first case since Reconstruction where blacks had appeared as lawyers in a courtroom in Mississippi. We found a black lawyer who lived in Meridian, Mississippi—James Burns. He owned a little grocery store, and he was scared to death. When we were in court, he sat with his back to us. He was making notes. He wanted to give the impression that he was just local counsel. He wanted to convey that he was not the lawyer bringing the suit. On the second day of the trial, Bob Carter said to him, 'Go out and see if our witnesses are out there.' He went out bent over completely—again, showing that he knew his place as a black man. When we went to have dinner, he would disappear; he did not want to take the chance of being killed with us.

"From time to time, the judge would rule in our favor, and once Bob spoke to the judge about a witness who was speaking very softly. He said, 'Could you ask that witness to speak up, please?' The black people in Jackson had never seen that before, and when Bob went to get his hair cut at the barbershop that evening everyone was reenacting this white man being made to speak up so a black man could hear. The final day, the judge was very polite. He addressed me as Mrs. Motley. The judge was from the Mississippi coast, and had no hostility toward black people. So, on the last day, when Bob told our lawyer to go out and get our witnesses, Burns for the first time in the entire trial walked out erect. I said to Bob, 'At least we have accomplished something in this case.'"

In the several TV movies made about the drama leading up to the *Brown* decision, the Inc. Fund is commonly portrayed as resembling a tabloid newsroom, filled with bantering black lawyers. The office jokes have become standards; one had it that Marshall called himself "HNIC"—"head nigger in charge." In Jack Greenberg's book *Crusaders in the Courts*, a history of the Inc. Fund that will be published this month, a different portrait emerges. Greenberg, now a Columbia Law School professor, started at the Inc. Fund several years after Connie Motley. For a while, they shared the same office. When Greenberg, as a naïve young white lawyer, first met Motley, according to his new book, he was startled when she quickly corrected his use of the term "Negress," then in common use. "Negress," she said, "was like using the word 'tigress' or 'lioness,' and was offensive to women." In one TV miniseries, *Separate but Equal*, the actor Ron Silver portrayed Greenberg, and Sidney Poitier portrayed Thurgood Marshall. Greenberg recently told me that he was nettled by the histrionics. "The idea that Thurgood was waving his arms around in court yelling and screaming and grimacing!" Greenberg said. "Thurgood didn't do that. In fact, no lawyer does that. Except William Kunstler." The real atmosphere was "lawyers at work," Greenberg recalled, the pedestrian stuff of "following precedents and filing motions for preliminary injunctions." It was difficult to tell the difference between the Inc. Fund office and any other office, except that its occupants talked about race all the time.

"What do you remember about the day of the Supreme Court's decision in *Brown* v. *Board of Education*?" I asked Judge Motley a few months ago. We were on a train on our way to Washington. It was the morning of the Supreme Court's memorial service for Thurgood Marshall, and Judge Motley had been asked to speak. At first, her memories were atmospheric—the pandemonium in the office, the joyous ringing of the telephones. That night, she recalled, she went home to her apartment on West End Avenue. She was proud of that apartment; the Motleys were the first black family to move into the building. Motley had big plans then for her two-year-old son, Joel—and, indeed, he ultimately graduated from Harvard

Law School and became a partner in an investment-banking firm. Motley's memory of the day of the *Brown* decision focused on Joel in his high chair. She had already realized, she told me, that the effect of *Brown* was going to be primarily psychological, and she informed her toddler that the Supreme Court had, that very day, undone segregation. She made no effort to explain it in terms a two-year-old might begin to comprehend, but she was convinced that Joel understood her.

When she got to the office the next morning, she learned that Walter White, the head of the NAACP, had had to cancel a lecture date in Selma, Alabama. "Thurgood called me and said, 'You go, Connie'—very terse. He did not say, 'I will help you with your speech,' or give me any ideas. You were supposed to do it on your own. If you made a mess, you made a mess. That was the way Thurgood was. So I went to Selma that Sunday. And the place was jammed. It was a small church, and one man had even come in an oxcart."

It was Connie Motley's first real exposure to southern black rural poverty. She recalled the drive from the airport in Birmingham to Selma, during which she looked out the window at tarpaper shacks and outhouses. She was not prepared for the starkness. "It sort of knocked me over," she said. The church was filled with people from all over Alabama, many of whom had saved their money to travel to hear Walter White. Thinking of that day in Alabama, she recalled that she knew immediately that the white people would fight *Brown* all the way. She saw her future in terms of a vast tapestry of court cases and problems, and worried about how the tiny Inc. Fund, with its minimal budget, could afford the years of litigation. On the flight back to New York, she recalled, her euphoria over the *Brown* decision faded, and she felt lost, with no idea what lay ahead.

As each *Brown* v. *Board of Education* milestone occurs, civil-rights legal scholars—Randall Kennedy among others—inevitably comment on the obliqueness of the Court's language, which led to years of legal maneuvers and the continued de-facto segregation that plagues inner-city schools. When the *Brown* decision came down, Motley recalls, it was initially viewed as a decision that prohibited segregation but not as one that required affirmative action from state officials. Connie Motley prepared many of the hundreds of court papers and arguments necessary to enforce *Brown*, yet she never became a darling of the civil-rights movement, perhaps because her skill as a litigator lay in her very thorough preparation and understanding of the arcana of the law.

Connie Motley first met Martin Luther King, Jr., in the Fifth Circuit Court of Appeals, in Atlanta. King was seen as a nuisance by the Inc. Fund, because his demonstrations had strained their ability to pursue school cases. In 1962, King had been enjoined by a court order from leading a march in Albany, Georgia. Motley arrived in Atlanta at one in the morning, in order to be in Judge Elbert Tuttle's court that day. Tuttle, an Eisenhower appointee, held relatively liberal views on race. He was born in California, and had once seen his mother leave her porch and stand at a bus stop with a black woman so that the bus would stop to pick her up. At the airport, Motley was met by the Legal Defense Fund's local counsel and, to her surprise, by William Kunstler, who was a private attorney at that time and had flown in from New York a few days before, claiming to represent Martin Luther King. Kunstler arranged with Motley and the other lawyers that he would make the first argument. "First of all, Judge Tuttle, let me introduce Mrs. Motley," Motley remembers him saying in court later that morning. Tuttle then said, "Mr. Kunstler, Mrs. Motley has been here so often that she could be a member of the court." The question at hand—whether the injunction against King's march was a preliminary one, and could be appealed—was a tricky point to argue. As Motley recalls it, Kunstler told Judge Tuttle, "Well, Mrs. Motley will argue that." With little preparation, Motley stood up and spoke. Tuttle overturned the injunction. "As I was walking out," she said, "who should be sitting in the front row but Martin Luther King!" Not long afterward, the Inc. Fund became King's primary counsel.

The envelope of papers that Connie Motley keeps in her chambers includes a copy of a letter written by James Meredith on January 29, 1961, to Thurgood Marshall:

> I am submitting an application for admission to the University of Mississippi, I am seeking entrance for the second semester which begins the 8th of February. I am anticipating encountering some type of difficulty with the various agencies here in the State which are against my gaining entrance into the school. . . . I am making this move in, what I consider, the interest of and for the benefit of (1) my country (2) my race (3) my family, and (4) myself.

Connie Motley is convinced that she was assigned the Meredith case because she was a woman. "Thurgood knew they treated black men a whole lot differently in Mississippi from the way they treated black women," she told Alfred Aman, the dean of the Indiana University–Bloomington School of Law, during an interview he conducted in 1988. "This is the last place in the world we wanted to hear from," she added, explaining that Marshall was worried about getting involved in Mississippi at that point, because the state seemed to be nearing an explosion, with Freedom Riders being arrested by the hundreds. By 1961, the Inc. Fund had grown to seven lawyers, and some of them were before the Supreme Court every couple of months. The office was already strained by its caseload, but Marshall knew that he had to make his last and best stand in Mississippi.

By then, Motley was well known in the Jackson federal court. She recalled that when she appeared to file her motion for Meredith, the judge, Sidney Mize, called to her from the bench, "Hi, Miz Motley!" "This was in the middle of another trial," she said. "He was very informal. When he took his recess, I told him I wanted to file my complaint against the University of Mississippi. Knowing there would be resistance, given the volatile situation in the state, he said to me, 'Why did you have to come now?'"

Motley was brisk with Meredith. She told him to get decent clothes and to shave his beard. He was a meticulous record keeper, Motley recalled. At one point, she subpoenaed his files from the university. The registrar, in an attempt to stall, said, "We didn't bring the records," whereupon Meredith said, "I have a copy of everything I sent." Motley had a vivid memory of the moment: "They were floored. They had never expected that here was this student who would have a copy of all their correspondence!" One of the many tactics that were used to keep Meredith out of the university was to threaten to arrest him for having registered to vote in

Jackson, where he had gone to college, rather than in his hometown, Kosciusko. Immediately, Motley flew to New Orleans, where the court of appeals judge on Meredith's case was sitting. "They are about to arrest Meredith," she told Judge John Minor Wisdom, and then suggested, "You could issue an injunction under the all-writs statute," a statute that permits a court to take whatever action is necessary to preserve its jurisdiction. Wisdom did so. Motley met Medgar Evers, the Mississippi field secretary of the NAACP, in New Orleans and, with him, drove straight to Jackson. "We got there at five minutes to six to prevent Meredith's arrest," she recalled.

For months, the Justice Department avoided weighing in on Meredith, because the new attorney general, Robert F. Kennedy, did not want a confrontation with Governor Ross Barnett. The litigation dragged on for a year and a half. Motley made twenty-two trips to Mississippi. For Joel Motley, then in grade school at Dalton, his mother's travel was part of a great crusade. "There was no question in our house that history was being made," he told me. "One day during the Meredith trial, Burke Marshall"—an assistant United States attorney general—"called. I remember he told my mother that he wanted her to do X, Y, and Z. She hung up the phone on him. She told us that she was happy to have his help, but he wasn't going to tell her how to run her case." On the day when Connie Motley decided that she would file a motion in federal district court to hold Governor Barnett in contempt, she drove to the Meridian, Mississippi, courthouse with Meredith and her secretary, in Medgar Evers's car. "While we were driving," she recalled, "Meredith said to me, 'Put those papers inside the *Times*. We are being followed. We don't want them to know who you are.' There we were, frightened to death, driving to Meridian. This occurred going through a wooded area. The state police just followed us all the way. They knew it was Medgar's car, because they had been following him for years." (Within a year, of course, Evers was murdered.) "When we got to court, my secretary, in her haste, wrote 'motion' instead of 'order.' Judge Mize was presiding over the court, with Harold Cox, another judge, who was the most antiblack human being I ever met. Judge Cox looked at our document and threw it at us. He said, 'Look at this, it says "motion"!' Judge Mize put his hand on Judge Cox's hand and said, 'Judge Cox, it is all over.' Mize was saying, in effect, 'You are a federal judge. You cannot take sides.'"

A few weeks before the fortieth anniversary of *Brown* v. *Board of Education*, I went to Columbia to visit Jack Greenberg. Greenberg has been on sabbatical this year, finishing *Crusaders in the Courts*, and I wondered whether the years he spent analyzing the Inc. Fund cases had given him a larger perspective on what he and Connie Motley and their colleagues accomplished. Greenberg, who is sixty-nine, is slightly built and appears younger than he is. I had noticed many black students on the campus; Greenberg recalled that when he entered Columbia Law School, in the 1940s, there was only one black in his class and she was from the Virgin Islands. Greenberg talked about Thurgood Marshall and his legacy, and that conversation led inevitably to the subject of Clarence Thomas. Greenberg simply shook his head sadly, as if he could hardly tolerate the fact that Thomas had taken Marshall's place on the bench.

I asked Greenberg about the many celebrations that I had been told he plans to speak at for the fortieth anniversary of *Brown*. He said, "I'll tell you exactly," and pulled out a small calendar and read off a list: It included forums at Princeton, the College of William and Mary, and Texas Southern University, and an event that the Legal Defense Fund, which now has a staff of twenty-five lawyers, will hold in Washington on May 16, at which the president will also speak. I told Greenberg about Connie Motley's trip to Indiana and how she was confronted by BLSA members who seemed to be trying to hold the Inc. Fund responsible for the breakdown in the black communities.

"None of these things are simple," Greenberg said. "We can't do anything about the pathologies of the ghetto: drugs, guns, single-parent households, and housing that has collapsed. But *Brown* has been an important factor in producing a large black middle class." As Judge Motley and I arrived in Washington for Thurgood Marshall's memorial service and walked through Union Station, she said, "When I first came to Washington, on that restrictive-covenants case, this was the only place Thurgood and I could eat." Motley and I had talked about some of her cases since she became a judge. In 1969, she had been vigorous in her decision to protect prisoners' right to due process in the *Sostre* case; in 1978, it was her ruling that allowed women reporters to enter the locker rooms of professional sports. But she said that it was her time at the Legal Defense Fund that was "lasting and significant." She later remarked that she was annoyed when the Indiana law students expected her to be an architect of social policy. "We were trying to eke out a legal victory. If you want to win a legal case, you had to win a legal argument," she said. It was a warm day in November—freakishly warm—and Judge Motley decided to take a taxi the short distance to the Court. In the taxi, she again brought up the subject of what had happened to her in Indiana. "Don't those students realize that they would not even be at Indiana if it weren't for Thurgood Marshall and the *Brown* decision?" she said.

I was sitting in the front seat of the taxi, whose driver happened to be black. When he heard the name Thurgood Marshall, he suddenly became attentive. He looked carefully in the rearview mirror at the judge. When we pulled up at the Supreme Court Building, it took Judge Motley a few moments to organize her papers in her briefcase and comb her hair. I noticed a sea of gray heads moving toward the entrance of the building, and she began to tell me which lawyer had helped with each case. The unpleasant questions posed by the Indiana students were forgotten. As we got out of the car, the taxi driver asked her, "Ma'am, did you really know Thurgood Marshall?"

"Yes," she said matter-of-factly.

"My God," he said.

THE MAN WHO
KNEW TOO MUCH

MAY 1996

*"I am a whistle-blower," he says. "I am notorious. It is a kind
of infamy doing what I am doing, isn't that what they say?"*

THE WITNESS

It was never Jeffrey Wigand's ambition to become a central figure in the great social chronicle of the tobacco wars. By his own
description, Wigand is a linear thinker, a plodder. On January 30,
when he and I arrange to meet at the sports bar at the Hyatt Regency in Louisville, he is in the first phase of understanding that he
has entered a particular American nightmare where his life will no
longer be his to control. His lawyer will later call this period "hell
week." Wigand has recently learned of a vicious campaign orchestrated against him, and is trying to document all aspects of his past.
"How would you feel if you had to reconstruct every moment of
your life?" he asks me, tense with anxiety. He is deluged with requests for interviews. TV vans are often set up at DuPont Manual,
the magnet high school where he now teaches. In two days Wigand,

249

the former head of research and development (R&D) at the Brown & Williamson Tobacco Corp., will be on the front page of the *Wall Street Journal* for the second time in a week. Five days from now, he will be on *60 Minutes.*

Wigand is trapped in a war between the government and its attempts to regulate the $50 billion tobacco industry and the tobacco companies themselves, which insist that the government has no place in their affairs. Wigand is under a temporary restraining order from a Kentucky state judge not to speak of his experiences at Brown & Williamson (B&W). He is mired in a swamp of charges and countercharges hurled at him by his former employer, the third-largest tobacco company in the nation, the manufacturer of Kool, Viceroy, and Capri cigarettes.

In the bar, Wigand sits with his security man, Doug Sykes, a former Secret Service agent. Wigand is worn out, a fighter on the ropes. He has reached that moment when he understands that circumstances are catapulting him into history, and he is frightened, off his moorings. He wears silver-rimmed aviator glasses, which he takes off frequently to rub his eyes. Although he has been on the *CBS Evening News* twice in the last five days, no one in the bar recognizes him. Wigand is fifty-three. He has coarse silver hair, a small nose, and a fighter's thick neck from his days as a black belt in judo. There is a wary quality in his face, a mysterious darkness that reminds me of photographs of the writer John Irving. Wigand wears the same clothes I have seen him in for days—jeans and a red plaid flannel shirt, his basic wardrobe for a $30,000-a-year job teaching chemistry and Japanese.

In front of us, on a large screen, a basketball game is in progress. "They kept me up until 2:00 a.m. last night. Just when I thought I was going to get some sleep, the investigators called me at midnight. At 6:00 a.m. I was gotten up again by someone from *60 Minutes* telling me I should relax. How am I supposed to relax?" Wigand stares at the TV screen. "You are becoming a national figure," I say. Wigand suddenly sputters with rage. "I am a national figure instead of having a family. Okay? I am going to lose economically and I am going to lose my family. They are going to use the trump cards on me."

I follow Wigand out of the Hyatt and down the street to a restaurant called Kunz's. A light snow is falling. By this time, Jeff Wigand and I have spent several days together, and I am accustomed to his outbursts. A form of moral outrage seems to have driven him from B&W, and he is often irascible and sometimes, on personal matters, relentlessly negative: "What does your brother think?" "Ask him." "Is your wife a good mother?" His expression hardens; he retreats into an inner zone.

"When you were in your thirties, how did you think your life was going to turn out?" I ask him. Wigand is no longer belligerent. His voice is quiet, modulated. "I thought I would be very successful. Affluent. I started at $20,000 a year and wound up at $300,000 a year. That was pretty nice."

All through dinner, Wigand keeps his cellular phone on the table. It rings as we are having coffee. He explodes in anger into the receiver: "Why do you want to know where I am? What do you want? What do you mean, what am I doing? It's ten o'clock at night. . . . What do you need to connect with me for? I am not a trained dog. You are going to have to explain to me what you are doing and why you are doing it so *I* can participate." Wigand narrows his eyes and shakes his head at me as if to signal that he is talking to a fool. He is beyond snappish now. I realize that he is speaking to one of his legal investigators, who has been putting in sixteen-hour days on his behalf, mounting a counterattack against his accusers. "You can't just drop into Louisville and have me drop what I am doing. No, you can't! I am not listening, okay? Fine. You tell him to find somebody else."

Wigand slams the telephone on the table. "Everyone on the legal team is pissed off because I am in Louisville. You know what the team can do! If he was going to come down today, why didn't he tell me he was coming?" We walk out of Kunz's and trudge back through the snow toward the Hyatt. Across from the hotel is the B&W Tower, where Wigand used to be a figure of prestige, a vice president with a wardrobe of crisp white shirts and dark suits. "I am sick of it. Sick of hiding in a hotel and living like an animal. I want to go home," he says with desperation in his voice.

Jeffrey Wigand and I met at an antismoking awards ceremony in New York. Wigand was receiving an honorarium of $5,000, and former surgeon general C. Everett Koop was going to introduce him. Wigand radiated glumness, an unsettling affect for a man who was in New York to be honored along with such other antismoking activists as California congressman Henry Waxman and Victor Crawford, the former Tobacco Institute lobbyist, who died soon after of throat cancer. "I am not sure I should be here," Wigand told me moments after we met. "Something terrible has happened to me. Brown & Williamson has gotten private records from the Louisville courthouse. A local TV reporter has come to my school to ask about my marriage. They are trying to ruin my life. When I get back to Louisville, I may not have a job. A public-relations man in New York named John Scanlon is trying to smear me. I have five sets of lawyers who are representing me, and no one can agree on a strategy." Then he said, without any special emphasis, "If they are successful in ruining my credibility, no other whistle-blower will ever come out of tobacco and do what I have done." One hour later he was on the stage accepting his award and giving a halting history of his conflict with B&W. "My children have received death threats, my reputation and character have been attacked systematically in an organized smear campaign," he said, his voice breaking.

When I saw Jeffrey Wigand for the first time in Louisville, he was at the end of one crisis and the beginning of another. We had been scheduled to meet for a first formal interview that evening, and I waited for him to call me. Out of necessity, Wigand has become a man of secret telephone numbers and relayed phone messages; there is an atmosphere of conspiracy around any meeting with him, with tense instructions and harried intermediaries. On my voice mail in the hotel, the messages grew increasingly dramatic. "This is Dr. Wigand's security man. He will call you at 4:00 p.m." "Marie, this is Dr. Wigand. Some problems have developed. I am not sure I can have dinner." At one point I picked up the telephone. "How are you?" I asked. "Let's put it this way: I've had better days." Then: "The FBI is coming to check out a death threat." Later: "My wife, Lucretia, wants me to leave the house. I am trying not to be served with papers." Finally: "I don't have a place to go."

By the time Wigand decided to move temporarily into the Hyatt, it was 10:30 p.m. I walked downstairs and knocked on his door. I was surprised by the change in his appearance in just one week. He leaned against the TV on the wall, diminished and badly shaken. "I have lost my family. I don't know what I am going to do," he said.

He had hurriedly packed a few shirts; he was missing even the lesson plans for his classes the next day at the high school. Before coming to the Hyatt, Wigand had broken down at home in the presence of an FBI agent who had come to investigate a death threat and a bullet that had been placed in the Wigands' mailbox the night before. Wigand said his wife told him, "You have put us all in danger, and I want you out of the house."

Over the next two weeks, he would hide in Room 1108 at the Hyatt, registered under another name. On January 26, his second night in exile, I joined him to watch himself as the lead story on the *CBS Evening News*. Wigand was fraught, particularly sour with one of his lawyers, Todd Thompson, when he walked into the room. "Don't you say hello to me, Jeff?" he asked. "I am angry at the world," Wigand answered. He was sitting at a small table. On his shirt was a button that read IF YOU THINK EDUCATION IS EXPENSIVE, TRY IGNORANCE. "I have no idea where my wallet and diary are!" he said. "Why should she have my assets? Why should I continue to pay her expenses?"

That same day the *Wall Street Journal* had published a front-page, thirty-three-hundred-word story with an extract from a lengthy deposition Wigand had given in late November about his experiences at B&W. The deposition would be used in a massive lawsuit filed by Michael Moore, the attorney general of Mississippi, against the major American tobacco companies. Wigand is a key witness in a singular legal attempt by seven states to seek reimbursement of Medicaid expenses resulting from smoking-related illnesses. Each year, 425,000 Americans die of such illnesses; through tax money that goes to Medicaid, the general population pays for a significant portion of the billions of dollars of health costs. If the state attorney general, with an assist from Jeffrey Wigand, were to succeed in proving that cigarettes are addictive, the cigarette companies could be forced into settling the hundreds of thousands of plaintiff actions that would result. A number of the lawyers representing the states are working on contingency—in some cases hoping to earn fees of 33 percent—and recently the *Wall Street Journal* raised the question "Should state governments be getting into bed with the contingency fee bar?"

Wigand is tentatively scheduled to testify late this spring. In his deposition, Wigand had talked about the dangers of a number of additives in cigarettes and pipe tobacco, the addictive properties of nicotine, and the alleged attempts at B&W to camouflage such information. The *Wall Street Journal* rested on the bed, as did a copy of the most recent death threat Wigand had received: "We want you to know that we have not forgotten you or your little brats. If you think we are going to let you ruin our lives, you are in for a big surprise! You cannot keep the bodyguards forever, asshole."

Wigand looked up to see his own face on TV. Mike Wallace was interviewing him.

WALLACE: Last August we talked with Jeffrey Wigand, previously the $300,000 research chief at Brown & Williamson. He is the highest-ranking executive ever to reveal what goes on behind the scenes at the highest level of a tobacco company.

WIGAND: We're in a nicotine-delivery business.

WALLACE: And that's what cigarettes are for?

WIGAND: Most certainly. It's a delivery device for nicotine.

The telephone rang. It was Wigand's father, and Wigand told him he was on CBS. There was no pleasure in his voice. Suddenly, a copy of the death threat that I had just read was on the screen. Wigand shouted, "How the hell did they get that? Don't I have any privacy at all?"

That night we had dinner at the revolving restaurant at the top of the Hyatt. As we sat down at the table, Wigand looked out the window. "I don't believe this," he said. "We are directly across from the Brown & Williamson Tower." I could see fluorescent light glowing on a single floor in the otherwise darkened building. "What is that?" I asked. "That's the eighteenth floor. The legal department. That is where they are all working, trying to destroy my life."

The restaurant revolves slowly, and each time the B&W Tower came into view, Wigand would grimace. "Look at that," he said. "They are still there, and they will be there tomorrow and they will be there on Sunday. . . . You can't schmooze with these guys. You kick them in the balls. You don't maim them. Don't take prisoners."

The antitobacco forces depict Jeffrey Wigand as a portrait in courage, a Marlon Brando taking on the powers in *On the Waterfront*. The protobacco lobbies have been equally vociferous in their campaign to turn Wigand into a demon, a Mark Fuhrman who could cause potentially devastating cases against the tobacco industry to dissolve over issues that have little to do with the dangers of smoking. According to New York public-relations man John Scanlon, who was hired by B&W's law firm to help discredit Wigand, "Wigand is a habitual liar, a bad, bad guy." It was Scanlon's assignment to disseminate a wide range of damaging charges against

Wigand, such as shoplifting, fraud, and spousal abuse. Scanlon himself, along with B&W, is now the subject of an unprecedented Justice Department investigation for possible intimidation of a witness. For First Amendment specialist James Goodale, the charges and countercharges B&W has attempted to level against Wigand represent "the most important press issue since the Pentagon Papers." Goodale, who represented the *New York Times* during that period, said, "You counteract these tactics by a courageous press and big balls."

The B&W executives appear to be convinced that they can break Wigand by a steady drumbeat of harassment and litigation, but they underestimate the stubborn nature of his character and the depth of his rage at what he says he observed as their employee. A part of his motivation is the need for personal vindication: Wigand is not proud that he was once attracted to the situation he came to find intolerable. According to Wigand's brother James, a Richmond, Virginia, endocrinologist, "If they think they can intimidate and threaten him, they have picked on the wrong person!"

It has become a dramatic convention to project onto whistle-blowers our need for heroism, when revenge and anger are often what drive them. There is a powerful temptation to see Jeffrey Wigand as a symbol: the little guy against the cartel, a good man caught in a vise. However, Wigand defies easy categorization. As a personality, he is prickly, isolated, and fragile—"peculiar as hell" in Mike Wallace's phrase—but there seems to be little doubt about the quality of his scientific information. Wigand is the most sophisticated source who has ever come forward from the tobacco industry, a fact that has motivated B&W to mount a multi-million-dollar campaign to destroy him. National reporters arrive in Louisville daily with questions for Wigand: How lethal are tobacco additives such as coumarin? What did B&W officials know and when? And what does it feel like, Dr. Wigand, to lose your wife and children and have every aspect of your personal life up for grabs and interpretation in the middle of a smear?

When Jeffrey Wigand tells the story of his life, he does not begin with his childhood. Instead, he starts with the events surrounding his forced exit from B&W and doesn't veer too far from that theme. For most of his life, Wigand defined himself as a man of science, but a scientist in the ethos of middle management, "a workaholic," and a hard-driving businessman. He is a corporate Everyman, part of a world of subsidiaries and spin-offs, golf on weekends and rides on the company plane. He uses phrases right out of the lexicon of business—"game plan," "troubleshooter." He was "director of corporate development at Pfizer," then a "general manager and marketing director" at Union Carbide in Japan. Later, as a senior vice president of marketing at Technicon Instruments, he was responsible for "a state-of-the-art plant" that "optimized" the "manufacturing facility" for biological compounds.

The son of a mechanical engineer, Jeffrey Wigand grew up in a strict Catholic home in the Bronx, the oldest of five children. When he was a teenager, the family moved to Pleasant Valley, a town in upstate New York near Poughkeepsie. Wigand's father stressed independence and insisted that his sons help build their new house. Wigand had to control his anger at his parents' strictness. According to James, their mother was "a cold individual" who had little understanding of children. "I am sure that my father will kill me if he reads this," James said, "but I felt that my parents believed that children were more to be tolerated. I always had the feeling how much was being done for us, how much we owed for this opportunity!"

A gifted chemistry and biology student, Jeff flourished in the quiet atmosphere of the science labs and hoped to study medicine. As a freshman at Dutchess Community College, he ran cross-country track and "worked as a scrub nurse at Vassar Brothers Hospital," James recalled. Then he suddenly announced to his parents that he was dropping out of college and joining the air force. "It was a rebellion to get away," James said. "My mother just about freaked out. . . . But if you make someone so suppressed, the anger kind of builds up."

It was 1961. Wigand was sent to Misawa, an American air base in Japan, where he ran an operating room. "I got hooked on the language and on martial arts," he said. He volunteered as an English teacher at a Catholic orphanage. He was sent briefly to Vietnam, he told me, although he brushed off the experience: "It was 1963, and nothing was going on." I wondered at the defensive tone in his voice. Later B&W would challenge whether he had been in Vietnam at all. (According to one investigator, he was there for about a month.)

When he came back to the States, he wrote a master's thesis on vitamin B12 and later earned a doctorate in biochemistry at the State University of New York at Buffalo. He was offered a $20,000-a-year job with the Boehringer Mannheim Corporation, a German health-care company. In 1970, at a judo class, Wigand met Linda, his first wife, a legal secretary from Eden, New York. Seven months after they married, in 1971, Linda developed multiple sclerosis. At the time, Wigand was still working for Boehringer Mannheim in New York, but he moved on to Pfizer and then was recruited for a lucrative position at Union Carbide. He was to form a subsidiary to test medical equipment in clinical trials in Japan. He was thirty-four years old, fluent in Japanese, basking in his new status.

Wigand is proud of his time at Union Carbide—"I was right at the top," he said—but Linda grew progressively weaker. "Jeff searched the world for specialists," recalled Conrad Kotrady, a Salt Lake City doctor who has known him since graduate school. "He attacked the problem as if it were an assignment, but then her condition became increasingly difficult for him." Wigand burrowed into his work, withdrawing from the agony of watching his wife disintegrate physically. In 1973 their daughter, Gretchen, was born.

Wigand has a quality his brother recalled as a kind of personal shutdown—an ability to close off his emotions when things get difficult. As Linda's condition worsened, Wigand distanced himself from her and his baby. "I really did not have a marriage," he told me. "If I said I didn't play around, I would be lying. Linda came back to the States, and something happened in my parents' house. She went home to Buffalo." Several years passed before he saw her or his daughter again, and eventually the marriage unraveled. Linda's parents believed that Wigand had abandoned their daughter, one friend recalled. "I thought Linda was dead," Wigand said quickly. "That's what a friend said." Wigand made little attempt to communicate with his daughter. It is Kotrady's belief that Wigand did not want to upset her by taking her away from a stable home with loving grandparents.

Wigand met his second wife, Lucretia, in 1981 at a sales conference at Ortho Diagnostic Systems, a subsidiary of Johnson &

Johnson, where he was a director of marketing. She was a sales rep. He was, he later remembered, attracted to her cool demeanor and willowy good looks. Lucretia had spent part of her childhood in Louisville, the daughter of two doctors who separated when she was eight. Lucretia's mother, at one time on the staff of the National Cancer Institute, used to tease Jeff about Lucretia's expensive tastes. They married in 1986.

Soon Wigand moved on to a grander position as a senior vice president at Technicon, responsible for marketing blood-testing equipment. Wigand was filled with ideas, but he was often testy. Bob Karlson, his mentor at Ortho, recalled pulling on his ear at meetings to tell Wigand to pipe down when he got out of hand. "I have a very bad problem—saying what's on my mind," Wigand told me. "I don't take too much crap from anybody."

He was a perfectionist who kept a file of correspondence with businesses he dealt with whose products were flawed. In one instance, he returned some hardware to a catalogue company. In another, he demanded reimbursement for a cleaning bill for water-damaged items. Later this file would be detailed and used against him as evidence in B&W's private investigation, suggesting that he had committed fraud. Wigand had a tendency not to share information, even with Lucretia. On the day before her thirtieth birthday, Wigand called her from the office: "My friends and I are coming home to celebrate." Later that afternoon, Lucretia used his car to go for pizza. "All of his office was in the backseat." She recalled asking, "Is there something you want to tell me?" As it happened, some of Technicon's upper-management team, including Wigand, had been dismissed. In 1987 he was made president of a small medical-equipment company called Biosonics in Fort Washington, Pennsylvania. Wigand recalled a power struggle with the owner of the company, who recently wrote an article in *Philadelphia Forum* about his experience with Wigand, accusing him of having bullied female employees and in one instance of having shined a light on his subordinates while he was asking about a company matter. Wigand denies both charges.

For one year Jeff Wigand did consulting work. He finally decided to pursue his dream of being a doctor, but Lucretia convinced him he was too old. Then he approached a headhunter, who asked if he would consider working for Brown & Williamson, the tobacco company. Lucretia was puzzled by the offer: "I said, 'Why do they want you? You know nothing about tobacco. You had—what?— seventeen years of health care.' It did not make sense."

From his first meetings with Alan Heard, the head of R&D for BAT Industries (formerly British American Tobacco), the conglomerate with $3 billion in annual profits that owns B&W, Wigand shut his eyes and ignored the Faustian arrangement. Heard said he wanted to develop a new cigarette to compete with Premier, a product made by the R. J. Reynolds Tobacco Company (RJR) that had little tar. The appeal was seductive for a man who prided himself on his research skills, and Wigand's title would be impressive: head of R&D. He would soon be paid more than he had ever earned in his life—$300,000 a year. His department would have a budget of more than $30 million and a staff of 243. Shortly after he began the interviews, Wigand took up smoking. He later said, "I was buying the routine. I wanted to understand the science of how it made you feel."

From the beginning, Lucretia encouraged the move to Louisville. Since her parents' divorce, her father had remarried a couple of times. Along with his medical practice, he owned tobacco land. A move back to Louisville with Wigand in an important position in that industry would probably impress Lucretia's father and might draw the family closer together. Besides, she had just had a baby, and she believed that life in Louisville would be a boon for the child. "I thought if I made big bucks she would be happy," Wigand told me.

When Wigand told his brother he was going to work for a tobacco conglomerate, James said, "You've got to be kidding." But Wigand was optimistic. "I thought I would have an opportunity to make a difference and work on a safer cigarette. I talked to a lot of my friends from college. They said, 'You know, you're never going to be able to come back. You can't go from tobacco back into health care.'"

THE FIRM

From Wigand's first days at B&W, it was apparent to him that there was a contradiction in his situation. On his good days he believed he was helping the world. On the other days he was a guy with a family who earned a large salary. He had a feisty, urban, go-getter personality in an unusual city; Louisville was a Velveeta town, clannish and sophisticated, once ruled by old families such as the Bingham publishing dynasty. At B&W, Wigand's intensity and uncongenial personality grated on many of his southern colleagues. Wigand believed that he was there to shake up the ossified atmosphere. Three months after he was hired, RJR withdrew Premier from the market because the taste was unpleasant, acrid, and synthetic. Had Wigand been shrewder, he might have thought that he was now in a trap. There was no real reason for a nontobacco man to remain at the company. But he attempted to keep his contrarian nature under wraps. He went to company parties, and Lucretia volunteered to help at the Hard Scruffle steeplechase, a charity event. It is conceivable that B&W had sized Wigand up psychologically. He surely appeared to be highly ambitious, money-hungry, a potential captive to the firm.

In Louisville, the Wigands bought a two-story, red brick house in a pleasant suburb. There was an allée of trees in the middle of the road, giving a sense of affluence. Wigand had two offices at B&W, one at the R&D laboratory and one in the office tower. When he toured the lab for the first time, he was startled, he told me, to observe how antiquated it seemed. "The place looked like a high-school chemistry lab from the 1950s with all sorts of old-fashioned smoking machines. There was no fundamental science being done." There was neither a toxicologist nor a physicist on staff, a fact that Wigand found very unsettling. How, he thought, could you be serious about studying the health aspects of tobacco or fire safety without the proper experts? According to documents that later wound up in the University of California at San Francisco library, even in the 1960s research had been done for B&W that tobacco activists say proved that cigarettes were addictive and caused cancer. However, Wigand says that he did not learn of those studies until after he left the company.

Shortly after Wigand was hired, he was sent to an orientation session on tobacco-litigation matters at Shook, Hardy & Bacon, a Kansas City law firm that specializes in defending lawsuits for the industry. The firm is reputed to have its own in-house scientists and tobacco researchers. Shook, Hardy & Bacon and B&W lawyers were aware of the dangers that the company's research could pose in a lawsuit. B&W lawyers had devised an ingenious method for avoiding discovery of sensitive information: have it "shipped offshore"—a practice one attorney referred to as "document management." It was the suggestion of Kendrick Wells, an attorney in B&W's legal department, that staff be told that this effort was "to remove deadwood," and that no one "should make any notes, memos or lists." Wigand later testified that another law firm, Covington & Burling, sometimes edited scientific information on additives.

Nine months after Wigand went to work, he attended a meeting of BAT scientists in Vancouver, British Columbia. The top R&D executives from BAT's worldwide tobacco subsidiaries were there to discuss health matters and the possibility of a nicotine substitute. There was a feeling of excitement among the scientists that they could reduce health risks for smokers. By then Wigand had grown used to the euphemisms of his new industry. He understood that "increased biological activity" in reports was code for cancer and other diseases. At the meeting, Wigand would later testify, roughly fifteen pages of minutes were taken by Ray Thornton, a British scientist. A copy was sent to Wigand, who circulated copies to upper management.

Soon after that, Wigand says, he was called into Kendrick Wells's office and asked to sign off on a three-page synopsis of the minutes—a reduction of about twelve pages. In a recent deposition

Wells testified that Raymond Pritchard, the then CEO of the company, had assigned Wigand to produce a revised set of minutes.

Within the industry, BAT is known as "the tough guy" for its ferocious litigation strategy. As a foreign corporation, it has never enjoyed quite as much political influence as the American tobacco companies, which donate vast sums of money to organizations as diverse as the African-American political caucuses, the Whitney Museum, and the political-action committees of dozens of candidates, especially Bob Dole. In the late 1970s the Federal Trade Commission (FTC) investigated the advertising practices of all the tobacco companies. In a nonpublic report later read at a congressional committee meeting, B&W's Viceroy cigarette was mentioned for a proposed test-marketing campaign that appeared to target minors. Several years later, a CBS anchorman in Chicago, Walter Jacobson, broadcast a segment about the report. B&W sued CBS, which paid a $3 million judgment after the case went all the way to the Supreme Court. B&W also clashed with RJR and Philip Morris over Barclay cigarettes and a false-advertising charge brought by the FTC. In 1987, B&W withdrew from the Tobacco Institute, an American tobacco lobbying group, for several years.

Although B&W employed five hundred people in Louisville, Wigand chafed at the bunker mentality. "It was an incestuous society," he said. "Wherever you went—to dinners, to parties—the B&W people stayed together. They never mixed." Many of the executives smoked, although in private they often talked about the risks. "Their whole corporate philosophy was 'Shit flows downhill.' You get paid very well. You have lots of nice benefits." Later he recalled, "I didn't trust anyone at B&W. I was a different animal."

Wigand felt that the scientific data at B&W was Stone Age, as he later told a friend. He brought new computers into the R&D facility and hired a physicist and a toxicologist. He worked on reverse engineering on Marlboros, attempting to discern their unique properties; he studied fire safety and ignition propensity.

After Vancouver, Wigand continued to push for more information. He began to hear mysterious names at company dinners—"Ariel" and "Hippo." "I did not drink at all then—only Diet Pepsi—and I would ask, 'What is that?' And suddenly people would clam up." As the head of R&D at B&W, he should logically have been aware of every aspect of the company's research. "There were essentially two research-and-development departments. They did the work on nicotine overseas." Wigand says he did not discover that Ariel and Hippo were research studies on health-related issues conducted in the 1970s at BAT in Switzerland until he read thousands of pages of documents taken from a law firm in downtown Louisville by a concerned paralegal named Merrell Williams, a Faulknerian personality with a doctorate in drama. "My perspective was like night and day," Wigand told me. "It was like being aware and not being aware. You look back on things that happened when you were present and you say, 'Hell, they knew about that all along.'"

Wigand began to keep an extensive scientific diary, both in his computer and in a red leather book. "I kept it day by day, month by month. I saw two faces, the outside face and the inside face. It bothered me. I didn't know the diary was going to be valuable." In one early entry, Wigand recalled, he recorded a promise made to him that he would be able to hire "a scientific and medical advisory committee." "Then, all of a sudden—poof!—it's gone."

Wigand's scientific ethics had been shaped during his years

working for Johnson & Johnson; he admired particularly the stringent standards enforced by CEO James Burke during the recall of shipments of Tylenol after a poisoning scare in 1982. At first he believed that Ray Pritchard was a man of honor like Burke. At lunch from time to time, he complained in private to Pritchard about Thomas Sandefur, then the company president. Wigand had come to believe that his safe-cigarette project was being canceled. He told *60 Minutes* that he had gone to ask Sandefur about it and that Sandefur had been harsh: "I don't want to hear any more discussion about a safe cigarette. . . . We pursue a safer cigarette, it would put us at extreme exposure with every other project." (On *60 Minutes*, B&W said this was false.)

Wigand made no secret of his lack of respect for Sandefur: "I wouldn't consider them all intellectual titans. Sandefur used to beat on me for using big words. I never found anybody as stupid as Sandefur in terms of his ability to read or communicate. . . . In terms of his understanding something and his intellectual capacity, Sandefur was just like a farm boy."

According to Wigand, Sandefur had a particular interest in B&W's manufacture of snuff. There were problems with bacterial fermentation, Wigand told me. "They could never get it fermented correctly. They could not get a consistent taste or particle size. They could not understand the tactility of soil bacteria and how it worked on the natural flora. What was the effect of ammonia to flora? Most moist snuff deteriorates after packaging. If you could find a way to sterilize it, you would slow up bacterial fermentation and have a safer product. No one had done this for four years."

Snuff was a critical product for B&W, Wigand said, because it is "start-up stuff for kids. . . . It was Sandefur's baby. You have to look at the age somebody starts smoking. If you don't get them before they are eighteen or twenty, you never get them." (Thomas Sandefur declined to make any comment for this article.)

According to the *Journal of the American Medical Association,* 3 million Americans under the age of eighteen consume one billion packs of cigarettes and 26 million containers of snuff every year. For a cigarette company, the potential for profits from these sales— illegal in all fifty states—is immense, more than $200 million a year.

Wigand came to feel increasingly that there was "no sense of responsibility" on the subject of teenagers and smoking. He was disturbed by a report that on the average children begin to smoke by fourteen. He was surprised, he told me, by Sandefur's lack of interest in such matters, and he grew visibly testy. "I used to come home tied in a knot. My kids would say to me, 'Hey, Daddy, do you kill people?' I didn't like some of the things I saw. I felt uncomfortable. I felt dirty.

"The last year and a half I was there, Brown & Williamson used to keep me isolated. How did they know I was trouble? I was asking some pretty difficult questions: How come there was no research file? . . . When they drink, they talk. I know a lot. My diary will reflect those meetings. I was not Thomas Sandefur's fair-haired boy."

He withdrew into a stolid isolation. Lucretia knew something was wrong, she later told me. When she asked him how things were going at the office, he would say, "Fine." If she pressed him, he would answer, "That's work, and I leave that at the office." His need to control his emotions caused him frequently to lose his temper at home, Lucretia remembered.

There was also a major additional problem at home, a hole in the center of his life. His older daughter with Lucretia had serious medical problems. According to Wigand, "Rachel was not diagnosed correctly from birth. Both specialists and general practitioners, including Lucretia's father, unequivocally stated that Rachel did not have any problem, even after substantive testing. I finally sought out a respected adult urologist, who made the diagnosis of spina bifida. This required spinal surgery." In a rage, Wigand threatened to sue the doctors who had not diagnosed her earlier. It is Wigand's opinion that his father-in-law never forgave him. (Neither Lucretia nor her father would comment on this subject.)

At work he grew increasingly vocal. After 1991, B&W's evaluations of him contained new corporate euphemisms. Wigand had "a difficulty in communication." He was becoming, as he later described it, a problem for Sandefur by sounding off at meetings. For Wigand, the critical moment occurred when he read a report from the National Toxicology Program. The subject was coumarin, an additive that had been shown to have a carcinogenic property that caused tumors in rats and mice. The makeup of coumarin was close to that of a compound found in rat poison, but until 1992 no one understood the possible dangers. The new report described its carcinogenic effect. When Wigand read this in late 1992, his first reaction was, "We have got to get this stuff out of the pipe tobacco." One of B&W's products was Sir Walter Raleigh. Wigand told *60 Minutes* that when he went to a meeting with Sandefur, Sandefur told him that removing it would affect sales. Wigand got the impression that Sandefur would do nothing immediately to alter the product, so he sought out his toxicologist, Scott Appleton. Wigand says he asked him to write a memo backing him up, but

Appleton refused, perhaps afraid for his job. (Appleton declined to comment.)

Driven by anger now, Wigand says, he determined to examine what happens when other additives are burned. He focused on glycerol, an additive used to keep the tobacco in cigarettes moist. He was involved in discussions about the nicotine patch and studied a genetically engineered, high-nicotine Brazilian tobacco called Y-1.

Wigand also began attending meetings of a commission on fire safety in cigarettes in Washington. He observed Andrew McGuire, an expert on burn trauma from San Francisco, who had won a MacArthur grant following his campaign for fire-retardant clothing for children. The commission met approximately forty times and had four R&D scientists from tobacco companies as members, including Alexander W. Spears, the future head of Lorillard. As far as McGuire knew, B&W was not represented. "I would look out and I would see all these men in suits listening to our discussions. I assumed that they were tobacco-company lawyers, monitoring what we were doing," McGuire said. Wigand had several conversations about his experiments with additives with other tobacco men attending the meetings, but he never met McGuire.

In the summer of 1992 Earl Kohnhorst, a senior executive at B&W, called Wigand into his office. Wigand had considered him a friend, and had urged him to stop smoking—as Wigand had. According to a memo Kohnhorst later wrote, the meeting was not friendly. Wigand apparently learned he was on notice, and Kohnhorst is said to have implied that he was difficult to work with and was talking too much.

Wigand says that his anger made it impossible for him to

censor himself; he had come to believe his worth as a scientist was being violated by his association with the tobacco company. He also believed that the other scientists in the company would share his values. Wigand was determined to be on the record with his research on additives. He recalled writing a memo for the files on the dangers of coumarin. He felt, he later said, that he was being diligent. In January 1993, it was announced that Thomas Sandefur, Wigand's nemesis, had been named CEO of B&W. On March 24, Wigand was fired and escorted from the building. He has testified that B&W never returned his scientific diary.

THE JOURNALIST AND THE WHISTLE-BLOWER

In the early spring of 1993, Lowell Bergman, an award-winning news producer at *60 Minutes,* found a crate of papers on the front steps of his house in Berkeley, California. Bergman's specialty at CBS was investigative reporting; he possessed a Rolodex of peerless snitches, CIA operatives, and corporate informants. The grandson of one of the first female leaders of the International Ladies Garment Workers Union, Bergman had a bemused, compassionate nature. He was close to fifty and had come to understand that life was a series of murky compromises. At the University of California at San Diego, he had studied with the political philosopher Herbert Marcuse and lived in a commune. Bergman's wife, Sharon Tiller, was a *Frontline* producer, and they had five grown sons between them.

Bergman often received anonymous letters and sealed court documents in his mailbox; it did not surprise him in the least, he told me, to find the box of papers on his porch. As always, Bergman was developing several pieces for Mike Wallace, the correspondent he worked with almost exclusively. They were close friends and confidants, but they argued ferociously and intimately, like a father and son. "Lowell can drive me crazy," Wallace told me. "Lowell would like to be the producer, the reporter, the correspondent, and the head of CBS News." Screaming messages and 6:00 a.m. phone calls were their standard operating techniques, but they shared a passion for corporate intrigue, and together had helped break the Iraqgate bank scandal in 1992 and examine the accusations of child abuse at McMartin Pre-School in Los Angeles in 1986. Shortly after the mysterious papers appeared on his steps, Bergman won a Peabody Award for a program on cocaine trafficking in the CIA.

At *60 Minutes,* the on-air personalities were involved in six or seven stories at the same time and took a deserved share of the credit for the show's singular productions, but the staff was well aware that the producers actually did the backbreaking reporting. In most cases, the producers had complete freedom to develop stories, and it was they, not the correspondents, who were in hotel rooms in Third World countries at all hours bringing along reluctant sources. Later, the correspondents stepped in. Only rarely did correspondents know the explicit details of stories other teams were developing.

When Bergman received the box of papers, he took a look at the hundreds of pages of material. "They were a shambles," he recalled, "but clearly from a nonpublic file." The papers were very technical and came from the Philip Morris company. The phrase "ignition propensity" was repeated often in them. "I had never heard that phrase before," Bergman said. He called his friend Andrew

McGuire, the only person he knew who had ever studied tobacco and fire. "Do you know anyone who can make sense of these papers for me?" Bergman asked. "I might have just the guy," McGuire said.

After being fired by B&W, Jeffrey Wigand remained optimistic for some time, Lucretia recalled. He came close to finding a lucrative job through a headhunter in Chicago. He gave as references Alan Heard and Ray Pritchard. He was surprised not to be hired immediately by another corporation, and soon he began to worry. He reportedly groused about his severance package to a friend at B&W, who repeated his remarks to his former boss. Several months later, Wigand learned that B&W was suing him for breach of contract. According to the suit, his medical benefits would be taken from him, a display of corporate hardball that would subsequently rebound. "If Brown &Williamson had just left me alone, I probably would have gotten a new job," Wigand said. He reluctantly signed an onerous, lifelong confidentiality agreement so stringent that he could be in violation if he discussed anything about the corporation. Wigand felt trapped, and he did not know what to do.

When I spoke with Lucretia Wigand in Louisville, she used an unusual phrase, "skeletons in the closet," to describe her fear of what would happen if Jeff went public with his experiences at B&W. "What do you mean, 'skeletons in the closet'?" I asked. In repose, Lucretia is elegant and steely. She looked at her divorce lawyer, Steven Kriegshaber, who shook his head as if to warn her not to speak. "The so-called spousal abuse—you were worried about that?" I asked. "Sure," she said softly.

Alcohol and rage are at the center of what happened on a bad night in the Wigand marriage in October 1994. The tension in the family had become overwhelming while Wigand was negotiating the punitive confidentiality agreement. Since Rachel had been diagnosed with spina bifida, the marriage had suffered enormous strain. "I felt that during Lucretia's pregnancy with Rachel she somewhat overabused alcohol," Wigand said. "She drinks quite heavily." (Lucretia denies this.) Wigand himself had at one time been a drinker, but he had stopped when he felt out of control. After he was fired, he told me, it was not surprising that he began to drink again. Lucretia, he said, was "stunned" when she heard that he had once again lost a job. She raged that he had not told even her of his growing unhappiness in the company. She was frightened that he would lose any claim to their medical package.

Wigand recalled her mood as sometimes dismissive and unsympathetic. There are contradictory versions of the evening. According to Wigand, Lucretia "hit me in the back with a wooden coat hanger and ran upstairs into the bedroom." Furious, he chased her and then called the police. According to Lucretia, "Because of the amount he drank, he does not remember most of the evening. . . . I tried to leave. He took my keys away and was grabbing me. . . . I picked up the phone to dial 911. He ripped the cord out of the wall. He smashed my nose with the palm of his hand. The kids were screaming, I was screaming. I ran down the hall and picked up another phone and dialed 911. Jeff left the house before the police arrived." Whatever happened that night, Lucretia and Jeffrey Wigand both blame B&W for placing an unbearable strain on their marriage, and say that this episode played no part in their later divorce. Soon after, according to a lawyer close to the case, Wigand became concerned enough about his drinking that he checked into a clinic for four days of evaluation—which would later, in a five-hundred-page dossier of allegations about his character, be reported as two weeks of hospitalization for treatment of anger.

Through an intermediary in the government, Wigand reached out tentatively to Andrew McGuire, whom he had observed in Washington. McGuire got a phone call: Would he speak to a former R&D executive? McGuire was intrigued. A tobacco-industry witness could be invaluable to him, since he was then pressing Congress to regulate fire safety. "I don't know if this guy is for real," the government official told McGuire, "but here is his home number. Call him." Wigand's voice on the phone was so strained and wary that McGuire wondered if he might not be a tobacco-industry spy. Nevertheless, he passed his name along to Lowell Bergman.

For weeks Bergman tried to get Wigand on the telephone. Each time a woman answered, and she would tell him, "He is not home." Finally she said, "He doesn't want to talk to you." Bergman had become fascinated by the court papers involving Philip Morris and was convinced he needed this particular chemist to make sense of them. He wanted a scientist, not an antitobacco advocate. In February 1994, he decided to go to Louisville. "I did the old 'call him at midnight' maneuver. He answered the phone and I said, 'If you are curious to meet me, I'll be sitting in the lobby at the Seelbach Hotel tomorrow at 11:00 a.m.'"

At 11:00 a.m. a gray-haired man in a windbreaker appeared and said, "Are you Lowell?" Bergman looked up to see a portrait of middle-aged anxiety. "I said to him, 'Let's go have a coffee.'"

It was the beginning of an extraordinary relationship. Bergman's presence in Wigand's life would eventually inspire him to come forward as a whistle-blower. For Bergman, Wigand would become a source who needed unusual protection and hand-holding—a fact that would ultimately jeopardize his position at CBS. "As a person, the guy I met had been raped and violated," Bergman said. Wigand told Bergman that he was suffering a "moral crisis." He said that he had always considered himself a scientist, and he called the type of research that went on at B&W "a display of craft."

"'Okay,'" Bergman recalled saying after their first day together, "'you can't talk to me about Brown & Williamson because of your severance agreement, but I have a problem. Can you analyze these documents for me?" He looked at two pages and said, "Wow!" After reading a few more pages about fire experiments, Wigand exclaimed, "Hey, they are way ahead of where we were."

Wigand agreed to examine the Philip Morris papers for Bergman. He was to be paid like any other consultant, about $1,000 a day. "I was bothered. Everything I had seen at the joint-venture meetings said it was not technologically feasible," he later told me. "I was pissed off! They had a fire-safe-product study on the shelf in 1986 and 1987, and they knew it!" (A spokesman for Philip Morris says the company has been unsuccessful in this so far but continues to do research.)

Wigand flew to New York for a day to attend a screening of a version of the projected program at CBS. At the end of March, CBS broadcast an exposé of the Hamlet project, which involved a fire-safe cigarette developed at Philip Morris. "I was angry when I saw it," said Wigand. "They knew all along it was possible to develop a fire-safe cigarette, and they even gave it a code name: Hamlet. Get it? 'To burn or not to burn.'"

At the end of the *60 Minutes* episode, Mike Wallace questioned on-camera a Philip Morris executive who had announced that his company was filing a $10 billion lawsuit against ABC for a *Day One* broadcast about alleged manipulation of nicotine levels in its cigarettes. ABC had problems: One of them was a source nicknamed Deep Cough, who was an executive at RJR. If Deep Cough's identity was to be kept a secret, she could not testify in a libel suit.

In April 1994, Henry Waxman, the California congressman, was holding public hearings on tobacco in Washington. Wigand watched the live coverage on C-SPAN of the testimony of top executives of the seven largest tobacco companies. He was in his den with Lucretia when he heard Thomas Sandefur say "I believe nicotine is not addictive." Wigand was furious. "I realized they were all liars. They lied with a straight face. Sandefur was arrogant! And that really irked me." Wigand, however, was hamstrung; he had the threat of a lawsuit hanging over his head. He could not criticize Sandefur publicly or his child might lose her medical insurance.

After Wigand started working as a confidential expert for CBS, his name began to circulate in antitobacco circles. He was soon called by the Food and Drug Administration. Would he consider advising FDA experts on cigarette chemistry? His identity would be protected. For Wigand, the invitation to Washington was a major step toward regaining his self-respect. By the time FDA commissioner David Kessler appeared before Congress in June 1994, he had reportedly been tutored by Wigand on ammonia additives and nicotine-impact boosting.

Wigand was invaluable; he even helped the FDA circumvent

a standard tobacco-industry tactic—"document dumping." If a company is subpoenaed for documents related to nicotine studies, it is common in the industry to respond "by driving a tractor-trailer to Washington and leaving ten tons of documents at your door," according to a close associate of the FDA. In this case, perhaps with an assist from Wigand, the FDA was able to ask B&W for specific papers.

That month, Wigand said, he received a threatening phone call. "Leave or else you'll find your kids hurt," the caller said. Wigand called Bergman in a panic. "I thought it could be a crank call," Bergman told me. "I knew Wigand was in a great quandary. He was bound up because of his contracts and yet he was filled with moral outrage." Bergman had been through this before with whistle-blowers. He even had a name for Wigand's mental state: "transition time." He remained patient and faxed amusing drawings to Wigand's children.

Soon Wigand told Bergman another death threat had come. Wigand was becoming distracted, unable to concentrate. He had started to drink again. "I used to come home and drink three fingers of booze every night," he told me. One day when he had his two young daughters in the car, he stopped to buy a bottle of liquor. "I am no goddamned angel. I can't hide what happened. I had one of those big jackets with the big pockets. Instead of getting a basket, I grabbed it and put it in my pocket. And then I realized I didn't have cash. And I said, 'Wait a minute,' and I ran out. And then somebody came running after me. They said, 'Somebody has been stealing in here before.' The truth of the matter is that I had the bottle in my pocket. Was it hidden? No. Was it exposed? Yes. My children, Rachel and Nikki, were in the car. I had $300 in cash in the car. I said, 'I have money. Look.' I made sure that I showed the cop the money. Was it intentional? It was two days after the death threat. I wasn't thinking. Why would I want to steal a ten-dollar bottle of booze? Give me a break. The whole thing was dismissed without adjudication. You can be arrested and charged with a lot of things in your life. Did you know that even Thomas Sandefur was once arrested and pleaded guilty on a DWI?"

Wigand did not tell Bergman about the episode, but Bergman sensed that something was very wrong. He worried about Wigand's state of mind. He was at the beginning of a long dance to create a sense of trust in his source, who he felt had an incredible story to tell. "Other whistle-blowers had come out of the tobacco industry to tell what they knew, but Wigand was singular. As an explorer, I felt, Wigand was Christopher Columbus," Bergman told me. The bottom line is that this was a man with significant information, but it wasn't just that he had to worry about the obvious, which is Brown & Williamson crushing him, but he had to worry about what would happen in his personal life."

A lawyer from the Justice Department went to Louisville in April to take Wigand's deposition on cigarette ignition. Privately, he complained that the lawyer did not ask the right questions. He also worried about his signed agreement with B&W and claims he took its legal department's advice to stick to the company line. He testified that there was no possibility of developing a safe cigarette and that, as far as he knew, B&W had never committed fraud—testimony that would later be used to challenge his credibility. By this time Wigand had become a shadow expert on the tobacco industry. He was hired by ABC's law firm Wilmer, Cutler &

Pickering to give technical advice in the $10 billion lawsuit Philip Morris had filed against ABC.

Wigand continued to tell Bergman that he could not talk about B&W until his severance package was completed, in March 1995. Wigand did not tell Bergman that he had signed a confidentiality agreement, but several of Bergman's finest pieces had been with sources who had been bound by such contracts. "The idea of some-body having a confidentiality agreement didn't even occur to me as a problem! That was my job, to get people to talk!"

In January 1995, Wigand began teaching school, much to Lucre-tia's surprise. He was making one-tenth the salary he had made at B&W, but he seemed quite happy. Meanwhile, Bergman had been feeling the heat from New York. Mike Wallace was getting antsy: "For God's sake, Lowell, when are you going to get this guy on tape?" In March, Bergman met with Wigand and his wife in Lou-isville. If Jeff went on-camera, Lucretia asked, what would they do if they got sued? Bergman said, "There may be antitobacco law-yers who would agree to represent you for free. But we don't even know yet if there is a story." Was there anything new to say on *60 Minutes*? Bergman next sent his associate producer to Louisville to do a preliminary interview with Wigand. She called Bergman after the interview and mentioned that Wigand had given her a copy of his B&W settlement agreement with the confidentiality clause. "He needs a lawyer," Bergman said.

In June 1994, the *New York Times* had run long articles based on thousands of pages taken from B&W—the cache of papers copied at a Louisville law office by Merrell Williams. Only in July 1995 did the University of California and tobacco expert Stanton Glantz put the documents on the Internet after successfully fighting off a serious lawsuit brought by B&W.

According to Bergman, "It took Jeff a long time to come out and decide that he wanted to tell his story. He used to say, 'Lowell, I want to do this, but I need support. I need my wife there. We can't do it yet, because Lucretia is not there.'" Wigand had continued to keep secrets from her: In May, the Wigands had come to New York as guests of *60 Minutes*. It was not obvious to Bergman that Wigand had not told Lucretia that he intended to be interviewed. "He expected me to explain it to her," Bergman told me. All summer long Wigand debated about his public role, and Lucretia grew increasingly panicky. Meanwhile, he continued to advise Wilmer, Cutler & Pickering regarding Philip Morris's suit against ABC. He was even asked to testify for ABC if the case should ever go to court. Bergman read his name on a wire-service story. "I called him and went ballistic! I said, 'Do you understand that B&W will now go to court to keep you from testifying? Soon every news outlet in America will be calling you.'" Bergman had begun to corroborate Wigand's story from the taped interview he had made; he knew that the Merrell Williams B&W documents supported Wigand's assertions about addiction, disease, and the role of various individuals. "I wasn't doing a personality profile. I wanted to find out what he knew that was different."

In July, Bergman began to get concerned. "I could see right up front that Jeff was going to wind up testifying. Philip Morris knew about him, the Justice Department knew about him, and so did the FDA. I called up Ephraim [Margolin, a lawyer friend who was advising Wigand by this time] and said, 'Your client may wind up with a court order not to speak. Let's get the guy's story on-camera and lock it up!' Ephraim had my verbal understanding that we wouldn't run it until he was ready. Jeff was worried about homesteading his house in case he lost a breach-of-contract suit. He showed up in New York and said, 'Ephraim wants you to write him a note.' So I did." The note stated that CBS would not run the interview without Wigand's permission, and that they would reconsider the matter on September 3. It was a harmless exercise, Mike Wallace later told me he believed, intended to keep a source happy and calm.

Bergman told me, "I knew it was going to take months to check out what he had to say. And I thought, Fuck! If he is going to testify in the ABC case, then it will be out there on Court TV in October or November. I had already yelled and screamed about him listing his name. I said, 'Great, you want to trust these people at ABC. What about this talk about ABC settling the lawsuit with Philip Morris?' I told him, 'The difference between ABC and CBS is that I will raise holy fucking hell if anything happens at CBS.'"

On September 12, Mike Wallace was asked to attend a meeting with Ellen Kaden, the CBS general counsel; Bergman; then-president of CBS News Eric Ober; *60 Minutes* executive producer Don Hewitt; and Phil Scheffler, Hewitt's second-in-command. "I think we have a problem," Kaden said, and used the phrase "tortious interference," which she said involved persuading someone to break a contract with another party. Because Wigand had a confidentiality agreement with B&W, she said, CBS could be "at a grave, grave risk." She was proposing something unprecedented in the history of CBS News—stopping an important history in midstream for fear of a lawsuit that hadn't been threatened. Hewitt, by disposition noisy and opinionated, was muted, as were Ober and Wallace. Hewitt later recalled that he had had no intention of "playing cards with a stacked deck." He advanced none of the First Amendment arguments considered routine, such as: How could you have a confidentiality agreement when there were thousands of pages of supporting documents on the Internet? And Hewitt made no offer to press the issue with his boss, Larry Tisch. Bergman, who was on his way to London to interview BAT executives, was told to cancel the trip.

Don Hewitt's relationship with Larry Tisch soured after Tisch got control of CBS in 1986. "I am not proud of it anymore, but Mike Wallace, Walter Cronkite, and I were the cheerleaders for Larry buying the network," he said. "The night Tisch bought CBS, we were all up at our friend Mollie Parnis's slapping him on the back." A week later, Hewitt went to see him. "I said, 'Larry, we have been pretty good friends, and now I need a favor.' I said, 'You have handed me all of this money. Tell me what to do with it. Lead me to a good financial adviser. Who knows better than you?' I got the brush-off. Later I heard he said, 'I not only pay the son of a bitch all that money—now he wants free business advice!'"

The relationship between Hewitt and Tisch, who are both seventy-three, grew icy, according to Hewitt, when Tisch realized that he could have no editorial influence on *60 Minutes*—an assertion that Tisch denies. In fact, the two men shared certain personality quirks: Hewitt was as voluble as Tisch and, like his new boss, had a desire for respectability. Hewitt's peppery letters and messages were famous in the city, as was Tisch's pose of modest conviviality. A few years after Tisch became CEO, *60 Minutes* produced a searing report on the American Israel Public Affairs Committee that Tisch didn't like. "He stopped talking to me at that point," Hewitt recalled. "I went to a reception that Warren Phillips [publisher of the *Wall Street Journal*] had at the River House, a room full of people like Punch Sulzberger and Kay Graham. I walked in and said to Larry, 'Hey, boss, how are you?' He said, 'Don't you "Hey, boss" me.' He turned his back and walked away! We next did a story on Temple Mount in which we say that the Jerusalem police got out of hand, and somebody tells me that when Larry was asked about it his answer was 'Don't ask me. Ask Horowitz and Wallach, the two self-hating Jews who changed their names.' . . . We were the most profitable broadcast in the history of television. The fucker got out of here with all that money only because we kept his company afloat." According to Tisch, "This is nonsense! Jesus! This poor fellow has a complex. So many things have been attributed to me that I never said. What would I care what Don Hewitt's last name was originally?"

In the midst of the furor over the Temple Mount piece, Hewitt said to Tisch, "Larry, you are, in effect, our publisher. It is up to you to defend us." Tisch answered, "I am not your publisher." "That episode with Temple Mount unsettled Larry," a close friend of his recalled. "He had no idea that as the new proprietor of CBS News he had to respect his news division and their editorial judgment."

After Tisch took over CBS, the news division was stripped of a good deal of its power and reputation. At a time when ABC was expanding its news operation, Tisch cut the CBS budget drastically.

He sold off the lucrative CBS record company, refused to invest in cable, and was outbid on broadcast rights to the NFL football games that were the lead-in to *60 Minutes*. "You have to understand," a friend of Tisch's told me, "Larry likes money. Money is a game for him!"

The relationship between CBS and Tisch's tobacco company, Lorillard, became a vexing problem for the news division. According to someone who knows Tisch well, when he bought Lorillard, in 1968, he viewed it only as a potential investment. "Years ago, the Tisch family was not afraid of liability. If he had asked his technical people, 'Am I in any danger?' he would have gotten the typical answer back: 'You can't prove anything in a liability case since the surgeon general forced the companies to put a warning on the packs.'" Tisch could not have forecast then the sweeping change in tort litigation, the possibility of immense jury awards. There was no imagining in 1968 how medical costs would soar in a few years. "None of this was on the horizon," Tisch told me. "I couldn't tell you today whether or not I would have bought Lorillard thirty years ago. . . . There is no clear-cut proof about addiction. I am not a scientist. I never smoked. I take a drink, but am I an addict? Liability suits? This is all pure speculation. I hate it when people tell me what I have been thinking."

Lorillard became an immense cash bonanza for the Loews Corporation—the parent company controlled by Tisch and his brother, Robert—earning approximately $700 million a year. For several of Tisch's friends, a key to his personality can be found in the controversy that tore apart New York University Medical Center in 1989. Tisch was the chairman of the university's board of trustees, and it was believed that he would give a substantial gift.

He announced that he and his brother would donate $30 million but with one proviso: The hospital would have to be renamed in their honor—a proposal that caused an outcry in the press. "Naming a hospital after tobacco men is just too ironic," Dr. William Cahan, a prominent surgeon at Sloan-Kettering, said in May 1989. "Around town, the University Hospital is becoming known as Lorillard General." But the hospital gave in to Tisch's demand. According to Tisch, "There was not a great a deal of negative feeling. I only received one or two letters about it. I thought the family was doing the right thing."

Lowell Bergman arrived at the Wigands' red brick house late in the afternoon on September 15. He was deeply concerned about the New York meeting and its ominous implications. His inner radar told him something was way off in the CBS decision, but he was a corporate employee. If he stormed out in a rage of protest, Wigand would be left unprotected. In the wake of ABC's recent settlement in the Philip Morris suit, Wigand felt doubly vulnerable and exposed, because his name was on the witness list. He said, "They're going to sue me, and I don't have any money." During dinner that night, Bergman received a phone call from Jonathan Sternberg, a CBS lawyer. "Leave that house right now," he told him.

At the end of September, Bergman spent a long weekend cutting a version of the B&W exposé. "I wanted to show Mike, Don, and Eric Ober exactly what it was CBS News wanted to kill." Bergman screened it for the three men that Monday. He recalled, "Hewitt was jumping up and down, yelling, 'Pulitzer Prize!'"

Soon after, Bergman ran into Phil Scheffler in the hall. The show's managing editor looked somber. "All he said to me was 'Stop!' in a loud, booming voice," referring to Bergman's reporting on Wigand.

In the research files of Nexis, the information-retrieval service, there are 220 newspaper and magazine stories that have mentioned "tortious interference" since CBS News made the decision not to allow the Wigand segment to go on the air. It is commonly believed that Tisch, who was in the midst of talks with Westinghouse concerning a merger with CBS, would not entertain the possibility of the threat of a tobacco-company lawsuit. Tisch had witnessed personally the consequences of tortious interference. In 1983 he had been brought onto the board of Getty Oil by Gordon Getty. Several months later he and Getty toasted a bid from Pennzoil to acquire Getty—a bid that would later be topped by Texaco. Pennzoil sued in a famous case in which Tisch testified, but Texaco was forced into temporary bankruptcy when Pennzoil won a record-breaking settlement. Still, Tisch denies that this experience had anything to do with the CBS decision. "What I went through had nothing to do with the B&W episode. I read about it in the paper, the same way you did," Tisch told me.

It was not widely known that a complex financial deal was going on at Lorillard about the time Bergman was trying to salvage the Wigand interview. At the end of 1994, the Federal Trade Commission had ruled that B&W had to sell off its discount, or value-brand, cigarettes—Montclair, Malibu, Crown's, Special 10's, Riviera, and Bull Durham—for antitrust reasons. Lorillard was a logical buyer because, although it controlled close to 8 percent of the tobacco market with brands such as Kent, Newport, and True, it was decidedly weak in the area of discount cigarettes. The potential acquisition of Montclair and the other brands would round out the Lorillard product line and increase cigarette sales by more than 5 billion units. While the acquisition was being studied inside Lorillard, Westinghouse was negotiating for a merger with CBS, and speculation within *60 Minutes* was focused on the effect a possible lawsuit would have on the merger.

By mid-October, the Liggett Group believed it was the high bidder for the B&W cigarettes, according to a source close to the case. Just before the deal was ready to close, the general counsel for Liggett suddenly could not get the B&W lawyers on the telephone. He was stunned when he discovered that B&W had sold the cigarette brands to Lorillard. George Lowy, an attorney who represented B&W in the divestiture, has said, "Lorillard's deal was financially superior." Liggett is considering bringing legal action against B&W. The FTC filing on the sale is unusual; some nine pages have been blanked out. The price of purchase and number of bidders are deleted. The deal was announced in late November, three weeks after *60 Minutes* killed its original story. But Tisch recently told me, "I don't know anything about it. I have nothing to do with Lorillard. I was spending my full time at CBS." Ironically, it is possible that the suit Liggett may bring would be for tortious interference.

In November, no one at *60 Minutes* was aware of the shuffle that was going on behind the scenes with the B&W brands. "I knew all kinds of litigation was possible," Bergman told me. "I kept saying to people, 'You are making news decisions in a corporate atmosphere where there is no appetite for this kind of story. There is possible perjury on the part of the son of the owner trying to sell an asset at a premium price where the consequences of the story might affect the stock price. Think how history might record this!'"

By brushing against Big Tobacco, Tisch, Wigand, Bergman, Hewitt, and Wallace were all soon lost in a thicket of hidden dangers. Wigand was still oblivious to the gathering perplexities and the corporate forces arrayed against him. As far as Wigand was concerned, said Bergman, "I was the face of *60 Minutes*. I was there holding his hand when his wife freaked out." As for Bergman, he had worked for a year and a half to bring in one of the most important stories of his career, and by doing so he had put his employer and his future in jeopardy. Hewitt and Wallace were millionaires many times over, yet their public acquiescence to CBS's reluctance to air their story threatened to tarnish their distinguished careers.

"In the end, I made the call to Wigand to tell him that management had made the decision to kill the show," Mike Wallace told me. "Lowell did not have the heart to do it." Bergman was distraught: "My work depends on my word. We had never indicated to Jeff that there would be any problem." The decision to kill the segment, Wallace said, marked "the first time in twenty-eight years that Don and I saw something differently." Hewitt, according to *60 Minutes* sources, was attempting both to please the authorities and to act like a newsman, a position that became known as "the Hewitt straddle" in the office. However angry Wallace was, he told friends he was too old to quit on principle, and he did not understand why Hewitt was siding with management.

Hewitt called a meeting of the staff. "This is not a First Amendment issue," he said, but several people in the room strongly disagreed with him. "General counsel believes we have broken the law." Suddenly Mike Wallace burst in and screamed at Hewitt, "I understand you have just said we should not have pursued the story!"—which Hewitt had not in fact said. "Who told you that? If that is what you think, I am quitting!" Hewitt said, and stormed out of the room.

In November, Hewitt decided to run a version of the B&W story without a Wigand interview. Wallace prepared a news piece for the Friday before the show was to run. It was Wallace's intention to broadcast management's decision, but when he saw the show, he realized his work had been cut by the CBS lawyers. In the hall he confronted Ellen Kaden. "Did you tell Larry Tisch about the Wigand interview? Is that why the piece was killed?" Kaden denied it. Wallace was relentless. "It doesn't make sense. You are his general counsel. Why would you not have told him?" Wallace later recalled that Kaden started to cry, a story she has denied. Kaden had sought advice from an outside counsel, First Amendment specialist Cameron DeVore, but she refused to show Wallace any of the memos he had written her. One former CBS executive surmised that no one at CBS management was willing to take responsibility for killing the Wigand interview, and Kaden was left to take the fall.

Hewitt told a *New York Times* reporter that the new version was "better, I think, than what we had before." When an Associated Press reporter called Bergman for comment, Bergman told him angrily, "The versions are apples and oranges." Wallace was enraged when he read a *Times* editorial accusing the program of betraying the legacy of Edward R. Murrow. "I don't know if things will ever go back to normal," one correspondent said. "The fact is," Wallace told me, "that Don and I had a difference of opinion about whether we should or should not push to get this thing on the air. It turned bloody and icy from time to time."

Except for Wallace, not one correspondent picked up the telephone to call Bergman. Wallace and Morley Safer were raging at each other. Safer even issued a statement to the press attacking Wallace and Bergman for making an agreement with Wigand. The feud at *60 Minutes* offered a rare view inside the psychodynamics of TV news. "It became poisonous and contagious, with many people wanting to hang Lowell," CBS producer George Crile said. In a fit of pique, Don Hewitt told several staffers to distance themselves from Bergman. Soon a reaction developed within the office. The staff felt as if it were living in a Potemkin village. Their very integrity rested on their ability to tell a story accurately, despite confidentiality agreements. Ellen Kaden would later tell friends that she was furious that Wigand's identity had been leaked to the *Daily News*. She blamed *60 Minutes* for it and for the attacks against her in the press. It was Kaden's belief that she was only doing her job, trying to prevent CBS from entering the nightmare of tobacco litigation that ABC had endured. She later recalled learning of the million pages of red paper that Philip Morris had delivered to ABC—the color red could not be photocopied—and noted with alarm that a Virginia judge had ruled that this was not an abusive tactic.

In Washington for an interview with President Clinton in mid-December, five *60 Minutes* correspondents rehearsed in a hotel room. Everyone agreed on areas and questions, but when the president arrived, the reporters started shouting as if it were a free-for-all. Mike Wallace demanded of one, "Why did you steal all of my lines?" The issue was Clinton, but the undercurrent was lethal, a shared understanding that tobacco and its implications were driving them apart. Soon after, the news of the CBS sale to Westinghouse was announced. Larry Tisch's Loews Corporation made nearly $1 billion on the sale. CBS general counsel Ellen Kaden made close to $5 million. And Eric Ober would receive around $4 million from severance and stock options.

"At Christmastime, I was disinvited from going to Lucretia's father's place," said Wigand. The debacle at *60 Minutes* was all that was needed to make their marriage collapse. A few weeks earlier, in late November, Wigand was leaving school when he noticed a car coming at him across the parking lot. "I thought it was the end," he later told me. In fact, it was another subpoena from B&W, demanding that he appear in court for violating his confidentiality agreement. Soon after, he flew to Mississippi to give a deposition in the state's case. "Are you aware that when you get back to Kentucky you could very well go to jail?" his lawyer Ephraim Margolin, a criminal-defense expert, reportedly asked him. "I better think about this," Wigand said. That afternoon Wigand was very late arriving at the courthouse in Pascagoula. Approximately fifteen lawyers from the tobacco companies were waiting, betting that he would not show up. Wigand took some time to make up his mind. "Fuck it. Let's do it," he finally said to Margolin. It was the real beginning of his new life, but Wigand worried about Lucretia. "She didn't understand what I was doing. All she cared about was that it disrupted her economic system."

"We were a quiet little company before all this happened," an executive for B&W's Kool brand tells me on a plane ride to Louisville. "Then we wound up on page one." I ask him the standard question in Tobacco Land: "Do you want your children to smoke?" He responds irritably, "I see where you are going with this. You are going to say that an unnamed Kool spokesman doesn't want his daughter to smoke. . . . I think tobacco has been singled out unfairly."

THE ATTACK

In late November, the litigator Stanley Arkin, one of more than a dozen lawyers working for B&W to head off the Justice Department's investigation into the tobacco industry, recommended that B&W hire public-relations man John Scanlon and Terry Lenzner, the former Watergate deputy counsel who is the head of Investigative Group Inc., a firm that specializes in legal work for corporate takeovers. Since his days as a liberal Republican lawyer, Lenzner has traveled philosophically from being someone who out of principle forced the Nixon administration to fire him to being an ambitious investigator in his fifties who would like to compete with Jules Kroll, a leader in the field. Like Arkin, Lenzner is attracted to the game of big-time corporate litigation, but, according to several former partners, his business has suffered recently. Lenzner's assignment was to prepare a lengthy dossier that B&W could use to torpedo Wigand's reputation with Jimmie Warren, the innovative Justice Department prosecutor running the investigation into the tobacco executives at Central Justice, the elite unit of the Justice Department that monitors national policies. "Wigand is the major witness against them in the federal grand jury both in Washington and New York," John Scanlon told me.

Scanlon and Arkin had worked together before. In 1989 they volunteered to help Covenant House, a shelter for teenage runaways in New York, defend Father Bruce Ritter, the director, against sexual- and financial-misconduct allegations—an ironic assignment for Scanlon, who at one time had wanted to be a priest. As part of the public-relations campaign, Covenant House held a press conference in which confidential information about Ritter's twenty-six-year-old male accuser was made public—a classic destroy-the-accuser technique. According to *Newsday*, the ploy backfired, however, in a groundswell of revulsion from New York social workers and resulted in more than five other boys' coming forward to make similar accusations against Father Ritter.

Scanlon is the foremost practitioner of what he calls "guerrilla PR." For columnist Murray Kempton, Scanlon is this generation's Roy Cohn—"a man proud of his infamies." During the McCarthy period, Roy Cohn was considered a master of the art of using false statements and exaggerations to impugn someone's reputation. As a young man, Scanlon was a passionate defender of left-wing causes, as far from the ethics of Cohn as it is possible to get. As he has gotten older, he has developed expensive tastes; he owns a million-dollar house in the Hamptons and another retreat in Ireland. Twenty years ago he began to build a business in corporate public relations. At first Scanlon's campaigns were a model of corporate responsibility: He helped create the gentle Mobil ads in the lower corner of the *New York Times* op-ed page in the 1970s.

His fees have always been high—he now charges $350 an hour—but his clients became increasingly controversial. He represented both Philip Morris and Lorillard in the landmark case of the late Rose Cipollone, whose husband sued, arguing that her death had been related to cigarette smoking.

Scanlon's friends do not pass judgment publicly on his clients, although in private many are strongly critical. "Loyalty is the vice of the New York establishment," columnist Liz Smith explained. For some reporters, Scanlon is an unreliable apologist. For others he is a bon vivant whose motivations are not so different from Jeffrey Wigand's when he signed up to work for B&W. (Scanlon has acted as a consultant for *Vanity Fair*, but is on a mutually agreed-upon leave of absence because of his relationship with B&W.)

Scanlon is part of the social network of prominent New Yorkers with country houses in the Hamptons. He occasionally hops a ride on a helicopter owned by financier Pete Peterson; the other passengers are Don Hewitt and his wife, Marilyn Berger. Very often on Sunday mornings, Scanlon, Peterson, and Hewitt have met for a catch-up conversation at the Candy Kitchen, a restaurant in Bridgehampton. Scanlon's clients find this access attractive.

B&W's campaign against Wigand surfaced in late December, when a *Washington Post* reporter phoned the office of Richard Scruggs in Pascagoula, Mississippi, and asked for a comment on Wigand's alleged history of spousal abuse and shoplifting as well as on his contradictory statements regarding fire safety and cigarettes. Scruggs, a law-school classmate of Michael Moore, the attorney general of Mississippi, made a fortune as an architect of the plaintiffs' suit against the asbestos companies in 1991. He flies a Learjet and has an estate in Pascagoula near his childhood home. As one of the chief lawyers representing Mississippi's case against the to-bacco companies, he has taken an interest in Wigand as a bonus witness and has become his personal lawyer, working pro bono at the invitation of Ephraim Margolin. Scruggs met Wigand in late October. "I was astonished when he told me his story," he recalled. Until he heard from the *Washington Post,* he told me, "I had never been engaged in a case involving a smear."

From Key West, Scruggs called Wigand, who was in Washington at the Justice Department. "Jeff was very, very upset," Scruggs recalled. On the telephone, Wigand gave Scruggs his account of the "abuse" and "shoplifting" episodes, but still Scruggs realized that he had a po-tential catastrophe on his hands. There was nothing that would be admissible in a court, but Scruggs dreaded the sound bite "Wigand is a wife beater" and knew it could potentially scare off the Justice Department. "There is no bigger lie than a half-truth," he later told me. Scruggs knew Wigand had few close friends, and was concerned about his growing isolated. Wigand had shut himself in his bedroom for sixteen hours. He believed he would lose his job because of the *Washington Post.* Later, Scruggs would say, "Jeff was despondent. I was worried he would unravel, and I didn't know what to do."

In New York, it was obvious to Mike Wallace and Lowell Bergman that a calculated attempt was being made to ruin Wigand's reputa-tion. Over the Christmas holidays, Scanlon took Don Hewitt aside at a party at the writer Avery Corman's and told him that Wigand was "a bad guy." Hewitt and Scanlon were not just longtime friends; Scanlon had advised CBS during the libel case brought against the network and Mike Wallace by General William Westmoreland in

1985. For weeks on the helicopter, Scanlon bombarded Hewitt and the Petersons with allegations against Wigand—he was a shoplifter, a wife beater. Hewitt was at first strongly influenced by Scanlon, he later recalled. "I hear that Wigand is a bad guy," Hewitt told Wallace. Scanlon had temporarily succeeded in diverting the story of B&W to a narrative about Wigand's personality. Months earlier, Bergman had run a crime check on Wigand, but since he had not been convicted of anything, neither incident had shown up on the computer. In January, Scanlon visited Wallace at *60 Minutes*. "He sat in my office and told me, 'Mike, don't worry—B&W is not going to sue you,'" Wallace recalled. "That is when I knew John was working for them." Wallace and Bergman motivated Hewitt by stoking his competitive streak. "*Dateline* is going to put Wigand on the air, and he is our guy," Wallace recalled telling Hewitt. "How can we let our guy appear on NBC?"

Scanlon made a blunder by overplaying his hand. Hewitt's and Wallace's sense of fair play was aroused. They are known for never allowing their personal histories to get in the way of a story, but after weeks of Scanlon's hammering at Wigand's credibility, his strategy backfired completely, Hewitt later told me. Once, on the helicopter, Hewitt had told him, "John, you are full of shit." Hewitt later remarked, "What I should have said to him was, 'Look, John, if you want to go out and work for tobacco companies defending people's right to smoke, more power to you. The next time someone calls you and asks you to break a guy's legs, tell them to hire a capo.'" By mid-January, Hewitt had made up his mind that Scanlon's campaign against Wigand had to be part of any coming *60 Minutes* report. "Mike and I never even discussed whether or not we should report it," Hewitt said.

"John was feeding me stuff all the time," Hewitt later told me. "He called me and told me the man was on a watch list at the liquor store. . . . He sent me two depositions done by Wigand. One of them, to the best of my knowledge, was under lock and key and sealed. . . . I kept egging him on. He was my pipeline to Brown & Williamson."

One night in January, I telephoned Scanlon at his house in Sag Harbor. "What can you tell me about Wigand?" I asked. Scanlon mentioned the contradictions in Wigand's testimony about fire-safe cigarettes, then warmed to his theme: Wigand, he said, "had been arrested for wife beating" and had been "shoplifting for a long period of time." He continued, "And then there's about twenty-five instances which he filed . . . insurance claims on lost luggage and hotel rooms broken into. . . . He's got a very, very shaky record." It seemed obvious that he was recalling the details of a written memo, although at that time I did not know of the five-hundred-page dossier.

"Who has dug this up?" I asked. "Terry Lenzner's group?"

"Yes," he said. "They're the investigators for B&W. . . . I have been hired to do what I always do, which is to try to find out what the story is and broker the story, and I'm convinced that without a single iota of doubt he is a liar."

I asked Scanlon if he had ever met Wigand or posed these allegations to him. "No. I've read his testimony. I don't have to ask him the questions." Scanlon paused. "You know, I have seen tape in which he says that he was an Olympic wrestler and a Vietnam fighter pilot." I asked him if I could see the tape. "Only off the record, and we wouldn't want it tied to us. We would have to have that firm agreement," he said. I said I could not enter into such an arrangement. "We may not be able to talk, then, because what they are trying to say is that this is a smear campaign." I said I was troubled by the implications of our conversation, the way the people who had compiled the allegations about Wigand were disseminating them to destroy his credibility. "Of course they are," Scanlon said. "I mean, he is an incredible witness. Why wouldn't they? I mean, if you had somebody testifying against you, and you knew they weren't credible, what would *you* do?"

THE COUNTERATTACK

The investigator Jack Palladino met Wigand at his house on the Colonel Anderson Parkway. In the world of hardball litigation, Palladino and his wife, Sandra Sutherland, are the Nick and Nora Charles of modern criminal investigation. Palladino wears $2,000 suits and splashy Balenciaga ties and speaks with a rapid-fire polish that hints of his childhood in Boston. At one time Palladino wanted to be a psychiatrist, and he has a persuasive narrative gift. Sutherland is the daughter of an Australian academic; her strength as an investigator is an intuitive sense of when something is amiss. They operate from the former I. Magnin mansion in San Francisco; they investigated the People's Temple in Jonestown in the 1980s and ran the counterattack against American Express's 1988 attempt to smear the banker Edmond Safra. They worked as well for the Clinton campaign in 1992, investigating accusations of Clinton's infidelities. The irony was that the couple usually work for Stanley Arkin, but this time they were on the other side. "I think Arkin would explain our working for Wigand as my sixties radical sympathies," Palladino said.

He was hired by Richard Scruggs to mount a counterattack, to disprove the charges in the dossier that B&W had hired Scanlon to disseminate to reporters. Palladino and his staff of seven investigators had to move quickly. An anonymous tip had already been sent to Joe Ward of the *Louisville Courier-Journal* and to Doug Proffitt, a TV personality in Louisville who specializes in tabloid investigations. The letter to Ward had a "gossipy tone," Ward told me, and said that Wigand had beat up his wife. Ward immediately suspected that it had come from the tobacco industry, and he chose to investigate further. Ward told me that even the police report had no context that he was comfortable with. Doug Proffitt, however, was less concerned. On the evening he was preparing a report on Wigand's marital problems, I telephoned him. He sounded elated that he had a scoop. "I got an anonymous tip which I'm sure came from the tobacco industry.... There's a side of this man that has never been told before."

Palladino met Wigand after Proffitt had aired his report. He was surprised, he told me later, that Wigand asked him to explain to his twenty-two-year-old daughter, Gretchen, the circumstances of the case, exactly how much was at stake. "He was in a paradoxical situation. At a time when the antitobacco forces wanted to make him a hero, he had isolated himself from everyone, including his own family," Palladino said. "Lock up all these papers and diaries before someone steals them," Palladino told him when he visited his home office. When Palladino relayed to Wigand the charges about him being detailed in phone calls to reporters, Wigand responded angrily, "What kind of bullshit is this?" Once Palladino realized what was happening to Wigand, he instructed the entire staff to put aside whatever they were working on and check every aspect of Wigand's past. "This is a war," Palladino said.

When Wigand meets me in the Hyatt coffee shop on Saturday morning, January 27, he is carrying a stack of newspapers. The testimony from his deposition about B&W is page-one news for the *Courier-Journal,* the *Lexington Herald-Leader,* and the *New York Times.* "You were on CNN this morning, Jeff," his security man says. "I bet you never thought, growing up on Bruckner Boulevard, that you would wind up on page one of the *Times*," I say. "That is bullshit," he says. "I don't care about front pages."

I am flying with Wigand to New York, where he will be interviewed again for *60 Minutes.* "Wallace and Hewitt outed me, all right?" he says angrily—a reference to the fact that his identity was leaked to the *New York Daily News*—as we walk toward the Hyatt parking garage. "And I intend to tell Mike what I think of him on the air." ("We are mystified that he thinks that," Wallace later said.) In the hotel driveway, as we wait in the car for the security man to join us, Wigand sees a man crossing quickly in front of us. "Holy shit, there is Kendrick Wells!" he yells. It is 8:00 a.m., and Wells, B&W's assistant general counsel for product litigation, is heading toward the company tower. "What in the world could they be doing so early on a Saturday?" Wigand asks nervously as we leave for the airport.

As Wigand and I were having dinner at the Hyatt the night before, the B&W lawyers apparently made a decision to attempt to counteract the publication of parts of the leaked deposition in the *Wall Street Journal.* Someone on the B&W legal team suggested that their entire five-hundred-page confidential dossier be sent immediately to the *Journal's* reporter, Suein Hwang. That would turn out to be a disastrous strategic error. No one at B&W had checked the accuracy of Lenzner's report, titled *The Misconduct of Jeffrey S. Wigand Available in the Public Record.* The list of allegations is dense and for most reporters immediately suspect. On the Sunday that Wigand taped at *60 Minutes,* Palladino met with Suein Hwang for seven hours, going over every charge in the report. "We didn't leave the Empire Diner until the early hours of the morning," Palladino later recalled. "The *Journal* editors decided they would investigate every allegation. When I got back to the hotel, I faxed my office: 'Drop everything and work on these charges.'"

The summary is divided into categories—Unlawful Activity; Possible False or Fraudulent Claims for Stolen, Lost or Damaged Property; Lies on Wigand's Résumés; Wigand's Lies Under Oath; Other Lies by Wigand; Mental Illness. The document is a smorgasbord of allegations, large and small. "On November 18, 1991, Wigand wrote to Coast Cutlery Company and returned an allegedly damaged knife for repair." "On March 19, 1992, Wigand wrote to Coach for Business requesting credit to his American Express card for two returned items." More serious for the Justice Department, the contradictions in his testimony on fire-safe cigarettes are detailed, which Wigand explains by the fact that time elapsed between his testimony in Washington, while he was still under a severance agreement with B&W, and what he was about to say about fire safety after analyzing the Hamlet project papers.

In Washington, even President Clinton has started to grapple with the problem of Jeffrey Wigand. Does he reach out and embrace him as he did the late Tobacco Institute lobbyist Victor Crawford? At the moment, Clinton is battle-weary, according to one source close to him. He has survived the controversy surrounding David Kessler, the vigorous head of the FDA, an inside battle in which Health and Human Services Secretary Donna Shalala and White House Deputy Chief of Staff Harold Ickes lined up for Kessler, and Patrick Griffin, the president's liaison to Congress, and Erskine Bowles, a deputy chief of staff, questioned Clinton's continued support of Kessler. Griffin pointed out that Kessler would bring down on Clinton the possible loss of four tobacco states—Kentucky, Virginia, and the Carolinas—and the enmity of the tobacco lobbies. Last year B&W hired the Whitewater special prosecutor, Kenneth Starr, to represent the company in its fight to prevent dissemination of the Merrell Williams documents. Recently a top White House official called the hiring of Kenneth Starr "a travesty" because of the possible conflict of interest in investigating the president as he attempts to regulate the tobacco industry.

If Clinton were to embrace Wigand, it would signal that the Justice Department had no reservations about his credibility, but as yet there has been no clear signal from Washington. David Kessler would not be interviewed for *60 Minutes* concerning his relationship with Wigand, perhaps because the FDA is careful to appear neutral as it attempts to change the laws and force tobacco to be regulated as a drug.

In New York we go to dinner at a Japanese restaurant with Jack Palladino. Wigand sits in a tatami room and orders baby eel in fluent

Japanese. Palladino tells him, "You are a very important man at the moment. You have got to get out of Louisville. You should be at a major foundation that is doing tobacco research." For Palladino, there is little about Wigand that reminds him of Edmond Safra, the banker—and the client of Stanley Arkin—he worked for who was also the victim of a smear. Safra was motivated by a sense of moral outrage, Palladino tells me, whereas Wigand's level of tension is a sign of pure fear. At dinner, he is without defenses. He says, "The only thing I have is my teaching. I will not give it up. I owe the kids." In the car on the way back to the hotel, Wigand is irritable. "I feel I am being corralled by these guys."

Wigand is tired in New York, and complains of chest pains. It is his intention to get a physical, including an EKG. He checks into the Shelburne, a modest hotel at Thirty-seventh Street, although *60 Minutes* has offered to put him up at the more posh Essex House, on Central Park South. "Do you know what it would be like if I were there with them?" he says. "They would be down my throat every second."

Wigand is scheduled for his second *60 Minutes* interview Sunday afternoon. In the morning he calls and says, "I have to have a Save the Children tie. This is what the whole thing is about—smoking and kids. Where can I get one?" His tone is intense, serious. "I won't go on the air without it," he says. I meet Wigand in his room at the Shelburne. Palladino has already arrived, and paces back and forth trying to boost Wigand's sense of self before he is filmed. "You are a man who is trying to tell the truth. They are trying to ruin your life. It is your story. You have to tell it the way you see it." Palladino coaches Wigand on TV technique: "Don't use too many nouns or proper names. Don't be too technical. What you want is for them—the TV audience—to suddenly look up from their cheese puffs and say, 'He is telling the truth.'" "I am a scientist," Wigand responds churlishly. "That is how I speak." "Yes," says Palladino, "but consider it this way: You are getting a chance to tell your story in front of an audience." While Palladino speaks, Wigand puts on a fresh shirt and takes a Save the Children tie from a Bloomingdale's box. He knots it while looking in the mirror and then visibly relaxes. "Okay, Jack," he says. "I feel better now."

"It's simple," Palladino says. "Just tell the truth. That is all you have."

On one occasion in Louisville, I go to see the B&W public-relations man Joe Helewicz, a former reporter for the *Baltimore Sun*. I am brought to a reception area, a large room filled with smoke. On several tables there are containers of B&W cigarettes, Kools and Capris. Near me a salesman from Pitney Bowes smokes a Kool and says, "I am supposed to be quitting, but I like coming here, because the cigarettes are free." After some time I am taken up to the eighteenth floor to wait for Helewicz. This is the inner sanctum of the B&W legal department, the floor that was lit until midnight five days earlier. The tension is palpable; men in suits are huddled in several corner offices. I am shown to an empty office to wait. The *Wall Street Journal* has scheduled an exposé of the Wigand investigation for the next day's paper. The publication of the B&W deposition excerpt in the *Journal* has also lifted any restriction on CBS—now owned by Westinghouse—to air its long-delayed report. In private, the new CBS News president, Andrew Heyward, tells Wallace that the story is "a priority." In New York, Bergman is scrambling with a CBS crew, freed at last by Ellen Kaden to complete a process he began in 1994. The crew has waited outside Scanlon's apartment building to ambush him. Scanlon stood in the snow and said, "Wigand is a habitual liar." Earlier, he had shouted at Bergman on the telephone, "You guys are going to hose me."

While I wait for Helewicz, I review my notes from the dinner I had with Wigand the night before. Wigand had been to see a divorce lawyer that afternoon, a fact that would be known twelve hours later at B&W headquarters.

From a window I look down at the exact table where Wigand and I had dinner in the Hyatt's revolving restaurant. Suddenly I hear loud voices coming from Room 1821, then occupied by John Kiser, a B&W lawyer:

"Things have been a little hectic here."

"We need a divorce specialist . . . "

"Wigand said no to child support."

"Let's do it all!"

"This will be blazed in the streets and the back alleys!"

"It has nothing to do with the law books!"

Sometime later I see Joe Helewicz. Within moments of our meeting, he tells me that, as far as he is concerned, Wigand is a liar and cheats at golf. "He's a paid mercenary," he says. "Is he talking to any other media besides CBS?" I do not answer, and he continues. "Why? Because they're not paying him. I don't know why you and a lot of others don't see it. Our business is out of favor. It's not politically correct. If somebody stands up to the tobacco business, they're a hero. Forget about the other side of the story."

I read to Helewicz parts of the conversation I have just over-heard and ask him if that language does not indicate a smear or un-ethical corporate behavior. "You picked up part of a conversation, and that's a characterization of a campaign, because you picked up a couple of sentences out of context!" he says, but he refuses to allow me to interview the lawyer whose office the conversation was held in. "I would take issue with the word 'smear' when what you are doing is putting out fact about a person who is lying about you and making vast allegations."

Japanese class begins at 8:00 a.m. in Room 312 at DuPont Manual in downtown Louisville. Wigand teaches a group of thirty-two stu-dents, who sit quietly after the bell and the Pledge of Allegiance on a closed-circuit TV. Wigand is adamant about not wanting to talk to his students about what he is going through. "I happen to love teaching," he says, "and I don't want to concern them." "*Hajime masu!*" he tells them. "Let's begin! We are going to do some *sumi* today—calligraphy. How many of you have brought brushes?" In front of his class, Jeff Wigand is transformed. He is open and generous, and the class responds with noisy delight. At the end of the session, Wigand's students surround him at a small table as he dips a special Japanese brush into calligraphy ink. "The maneu-ver is very loose, all from the shoulder—you have to relax to do it right," he says. "It is about *flow*." His shoulder loosens, and his hand begins moving the brush across a page. He makes a small box, a long line, a special dot, a flourish. "You see this symbol in Japanese restaurants. Does anyone know what it is? This is known as 'happi-ness forever,'" he tells them. "It is all a matter of control."

Soon after the *Wall Street Journal* published its front-page article harshly skeptical of the five-hundred-page dossier, Wigand moved into a two-bedroom apartment in Louisville. "I will feel better when I have my things around me," he said. He was particularly concerned about his computer, which contained one version of his B&W scientific diary. During a routine FBI investigation of his most recent death threat, Wigand grew outraged that his privacy was being invaded. He had words with one agent, who reacted by obtaining a search warrant and impounding his computer, telling lawyers close to the case that Wigand was "a suspect" in the matter, although there was no evidence of any kind to suggest that Wigand had sent himself a death threat.

"They are not going to leave me alone," Wigand told me in early February. It was the day after the most recent episode—a break-in at the office of Joe Mobley, his divorce lawyer. "There have been a few fireworks," Mobley told me. "Four days after my employment, I did have a 'toss,' as they say in the vernacular. Nothing was taken, but the contents of my desk were thrown all over the floor." For Palladino, the break-in was "clearly a message." The clue, he said, was unmistakable: a pile of burned matches near the door.

According to the *American Lawyer*, there are now nearly two hundred law firms working on more than twenty-five major tobacco cases, and Wigand could be an expert witness in all of them. His testimony has been sought for five ongoing investigations in the Justice Department. Wigand's lawyers announced in early February that he is countersuing B&W for invading his privacy, and he has charged that B&W abused the legal process by seeking to block his testimony. Like a Mob witness, Wigand has entered a shadowland of litigation. For investigators and lawyers, he has lost his former identity and is now referred to as "the client": "I am having dinner with the client." "The client has to be in New York for a meeting." There was recently a bomb threat at DuPont Manual.

There is no question that Wigand's presence in the middle of the tobacco wars is an accident, without grand design. "I just wanted to get the story out," he told Lowell Bergman after the *60 Minutes* segment aired. It is possible that his testimony could cause several former CEOs to be indicted for perjury, including Thomas Sandefur and Andrew Tisch. "I can't give you twenty-five reasons why I did it," he told me recently, but since Wigand appeared in the arena, there has been a revolution in tobacco history. Over St. Patrick's Day weekend, he was back in New York, far more sanguine than he had been in late January. That week Richard Scruggs had negotiated a remarkable settlement with the Liggett Group, which, in an unprecedented move, broke ranks with the other four U.S. tobacco giants and agreed to settle the states' claims and to accept proposed FDA marketing regulations. The Liggett breakthrough was the inspiration of majority shareholder Bennett LeBow, a Wall Street buccaneer who, in alliance with corporate raider Carl Icahn, is hoping to take over RJR Nabisco. Liggett's settlement created a selling frenzy on Wall Street, and Philip Morris's stock plunged 16 percent in five days. Big Tobacco was suddenly like South Africa in the 1980s, as the giant structure began to crack. In March three more whistle-blowers came forward—former employees of Philip Morris. Shortly before Scruggs began negotiating with

LeBow's lawyers, Ian Uydess, a scientist, was in Washington at the FDA alleging in a twenty-four-page affidavit that Philip Morris had routinely adjusted nicotine levels. Meanwhile, the *Courier-Journal* reported that of the seven top executives who testified before Congress in 1994 that nicotine was nonaddictive, only one remains in place. Recently, Governor Kirk Fordice of Mississippi has gone to court to try to stop his own attorney general, Michael Moore, from pursuing antitobacco litigation, implying he was opportunistic, a captive of plaintiffs' lawyers.

While Scruggs was fielding calls about the Liggett settlement, Wigand learned that the drawers in his home office had been jimmied open and his 1993 diary had vanished. Wigand was in New York to meet with Scruggs and Margolin to discuss an unusual tort suit—the intentional infliction of emotional harm—they are considering filing against John Scanlon and others involved in the B&W dossier. Scanlon, meanwhile, soldiered on for B&W. "There will be a third act, and Jeff Wigand will be unmasked," he told me. Ellen Kaden remained angry; she could not see that she had set off a historic process by being concerned about tortious interference. In Washington, D.C., at the end of March, a U.S. district judge seemed to override the Kentucky restraining order by granting an emergency order allowing Wigand to testify before a federal grand jury without briefing B&W first.

Wigand reached a point where nothing surprised him anymore, so he hardly reacted when he looked across the dining room at the Essex House and noticed Ian Uydess, the tall, balding new whistle-blower from Philip Morris, having breakfast. The two men nodded at each other—Uydess had once applied to Wigand for a job—but they avoided direct conversation, perhaps in order to prevent any suggestion of conspiracy. Later, Uydess told me that he believed his own role was relatively minor, and that Wigand was the person "with real courage."

"None of this would have happened without Jeff and Merrell Williams," Scruggs told me. "In early November it looked like Big Tobacco had silenced the press. Now who knows what will happen?" At Hatsuhana, a smart Japanese restaurant in midtown Manhattan, Scruggs toasted Wigand. "You are an important man. I salute you." Wigand smiled, but his response was muted. I thought of a remark he had made to me on a plane in January: "I wish I could see the horizon." When we got to New York that day, there was a driving rain, with gales of wind. Wigand and I ran through the parking lot to a car. He was suddenly released, laughing convulsively. "Maybe this is a sign," he told me.

HOW DONALD TRUMP AND ROY COHN'S RUTHLESS SYMBIOSIS CHANGED AMERICA

AUGUST 2017

"Pro-Americanism is a common thread for McCarthy, Goldwater, Nixon, [and] Reagan. The heir to that tradition is Donald Trump. When you combine that with the bare-knuckled tactics of Roy Cohn—or a Roger Stone—that is how you win elections. So Roy has an impact on Donald's understanding of how to deal with the media—attack, attack, attack, never defend."

"Donald calls me fifteen to twenty times a day," Roy Cohn told me on the day we met. "He is always asking, 'What is the status of this . . . and that?'"

It was 1980. I had been assigned to write a story on Donald Trump, the brash young developer who was then trying to make a name for himself in New York City, and I had come to see the man who, at the time, was in many ways Trump's alter ego: the wily, menacing lawyer who had gained national renown, and enmity, for his ravenous anticommunist grandstanding.

Trump was thirty-four and using the connections of his father, Brooklyn and Queens real-estate developer Fred Trump, as he navigated the rough-and-tumble world of political bosses. He had recently opened the Grand Hyatt Hotel, bringing life back to a dreary area near Grand Central Terminal during a period when the city had yet to fully recover from near bankruptcy. His wife, Ivana, led me through the construction site in a white wool Thierry Mugler jumpsuit. "When will it be finished? When?" she shouted at workers as she clicked through in stiletto heels.

The tabloids couldn't get enough of the Trumps' theatrics. And as Donald Trump's Hyatt rose, so, too, did the hidden hand of his attorney Roy Cohn, always there to help with the shady tax abatements, the zoning variances, the sweetheart deals, and the threats to those who might stand in the project's way.

Cohn was best known as a ruthless prosecutor. During the Red Scare of the 1950s, he and Wisconsin senator Joe McCarthy, the fabulist and virulent nationalist crusader, had hauled dozens of alleged "communist sympathizers" before a Senate panel. Earlier, the House Un-American Activities Committee had skewered artists and entertainers on similar charges, resulting in a trail of fear, prison sentences, and ruined careers for hundreds, many of whom had found common cause in fighting fascism. But in the decades since, Cohn had become the premier practitioner of hardball deal-making in New York, having mastered the arcane rules of the city's Favor Bank (the local cabal of interconnected influence peddlers) and its magical ability to provide inside fixes for its *machers* and rogues.

"You knew when you were in Cohn's presence you were in the presence of pure evil," said lawyer Victor A. Kovner, who had known him for years. Cohn's power derived largely from his ability to scare potential adversaries with hollow threats and spurious lawsuits. And the fee he demanded for his services? Ironclad loyalty.

Trump—who would remain loyal to Cohn for many years—would be one of the last and most enduring beneficiaries of Cohn's power. But as Trump would confide in 1980, he already seemed to be trying to distance himself from Cohn's inevitable taint: "All I can tell you is he's been vicious to others in his protection of me," Trump told me, as if to wave away a stench. "He's a genius. He's a lousy lawyer, but he's a genius."

BLEAK HOUSE

On the day I arrived at Cohn's office, in his imposing limestone town house on East Sixty-eighth Street, his Rolls-Royce was parked outside. But all elegance stopped at the front door. It was a fetid place, a shambles of dusty bedrooms and office warrens where young male assistants made their way up and down the stairs. Cohn often greeted visitors in a robe. On occasion, IRS agents were said to sit in the hallway and, knowing Cohn's reputation as a deadbeat, were there to intercept any envelopes with money.

Cohn's bedroom was crowded with a collection of stuffed frogs that sat on the floor, propped against a large TV. Everything about him suggested a curious combination of an arrested child and a sleaze. I sat on a small sofa covered with dozens of stuffed creatures that exploded with dust as I tried to move them aside. Cohn was compact, with a mirthless smile, the scars from his plastic surgeries visible around his ears. As he spoke, his tongue darted in and out; he twirled his Rolodex, as if to impress me with his network of contacts. The kind of law Cohn practiced, in fact, needed only a telephone. (*The New Yorker* would later report that his longtime switchboard operator taped his calls and kept notes of conversations.)

Who did not know Roy Cohn's backstory, even in 1980? Cohn—whose great-uncle had founded Lionel, the toy-train company—grew up as an only child, doted on by an overbearing mother who followed him to summer camp and lived with him until she died. Every night he was seated at his family's Park Avenue dinner table, which was an unofficial command post of the Favor Bank bosses who'd helped make his father, Al Cohn, a Bronx county judge, and later a State Supreme Court judge. (During the Depression, Roy's uncle Bernard Marcus had been sent to prison in a bank-fraud case, and Roy's childhood was marked by visits to Sing Sing.) By high school, Cohn was fixing a parking ticket or two for one of his teachers.

After graduating from Columbia Law School at twenty, he became an assistant U.S. attorney and an expert in "subversive activities," allowing him to segue into his role in the 1951 espionage trial of Julius and Ethel Rosenberg. (Cohn persuaded the star witness, Ethel Rosenberg's brother, David Greenglass, to change his testimony; in Cohn's autobiography, written with Sidney Zion, Cohn claimed that he had encouraged the judge, already intent on sending Julius to the electric chair, to also order Ethel's execution, despite the fact that she was a mother with two children.) Come 1953, this legal prodigy was named McCarthy's boy-wonder chief counsel, and the news photos told the tale: the sharp-faced, heavy-lidded twenty-six-year-old with cherubic cheeks, whispering intimately into the ear of the bloated McCarthy. Cohn's special skill as the senator's henchman was character assassination. Indeed, after testifying in front of him, an engineer with the Voice of America radio news service committed suicide. Cohn never showed a shred of remorse.

Despite McCarthy's very public demise when the hearings proved to be trumped-up witch hunts, Cohn would emerge largely unscathed, going on to become one of the last great power brokers of New York. His friends and clients came to include New York's Francis Cardinal Spellman and Yankees owner George Steinbrenner. Cohn would become an occasional guest at the Reagan White House and a constant presence at Studio 54.

By the time I met with Cohn, he had already been indicted four times on charges ranging from extortion and blackmail to bribery, conspiracy, securities fraud, and obstruction of justice. But he had been acquitted in each instance and in the process had begun to behave as if he were somehow a super-patriot who was above the law. At a gay bar in Provincetown, as reported by Cohn biographer Nicholas von Hoffman, a friend described Cohn's behavior at a local lounge: "Roy sang three choruses of 'God Bless America,' got a hard-on and went home to bed."

Cohn, with his bravado, reckless opportunism, legal pyrotechnics, and serial fabrication, became a fitting mentor for the young real-estate scion. And as Trump's first major project, the Grand Hyatt, was set to open, he was already involved in multiple controversies. He was warring with the city about tax abatements and other concessions. He had hoodwinked his very own partner, Hyatt chief Jay Pritzker, by changing a term in a deal when Pritzker was unreachable—on a trip to Nepal. In 1980, while erecting what would become Trump Tower, he antagonized a range of arts patrons and city officials when his team demolished the Art Deco friezes decorating the 1929 building. Vilified in the headlines—and by the Establishment—Trump offered a response that was pure Roy Cohn: "Who cares?" he said. "Let's say that I had given that junk to the Met. They would have just put them in their basement."

For author Sam Roberts, the essence of Cohn's influence on Trump was the triad: "Roy was a master of situational immorality.... He worked with a three-dimensional strategy, which was: 1. Never settle, never surrender. 2. Counter-attack, counter-sue immediately. 3. No matter what happens, no matter how deeply into the muck you get, claim victory and never admit defeat." As columnist Liz Smith once observed, "Donald lost his moral compass when he made an alliance with Roy Cohn."

WHEN DONALD MET ROY

Let's go back further still, to 1973. Trump, twenty-seven, was living in a rent-controlled studio, wearing French cuffs, and taking his dates to the Peacock Alley, the bar in the lobby of the Waldorf Astoria. At the time, the lockbox of Establishment New York was tightly closed to the Trumps of Queens, despite their mansion in Jamaica Estates.

Riding around Brooklyn in a Rolls-Royce, Trump's mother, Mary, collected quarters from laundry rooms in various Trump buildings. Trump's father, Fred, had already beaten back two scandals in which he was accused of overcharging and profiteering at some of his government-financed apartment complexes, and was now facing an even more explosive charge—systemic discrimination against black and other minority tenants. The Trumps, however, were connected to Favor Bank politicians in the Brooklyn Democratic machine, which, in tandem with the Mob bosses, still influenced who got many of the judgeships and patronage jobs. It was twilight in a Damon Runyon world, before the reformers moved in.

As Donald Trump would later tell the story, he ran into Cohn for the first time at Le Club, a members-only nightspot in Manhattan's East Fifties, where models and fashionistas and Eurotrash went to be seen. "The government has just filed suit against our company," Trump explained, "saying that we discriminated against blacks. . . . What do you think I should do?"

"Tell them to go to hell and fight the thing in court and let them prove you discriminated," Cohn shot back. The Trumps would soon retain Cohn to represent them.

The evidence was damning. At thirty-nine Trump-owned properties, according to the Department of Justice lawsuit, widespread practices were used to avoid renting to blacks, including implementing a secret code. When a prospective black renter would apply for an apartment, the paperwork would allegedly be marked with a C—indicating "colored" (a charge that, if true, would constitute a violation of the Fair Housing Act). Nevertheless, the Trumps countersued the government. "It just stunned me," the lawyer and journalist Steven Brill recently recalled. "They actually got reporters to appear for a press conference where they announced that they were suing [the Justice Department] for defamation for $100 million. You couldn't get through your second day of law school without knowing it was a totally bogus lawsuit. And, of course, it was thrown out."

A race-discrimination case of this magnitude might have sunk many a developer, but Cohn persisted. Under his guidance, the Trumps settled by agreeing to stipulations to prevent future discrimination at their properties—but came away without admitting guilt. (With that, a Trump strategy was launched. Decades later, when questioned about the case in one of the presidential debates, Trump would declare, "It was a federal lawsuit—[we] were sued. We settled the suit . . . with no admission of guilt.")

Cohn continued to go on the attack for the Trumps. "I was a young reporter just starting my first job, at the *New York Post* [in 1974]," book publisher David Rosenthal told me. "I was working on illegal campaign contributions and I started looking at the records that had come from a group of buildings in Brooklyn, which showed massive donations to [Democrat] Hugh Carey, then running for governor of New York. They had all come from buildings that I had traced to Fred Trump. . . . My story was published and my editors were thrilled.

"The next day, my phone rang and it was Roy Cohn. 'You piece of shit! We are going to ruin you! You have a lot of fucking nerve!'" Shaken, Rosenthal, then twenty-one, went to his editors. "Their jaws dropped. I thought I was finished. I was sure Cohn's next call would be to Dolly Schiff, the owner of the paper. Of course, the call never came. The story was true. They had skirted the New York finance laws."

For about a decade, the tax abatements and legal loopholes that Trump was able to finesse came about, in large part, because of Cohn. The time he spent on Trump matters was not reduced to "billable hours," wrote the late investigative journalist Wayne Barrett in *Trump: The Greatest Show on Earth*. Instead, Cohn asked for payment only when his cash supply ran low.

Steve Brill again saw Cohn's stamp when Trump struck back, defending the case against Trump University. It was, Brill asserted, "a scam against the very people who [eventually] voted for Trump—the middle and lower middle class. . . . The first thing Trump does is sue one of the plaintiffs. She wins and the judge awards her $800,000 in legal fees, and Trump appeals, and in that decision he's compared to Bernie Madoff. . . . This strategy was pure Cohn: 'Attack your accuser.'"

After Brill's investigation was published, Brill said, he received a call from one of Trump's lawyers. "I understand you may do a follow-up," he told Brill, adding a bit of advice: "Just be careful." "Thanks," Brill replied. "And let me give you some advice: 'You better get the check because this guy is never going to pay you.' Being a deadbeat was also pure Cohn." (A White House spokesperson says this claim is totally false.)

BOYS FROM THE BOROUGHS

How to explain the symbiosis that existed between Roy Cohn and Donald Trump? Cohn and Trump were twinned by what drove them. They were both sons of powerful fathers, young men who had started their careers clouded by family scandal. Both had been private-school students from the boroughs who'd grown up with their noses pressed against the glass of dazzling Manhattan. Both squired attractive women around town. (Cohn would describe his close friend Barbara Walters, the TV newswoman, as his fiancée. "Of course, it was absurd," Liz Smith said, "but Barbara put up with it.")

Sometime during the 2016 presidential campaign, Brill noticed that Donald Trump was using Cohn's exact phrases. "I began to hear, 'If you want to know the truth,' and 'that I can tell you . . .' and 'to be absolutely frank'—a sign that the Big Lie was coming," Brill said.

Cohn—possessed of a keen intellect, unlike Trump—could keep a jury spellbound. When he was indicted for bribery, in 1969, his lawyer suffered a heart attack near the end of the trial. Cohn deftly stepped in and did a seven-hour closing argument—never once referring to a notepad. He was acquitted. "I don't want to know what the law is," he famously said, "I want to know who the judge is."

When Cohn spoke, he would fix you with a hypnotic stare. His eyes were the palest blue, all the more startling because they appeared to protrude from the sides of his head. While Al Pacino's version of Cohn (in Mike Nichols's 2003 HBO adaptation of Tony Kushner's *Angels in America*) captured Cohn's intensity, it failed to convey his childlike yearning to be liked. "He was raised as a miniature adult," Tom Wolfe once observed.

Cohn liked to throw parties crowded with celebrities, judges, Mob bosses, and politicians—some of whom were either coming from or on their way to prison—causing Cohn's close friend the comedian Joey Adams to remark, "If you're indicted, you're invited." But it was Cohn's circle of legal aides and after-hours pals that also held sway. "Roy loved to surround himself with attractive straight men," said divorce attorney Robert S. Cohen, who, before taking on clients such as Michael Bloomberg—and both of Trump's ex-wives (Ivana Trump and Marla Maples)—began his career working for Cohn. "[Roy had] a coterie. If he could have had a relationship with any of them, he would have."

Cohn's cousin David L. Marcus concurred. Soon after graduating from Brown in the early eighties, Marcus recalled, he sought Cohn out. While they had encountered each other over the years at family gatherings, Marcus's parents had despised Cohn since his McCarthy days, and a chill had set in. But Cohn, intrigued by the attention of his long-lost cousin, welcomed him. Marcus, a journalist who would later share a Pulitzer Prize, recently said that he was astonished by the atmosphere of creepy intimacy that, in those days, seemed to perfume Cohn's attitude toward his acolytes, including one in particular. "There was a party in the mid-1980s, where Mailer was, and Andy Warhol, [when] in walked Trump," recounted Marcus. "Roy dropped everyone else and fussed over him . . . Roy had that ability to focus on you. I felt that Roy was attracted to Trump, more than in a big-brotherly way.

"Donald fit the pattern of the hangers-on and the disciples around Roy. He was tall and blond and . . . frankly, *über*-Gentile. Something about Roy's self-hating-Jewish persona drew him to fair-haired boys. And at these parties there was a bevy of blond guys, almost midwestern, and Donald was paying homage to Roy . . . I wondered then if Roy was attracted to him."

"Thwarted loves obsessed Roy Cohn's life," added a lawyer who first met Cohn in the sixties, characterizing some of the men, both gay and straight, in Cohn's orbit. "He would become sexually obsessed with cock-tease guys who would sense his need and not shun him. These were unrequited relationships. The way he would expiate the sexual energy was possessive mentoring. Introducing them to everyone in town and taking them places."

Seeing Trump and Cohn enter a room together had a hint of vaudeville. Donald, standing six feet two inches, would typically enter first, with a burlesque macho-man's gait, walking as if he led from his toes. A few feet behind would be Cohn, skinny, eyes darting, his features slightly caved in from plastic surgery. "Donald is my best friend," Cohn said back then, shortly after he had thrown a thirty-seventh-birthday party for Trump. And over the years, several who knew Cohn would remark on Donald Trump's resemblance to the most infamous of Roy Cohn's blond, rich-boy obsessions: David Schine.

PATRIOT GAMES

Consider the episode—and the compulsion—that ended Roy Cohn's time in the capital and Joe McCarthy's Senate career. In the mid-fifties, Cohn was in the headlines for the malicious circus of the hearings. Scores of witnesses were being bullied by Cohn or McCarthy or both. "Are you now or have you ever been a member of the Communist Party?" Cohn demanded in his nasal honk, a spectacle replayed in the evenings on TV and radio.

It was amid this high drama that a young man had come into Cohn's life. The heir to a hotel-and-movie franchise, the feckless David Schine had reportedly pulled Ds in his first year at Harvard. But in 1952, he wrote a pamphlet on the evils of communism and was soon introduced to Cohn. It was, for Cohn, a *coup de foudre*, and Schine came on the McCarthy committee as an unpaid "research assistant." Dispatched on a tour of Europe to investigate possible subversion at army bases and American embassies—which included ridding the consular libraries of "subversive literature" (among them works by Dashiell Hammett and Mark Twain)— the pair were dogged by rumors that they were lovers. (Cohn told friends that they were not.) Whispers also began to swirl about McCarthy's sexual orientation.

In lavender Washington, Cohn was known as both a closeted homosexual and homophobic, among those leading the charge against supposedly gay witnesses who he and others believed should lose their government jobs because they were "security risks." When Schine was drafted as a private and not a commissioned officer, Cohn threatened he would "wreck the army." McCarthy even mentioned to Robert T. Stevens, the secretary of the army, that "Roy thinks Dave ought to be a general and operate from a penthouse in the Waldorf Astoria." President Dwight Eisenhower, meanwhile, angered by McCarthy's attacks and fearful that the senator's zealotry was severely damaging the president's agenda and the GOP itself, sent word to the army counsel to write a report on Cohn's harassment tactics. According to historian David A. Nichols, the president secretly ordered the document to be released to key legislators and the press, and the revelations were explosive, resulting in the Army-McCarthy hearings.

Over thirty-six days, 20 million Americans watched. It was all there: Cohn and Schine's jaunt to Europe, Cohn's ultimatums, McCarthy's smears. The high point came when the army's sly Boston lawyer, Joseph Welch, shook his head in pained disbelief at McCarthy's attempt to slander one of Welch's own assistants, imploring the senator, "Have you no sense of decency, sir, at long last . . . ?" Within weeks, Cohn was banished and McCarthy was soon censured.

Cohn played it as a win. After the debacle, he returned to New York and attended a party thrown in his honor at the Hotel Astor. It would be the first example of his ability to project victory from defeat and induce moral amnesia upon a mesmerized New York—a gambit not dissimilar to those later utilized by his confrère Donald Trump.

Another of Cohn's tactics was to befriend the town's top gossip columnists, such as Leonard Lyons and George Sokolsky, who would bring Cohn to the Stork Club. He was irresistible to tabloid writers, always ready with scandal-tinged tales. "Roy would be hired by a divorce client in the morning and be leaking their case in the afternoon," *New Yorker* writer Ken Auletta recalled. Columnist Liz Smith said she learned to distrust most items he gave her. A similar reliance on the press would also become a vital component of the young Trump's playbook.

"[Roy] would call me up and it was always short—'George, Roy,'" said former *New York Post* political reporter George Arzt, who was later Mayor Ed Koch's press secretary. "He would drop a dime on someone, hoping I would print it."

My initiation to the louche world of Roy Cohn came in 1980—at a lunch with Trump in the room upstairs at the "21" Club, the first time I had been there. "Anybody who is anybody here sits between the columns," Trump told me. I was expecting our meal to be one-on-one, but a guest joined us that day. "This is Stanley Friedman," Trump said. "He is Roy Cohn's law partner." The lunch agenda, not surprisingly, turned into a sales pitch, with Friedman offering a monologue on what Roy Cohn had already done for Trump. (Friedman, in pure Tammany Hall style, worked for the city while assisting Cohn, and would later go to prison for taking kickbacks in a parking-ticket scandal.)

"Roy could fix anyone in the city," Friedman told me that day. "He's a genius. . . . It is a good thing Roy isn't here today. He would stab all the food off your plate." A Cohn quirk was to rarely order food and, instead, commandeer the meals of his dining partners. I wrote then about the moment when hotel titan Bob Tisch came by the table. "I beat Bob Tisch on the convention site," Trump said loudly. "But we're good friends now, good friends. Isn't that right, Bob?"

Trump, at the time, was developing a sullen moxie that rivaled Cohn's. The lawyer Tom Baer, for instance, did not know what to expect when he got a call one day to meet with Trump. Baer had been recently appointed by Mayor Koch to represent the city in all aspects of what was to become its new convention center, and Baer was trying to line up possible partnerships. "Donald said, 'I would be willing to contribute the land,'" Baer would remember. "'I think it is only fair that it be named Trump Center'"—after his father.

"I called Ed Koch, and he said, 'Fuck him! Fuck him.' I said, 'I don't talk that way.' He said, 'I don't care how you talk! Fuck him!' So, I used my best lawyerese, and I called him back and said, 'The mayor is so grateful for your offer. But he is not inclined to agree.'" Some time later Trump went to Deputy Mayor Peter Solomon and reportedly proposed a deal entitling him to a $4.4 million commission. (He eventually got $500,000.) Recalled Baer, "He spoke to the representatives of the governor [too]. He wasn't going to be

deterred because *pisher* Tom Baer told him he couldn't do it. . . .
Koch [just shook his head and] thought, This guy is ridiculous."

"YOU NEED TO SEE DONALD"

"Come and make your pitch to me," Roy Cohn told Roger Stone
when they met at a New York dinner party in 1979. Stone, though
only twenty-seven, had achieved a degree of notoriety as one of
Richard Nixon's political dirty-tricksters. At the time, he was running Ronald Reagan's presidential campaign organization in New
York, New Jersey, and Connecticut, and he needed office space.

Stone appeared on East Sixty-eighth Street to find Cohn, just
awakened, in his robe, sitting with one of his clients, Mob boss "Fat
Tony" Salerno, of the Genovese crime family. "In front of [Roy]
was a slab of cream cheese and three burnt slices of bacon," Stone
remembered. "He ate the cream cheese with his pointing finger. He
listened to my pitch and said, 'You need to see Donald Trump. I will
get you in, but then you are on your own.'"

"I went to see him," Stone told me, "and Trump said, 'How do
you get Reagan to 270 electoral votes?' He was very interested [in
the mechanics]—a political junkie. Then he said, 'Okay, we are
in. Go see my father.'" Out Stone went to Avenue Z, in Coney Island, and met Fred Trump in his office, which was crowded with
cigar-store Indians. "True to his word, I got $200,000. The checks
came in $1,000 denominations, the maximum donation you could
give. All of these checks were written to 'Reagan For President.'
It was not illegal—it was bundling. Check trading." For Reagan's
state headquarters, the Trumps found Stone and the campaign a

decrepit town house next to the "21" Club. Stone was now, like Donald Trump, inside the Cohn tent.

And Stone soon seized the moment to cash in. After Reagan was elected, his administration softened the strict rules for corporations seeking government largesse. Soon Stone and Paul Manafort, Trump's future campaign manager, were lobbyists, reaping the bonanzas that could flow with Favor Bank introductions. Their first client, Stone recalled, was none other than Donald Trump, who retained him, irrespective of any role Manafort might have had in the firm, for help with federal issues such as obtaining a permit from the Army Corps of Engineers to dredge the channel to the Atlantic City marina to accommodate his yacht, the *Trump Princess.*

"We made no bones about it," Stone recently said. "We wanted money. And it came pouring in." Stone and Manafort charged hefty fees to introduce blue-chip corporations—such as Ronald Perelman's MacAndrews & Forbes and Rupert Murdoch's News Corp.—to their former campaign colleagues, some of whom were now running the Reagan White House. It was all cozy and connected—and reminiscent of Roy Cohn.

By 2000, Stone had offered his talents to a new candidate: Trump himself. That year Stone traveled the country to help Trump explore the viability of running as a Reform Party candidate. But at a stop in Florida, things halted abruptly. "I'm tired," Stone recalled Trump telling him. "Cancel the rest of this. I am going to my room to watch TV." In Stone's view, "His heart was never in it." (A White House spokesperson disputes this account.)

"You have to let Donald be Donald," Stone explained. "We have been friends for forty years. . . . Look what happened with the 'birther' push. You don't want to hear this, but when he started that campaign seven out of ten Republicans at the time believed that Obama was born in Kenya. And, let's face it, many still question it. Donald still believes it." (In fact, candidate Trump released an official statement two months before Election Day asserting, unequivocally, that "Barack Obama was born in the United States.")

Stone's modus operandi, even to this day, has seemed to be vintage Cohn. Fired by Trump for what one of his spokesmen called Stone's desire "to use the campaign for his own personal publicity," Stone went into overdrive, fighting back and scheduling interviews in which he praised candidate Trump. (Stone denied he was fired and says he resigned.) Stone recently expressed concern that Jared Kushner's inexperience and façade of centrist policies might very well scuttle the already beleaguered Trump presidency. And he fretted about Trump's daughter Ivanka as well, saying that he found it "disturbing" when Saudi Arabia and the United Arab Emirates, in May, pledged $100 million to a World Bank women's entrepreneurial fund—a project she had promoted.

Yet Stone would not concede that his decades-long relationship with Trump had become strained, even though Stone, along with some members of the administration, are facing allegations that they've had questionable contacts with a variety of Russian nationals. (All have denied any wrongdoing.) "There is nothing to any of this," Stone claimed. "Donald knows he has my loyalty and friendship. I leave a message when I want to speak with him."

All along there had been something deeper connecting Stone and Trump and Roy Cohn: the climate of suspicion and fear that had helped bring all three to power. Although Stone, like many around Cohn in the seventies and eighties, was too young to have observed how Cohn helped poison America in the McCarthy years, Stone had learned at the feet of Richard Nixon, the ultimate American paranoid. And the politics of paranoia that Cohn and Stone had cynically mastered would eventually make them kindred spirits. Just as the two of them had come to prominence by exploiting a grave national mood (Cohn in the fifties, Stone in the seventies), it was this same sense of American angst, resurgent in 2016, that would ultimately help elect Donald Trump.

"Pro-Americanism," Stone said, "is a common thread for McCarthy, Goldwater, Nixon, [and] Reagan. The heir to that tradition is Donald Trump. When you combine that with the bare-knuckled tactics of Roy Cohn—or a Roger Stone—that is how you win elections. So Roy has an impact on Donald's understanding of how to deal with the media—attack, attack, attack, never defend."

THE LONG GOOD-BYE

Roger Stone was there in 1982 when Roy Cohn was at his peak. At the time, Cohn was trying to help Trump realize his dream of opening casinos in Atlantic City. Crucial to his success would be a sympathetic New Jersey governor. And Cohn and Stone were working hard to elect their candidate: Republican Tom Kean. Stone, as it turned out, was Kean's campaign manager, and after Kean won in a close race, Stone would remain as an unofficial adviser.

Trump began to purchase boardwalk real estate. He built one casino and bought another. His prospects looked bright. But Cohn's downfall was imminent. Word would soon begin to circulate that Cohn was battling AIDS. He denied it. He was also battling disbarment—under a cloud of fraud and ethical-misconduct charges. (Cohn, along with other misdeeds, had stiffed a client on a loan and altered the terms of a virtually comatose client's will—in his hospital room—making himself its coexecutor.)

Cohn tried to keep up a good face. But Trump, among other clients, began to shift his business elsewhere. "Donald found out about [Cohn's condition] and just dropped him like a hot potato," Cohn's personal secretary, Susan Bell, was quoted as saying. (A White House spokesperson says this claim is totally false.)

Cohn sensed his growing isolation. And for whatever reason, he decided, according to journalist Wayne Barrett, to help the efforts of Trump's sister Maryanne Trump Barry, who was seeking an appointment to the federal bench. "Maryanne wanted the job," Stone would recall. "She did not want Roy and Donald to do anything. She was attempting to get it on her own."

Stone remembered that when it appeared someone else was in line for the job Cohn approached Reagan's attorney general, Ed Meese, for help. In the end, Barry got the plum post. "Roy can do the impossible," Trump reportedly said when he heard the news. The next day, Barrett noted, Barry called Cohn to thank him. (According to the *Times*, Trump, when asked in 2015, said his sister "got the appointment totally on her own merit." For herself, Barry admitted to Trump-family biographer Gwenda Blair, "There's no question Donald helped me get on the bench. I was good, but not that good.")

By 1985, Cohn was seriously ill—"I have liver cancer," he contended—and he started calling in his last markers. He phoned *New York Times* columnist William Safire, whom he'd known since

Safire's days as a publicist. And, sure enough, Safire ran a piece attacking the "buzzards of the bar" who had "dredged up" fraud charges to get even with Cohn, "[the] hard-hitting anti-legal-establishment right-winger at a time when he is physically unable to defend himself." Roger Stone would recall Trump phoning him and asking, "'Have you seen Bill Safire's column?' He called me to point it out to me. He said, 'This is going to be terrific for Roy.'"

Cohn also had asked a favor of Trump: Could he give him a hotel room for his lover, who was dying of AIDS? A room was found in the Barbizon Plaza Hotel. Months passed. Then Cohn got the bill. Then another. He refused to pay. At some point, according to the *New York Times'* Jonathan Mahler and Matt Flegenheimer, Trump would present Cohn with a thank-you gift for a decade of favors: a pair of diamond cuff links. The diamonds turned out to be fakes.

Relations between the two became progressively strained. And the dying Cohn, as Barrett would describe him in those waning days, would say, "Donald pisses ice water."

That said, Trump did come out to testify on Cohn's behalf at his 1986 disbarment hearing, one of thirty-seven character witnesses, including Barbara Walters and William Safire. But none of it mattered. Cohn, after putting up a four-year fight, was kicked out of the New York Bar for "dishonesty, fraud, deceit, and misrepresentation." Cohn's nefarious practices had finally caught up with him.

Trump, by then a presence in Atlantic City, was setting his sights on a third casino. Roy Cohn, in contrast, would die almost penniless, given how much he owed the IRS. And his funeral made it clear what Cohn and his friends and family had felt, in the end, about Trump. The real-estate developer was not one of the speakers. He was not asked to be a pallbearer. Trump, in Barrett's account, did show up, however, and stood in the back.

Thirty years later, on the day after Donald J. Trump was elected president, Roger Stone was one of the callers who got through to his old friend at Trump Tower. "Mr. President," said Stone. "Oh, please, call me Donald," Stone remembered Trump saying.

A few moments later, Trump sounded wistful. "Wouldn't Roy love to see this moment? Boy, do we miss him."

Acknowledgments

Thank you, most of all, to the many who have so generously shared their stories with me over decades of reporting. You have given me the gift of your trust, and for that, my gratitude is unending.

At Simon & Schuster, thank you to Jofie Ferrari-Adler, the most generous and thoughtful of editors, who suggested the idea of this collection. Thank you to Al Madocs, Elisa Shokoff at Simon & Schuster Audio, and Julianna Haubner. And as well to Jonathan Karp, Simon & Schuster's president and publisher. At *Vanity Fair*, many thanks to Graydon Carter, Tina Brown, Wayne Lawson, Mark Rozzo, and David Friend for years of guidance. A special thank-you to Mary Flynn, Simon Brennan, and Robert Walsh, whose factual and legal reviews have enhanced every story we worked on together for years of late night emails and dawn closings. I am especially grateful to my agents, Amanda Burden and Ron Bernstein, for our long collaboration and friendship. My deep gratitude to the director Matt Heineman, the producer Marissa McMahon, the writer Arash Amel, and the actress Rosamund Pike, whose tenacity and passion brought *A Private War* to the screen. And to the director Michael Mann and writer Eric Roth, for their searing adaptation of *The Man Who Knew Too Much* into *The Insider*. My deep appreciation to both Michael Mann and Matt Heineman for allowing me take part in their process.

And as always, none of this would have been possible without the love and support of my closest friends and my beloved Casey, Adam, James and Kat, and Lucy and Milo. And always, to Ernie, who has encouraged and loved me through it all.